Garfield
bigger
than life

BY: JIM DAVIS

Ballantine Books · New York

A Ballantine Book
Published by The Random House Publishing Group
Copyright © 1981, 2002 by PAWS Incorporated. All Rights Reserved.

Published in the United States by Ballantine Books, an imprint of The Random House Publishing Group, a division of Random House, Inc., New York, and simultaneously in Canada by Random House of Canada Limited, Toronto. Originally published in a slightly different form by The Random House Publishing Group, a division of Random House, Inc., in 1981.

Ballantine and colophon are registered trademarks of Random House, Inc.

"GARFIELD" and the GARFIELD characters are registered and unregistered trademarks of PAWS, Inc.

www.ballantinebooks.com

Library of Congress Catalog Card Number: 2001119050

ISBN 0-345-45027-2

Manufactured in the United States of America

First Ballantine Books Edition: November 1981
First Colorized Edition: March 2002

9 8 7 6 5 4

how to draw Garfield
1.
PASTA SPOTTERS
DAISY SNIFFER
2.
CAN OPENER SENSORS
SMIRK
SMIRK RETAINERS
3.
STROKING SURFACE
LASAGNA STORAGE UNITS
TWITCHER
4.
HAIR BALL CATCHER
DIRT DRAGGER
CHAIR SHREDDERS
5.
NOT JUST ANOTHER PRETTY FACE
STRIPES
NOW ADD THE PERSONALITY
JIM DAVIS

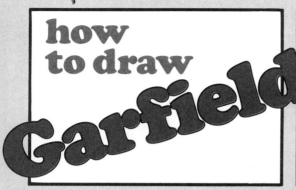

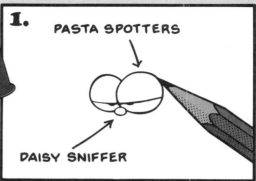

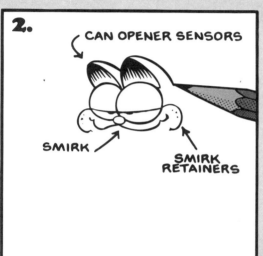

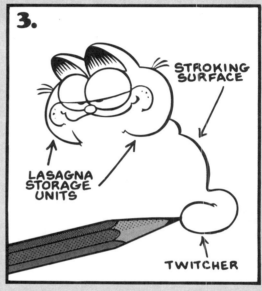

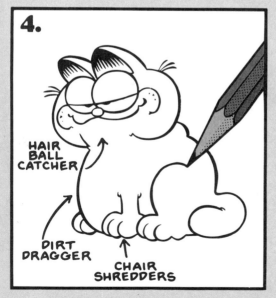

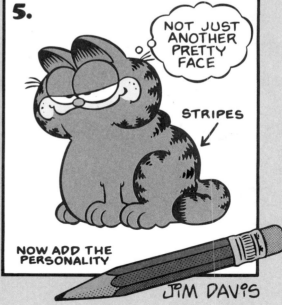

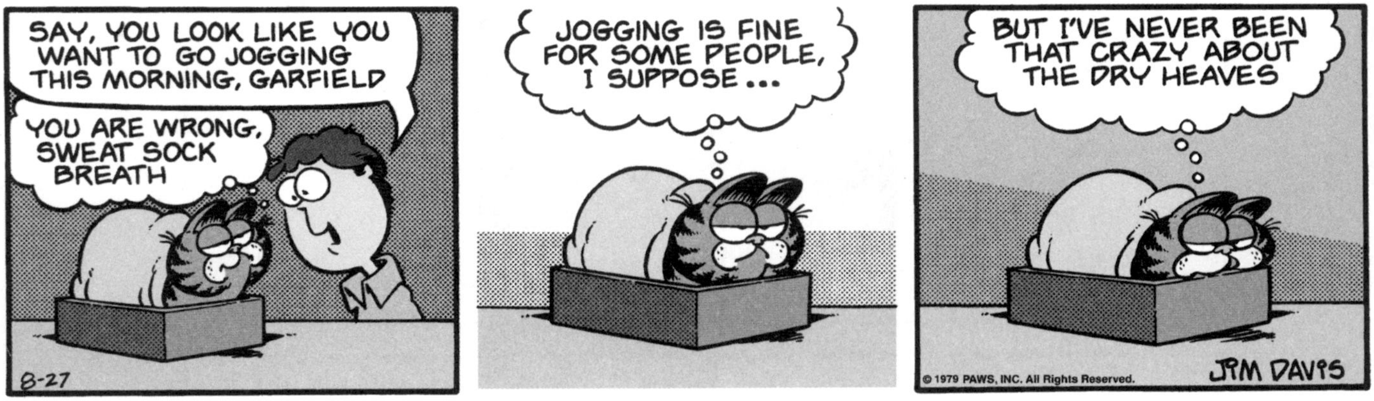
SAY, YOU LOOK LIKE YOU WANT TO GO JOGGING THIS MORNING, GARFIELD
YOU ARE WRONG, SWEAT SOCK BREATH
8-27
JOGGING IS FINE FOR SOME PEOPLE, I SUPPOSE...
BUT I'VE NEVER BEEN THAT CRAZY ABOUT THE DRY HEAVES
© 1979 PAWS, INC. All Rights Reserved.
JIM DAVIS

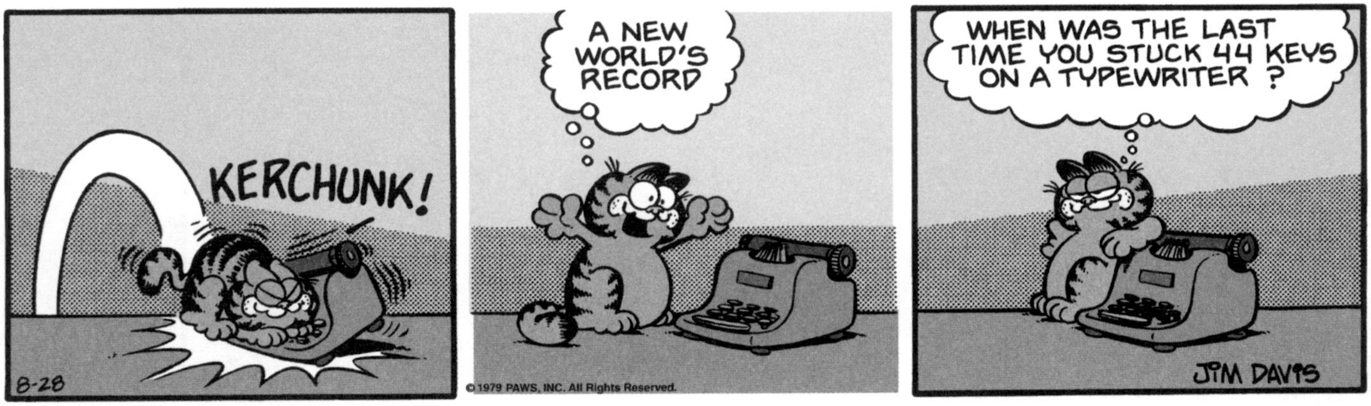
KERCHUNK!
8-28
A NEW WORLD'S RECORD
© 1979 PAWS, INC. All Rights Reserved.
WHEN WAS THE LAST TIME YOU STUCK 44 KEYS ON A TYPEWRITER ?
JIM DAVIS

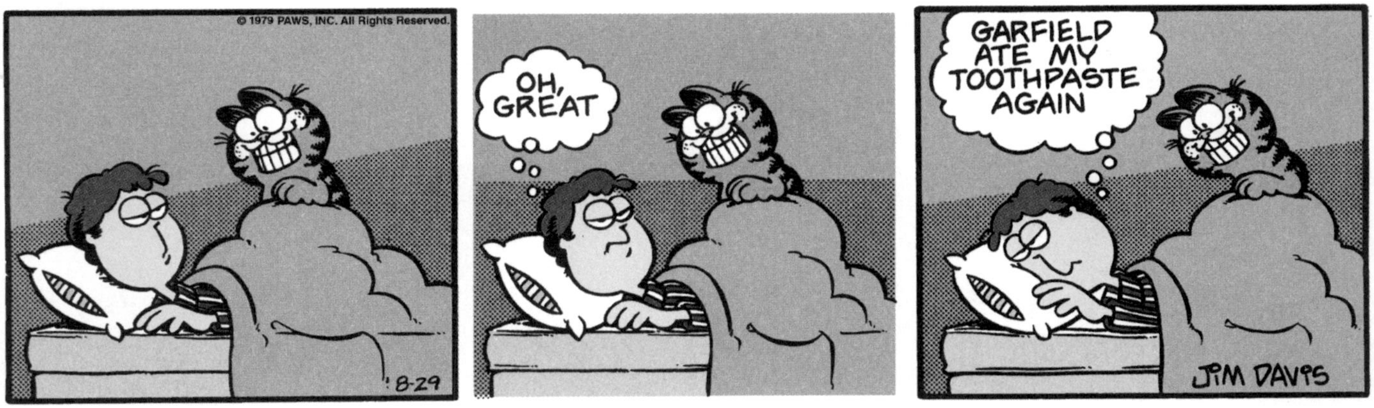
© 1979 PAWS, INC. All Rights Reserved.
8-29
OH, GREAT
GARFIELD ATE MY TOOTHPASTE AGAIN
JIM DAVIS

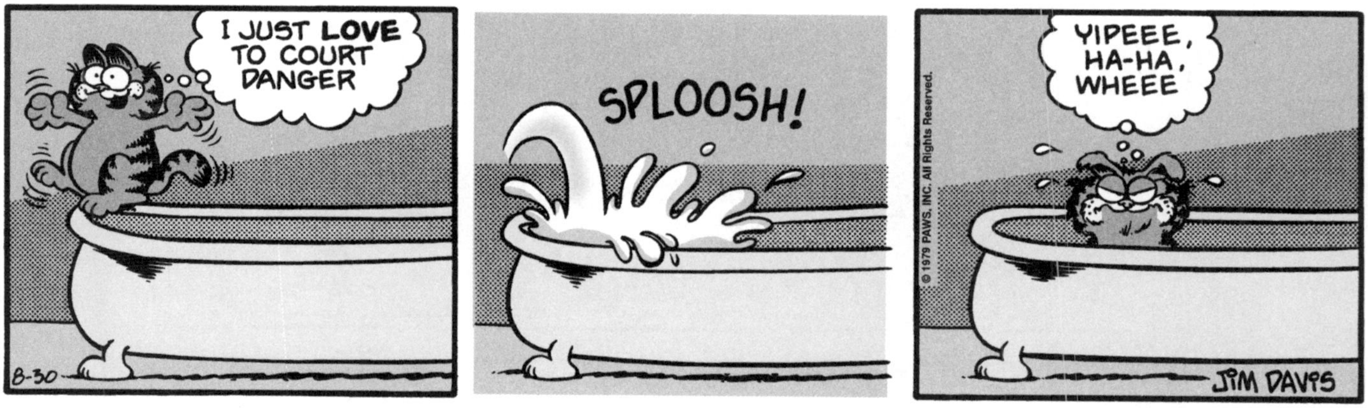
8-30
I JUST **LOVE** TO COURT DANGER
SPLOOSH!
© 1979 PAWS, INC. All Rights Reserved.
YIPEEE, HA-HA, WHEEE
JIM DAVIS

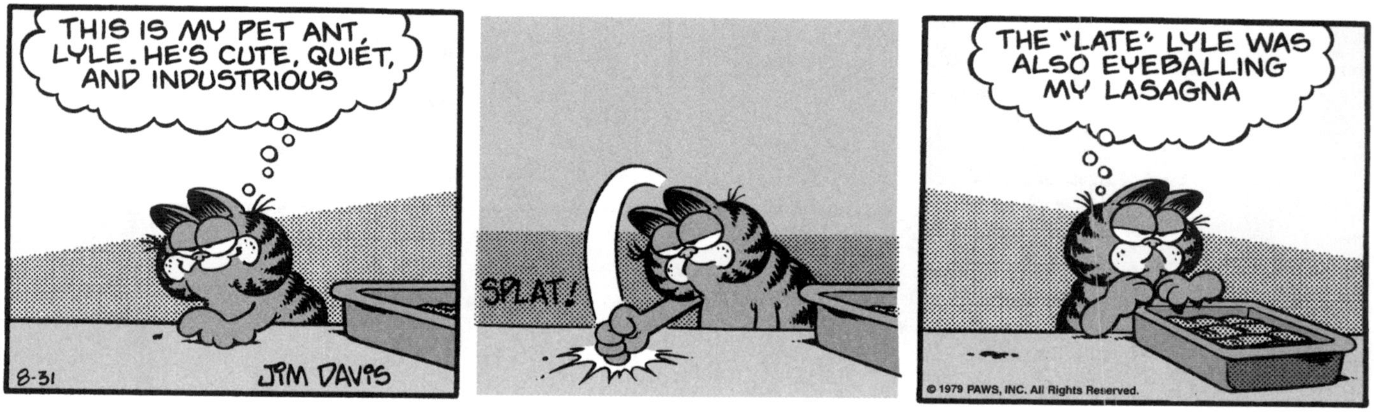
THIS IS MY PET ANT, LYLE. HE'S CUTE, QUIET, AND INDUSTRIOUS
8-31
JIM DAVIS
SPLAT!
THE "LATE" LYLE WAS ALSO EYEBALLING MY LASAGNA
© 1979 PAWS, INC. All Rights Reserved.

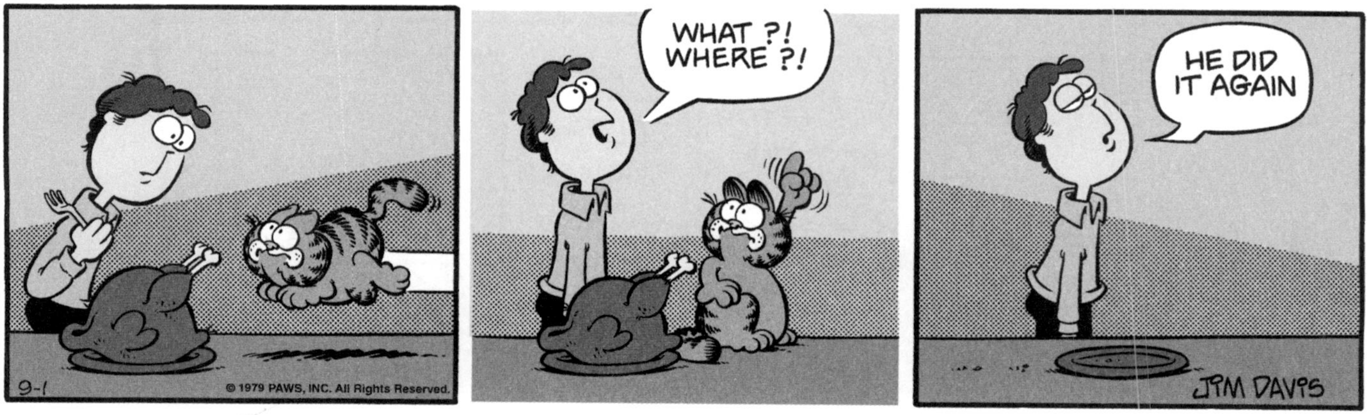
9-1
© 1979 PAWS, INC. All Rights Reserved.
WHAT ?! WHERE ?!
HE DID IT AGAIN
JIM DAVIS

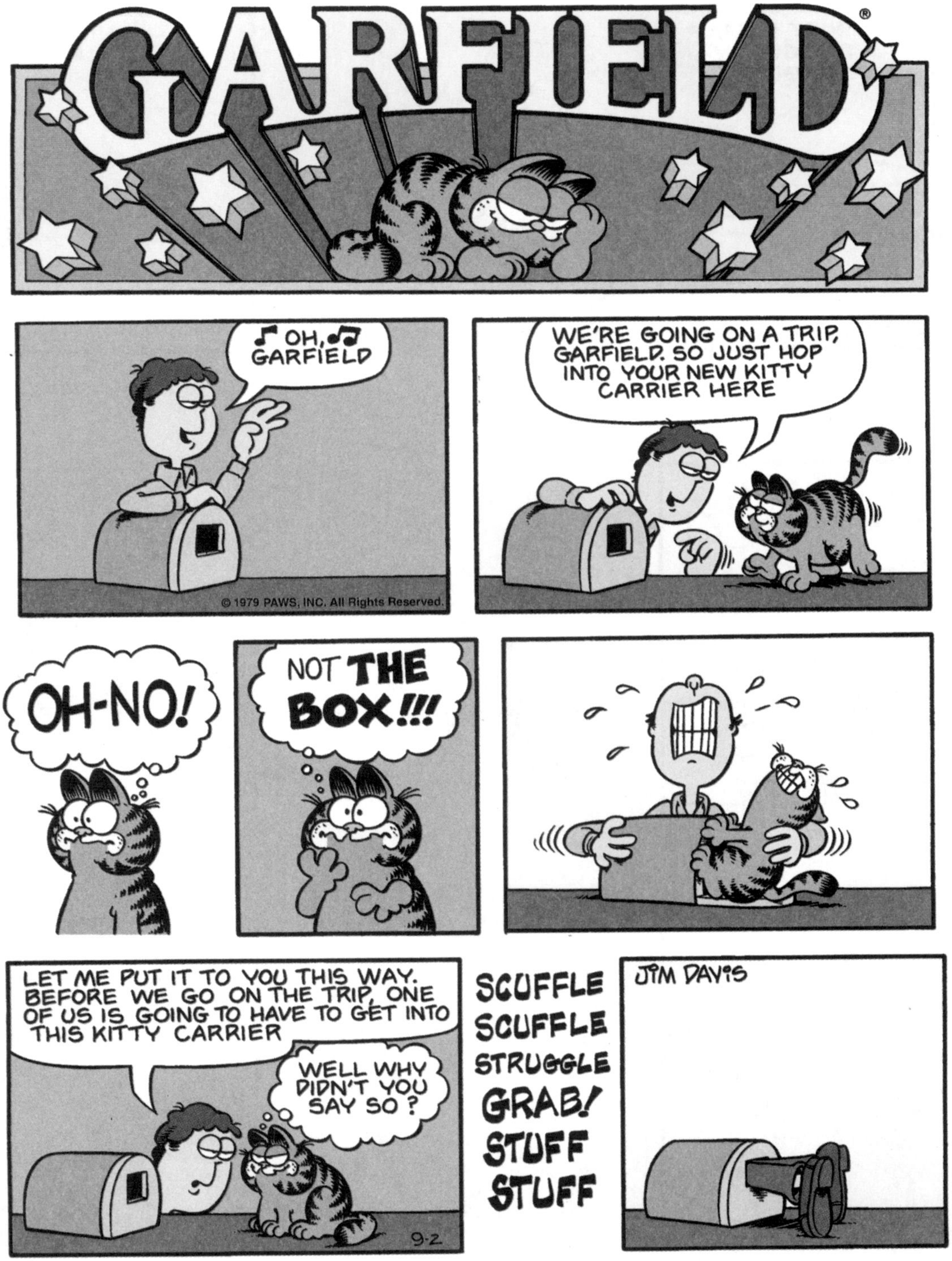
GARFIELD®
♪ OH, ♫ GARFIELD
© 1979 PAWS, INC. All Rights Reserved.
WE'RE GOING ON A TRIP, GARFIELD. SO JUST HOP INTO YOUR NEW KITTY CARRIER HERE
OH-NO!
NOT THE BOX!!!
LET ME PUT IT TO YOU THIS WAY. BEFORE WE GO ON THE TRIP, ONE OF US IS GOING TO HAVE TO GET INTO THIS KITTY CARRIER
WELL WHY DIDN'T YOU SAY SO ?
9-2
SCUFFLE
SCUFFLE
STRUGGLE
GRAB!
STUFF
STUFF
JIM DAVIS

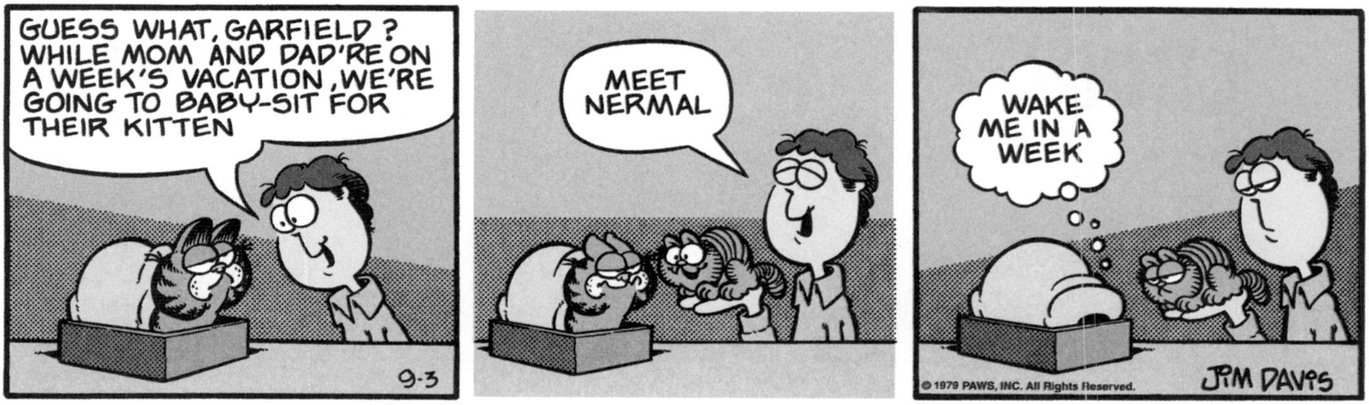
GUESS WHAT, GARFIELD? WHILE MOM AND DAD'RE ON A WEEK'S VACATION, WE'RE GOING TO BABY-SIT FOR THEIR KITTEN
9-3
MEET NERMAL
WAKE ME IN A WEEK
© 1979 PAWS, INC. All Rights Reserved.
JIM DAVIS

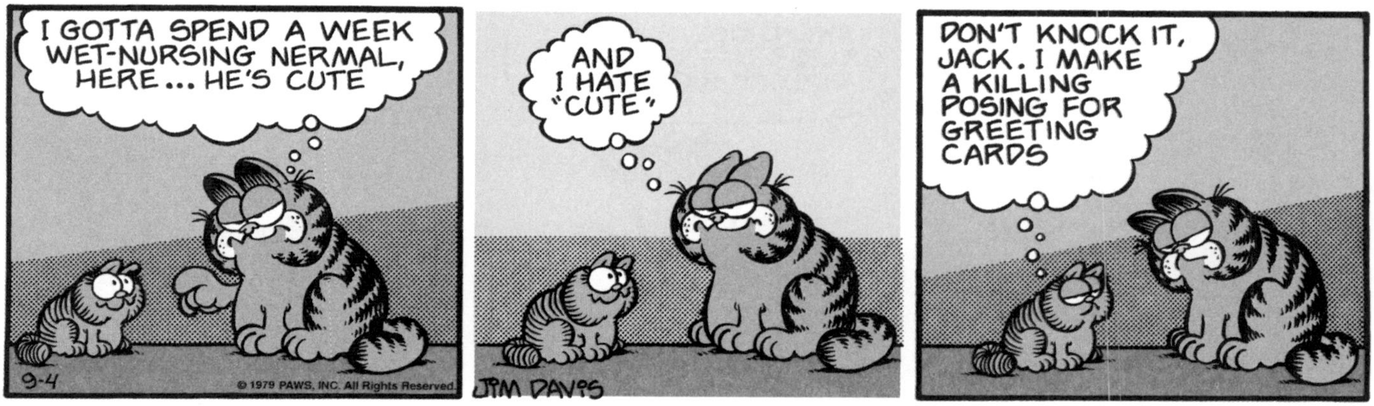
I GOTTA SPEND A WEEK WET-NURSING NERMAL, HERE... HE'S CUTE
9-4
© 1979 PAWS, INC. All Rights Reserved.
AND I HATE "CUTE"
JIM DAVIS
DON'T KNOCK IT, JACK. I MAKE A KILLING POSING FOR GREETING CARDS

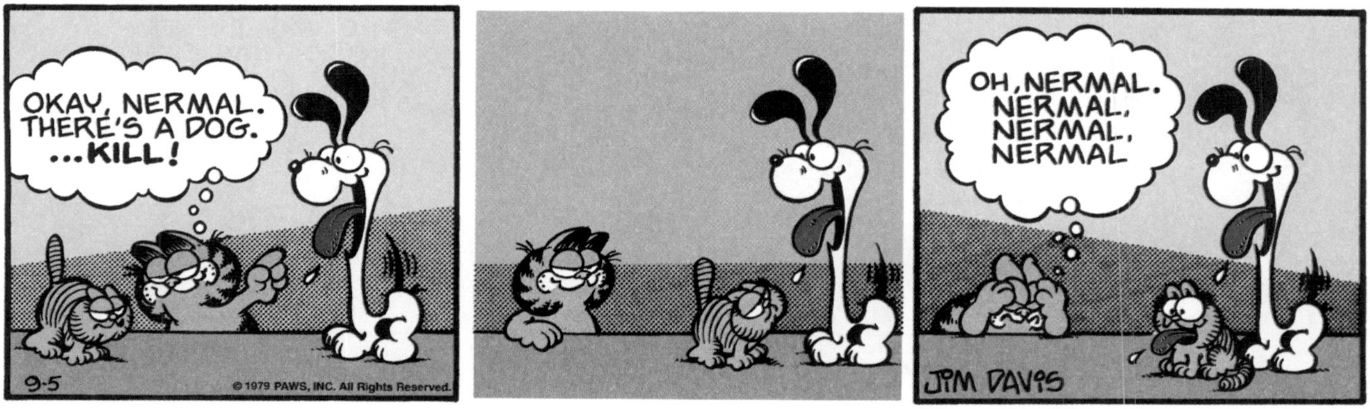
OKAY, NERMAL. THERE'S A DOG. ...**KILL!**
9-5
© 1979 PAWS, INC. All Rights Reserved.
OH, NERMAL. NERMAL, NERMAL, NERMAL
JIM DAVIS

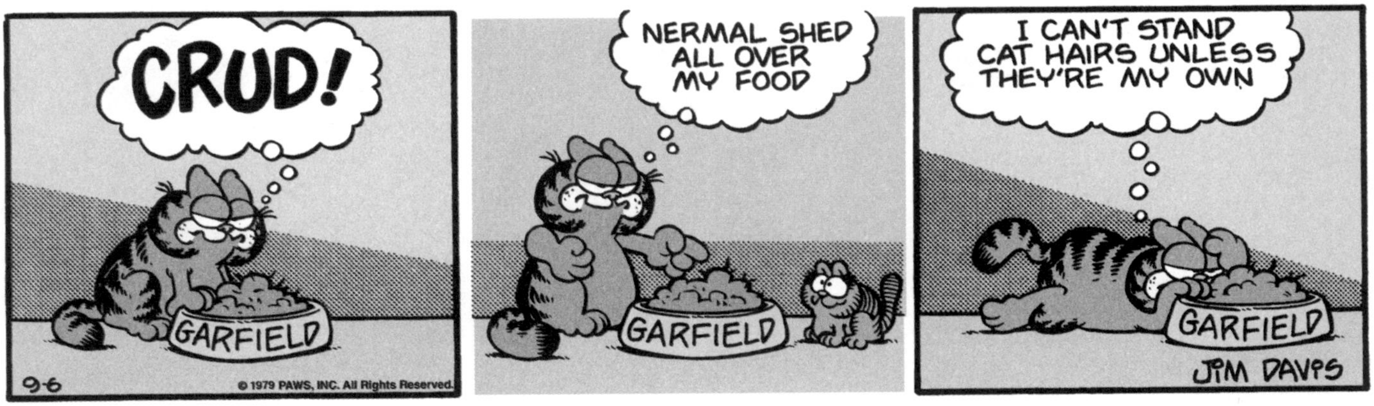
CRUD!
GARFIELD
9-6
© 1979 PAWS, INC. All Rights Reserved.
NERMAL SHED ALL OVER MY FOOD
GARFIELD
I CAN'T STAND CAT HAIRS UNLESS THEY'RE MY OWN
GARFIELD
JIM DAVIS

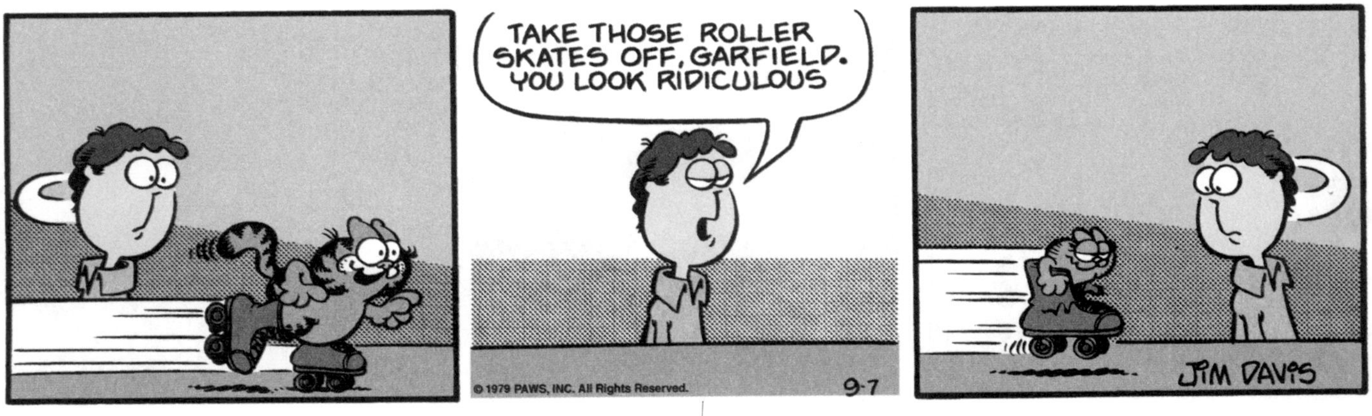
TAKE THOSE ROLLER SKATES OFF, GARFIELD. YOU LOOK RIDICULOUS
© 1979 PAWS, INC. All Rights Reserved.
9-7
JIM DAVIS

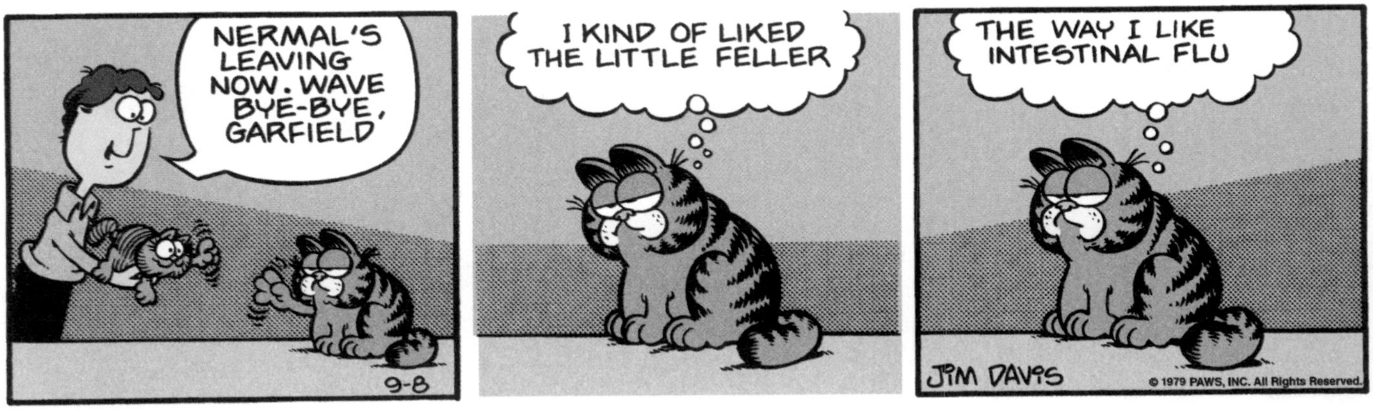
NERMAL'S LEAVING NOW. WAVE BYE-BYE, GARFIELD
9-8
I KIND OF LIKED THE LITTLE FELLER
THE WAY I LIKE INTESTINAL FLU
JIM DAVIS
© 1979 PAWS, INC. All Rights Reserved.

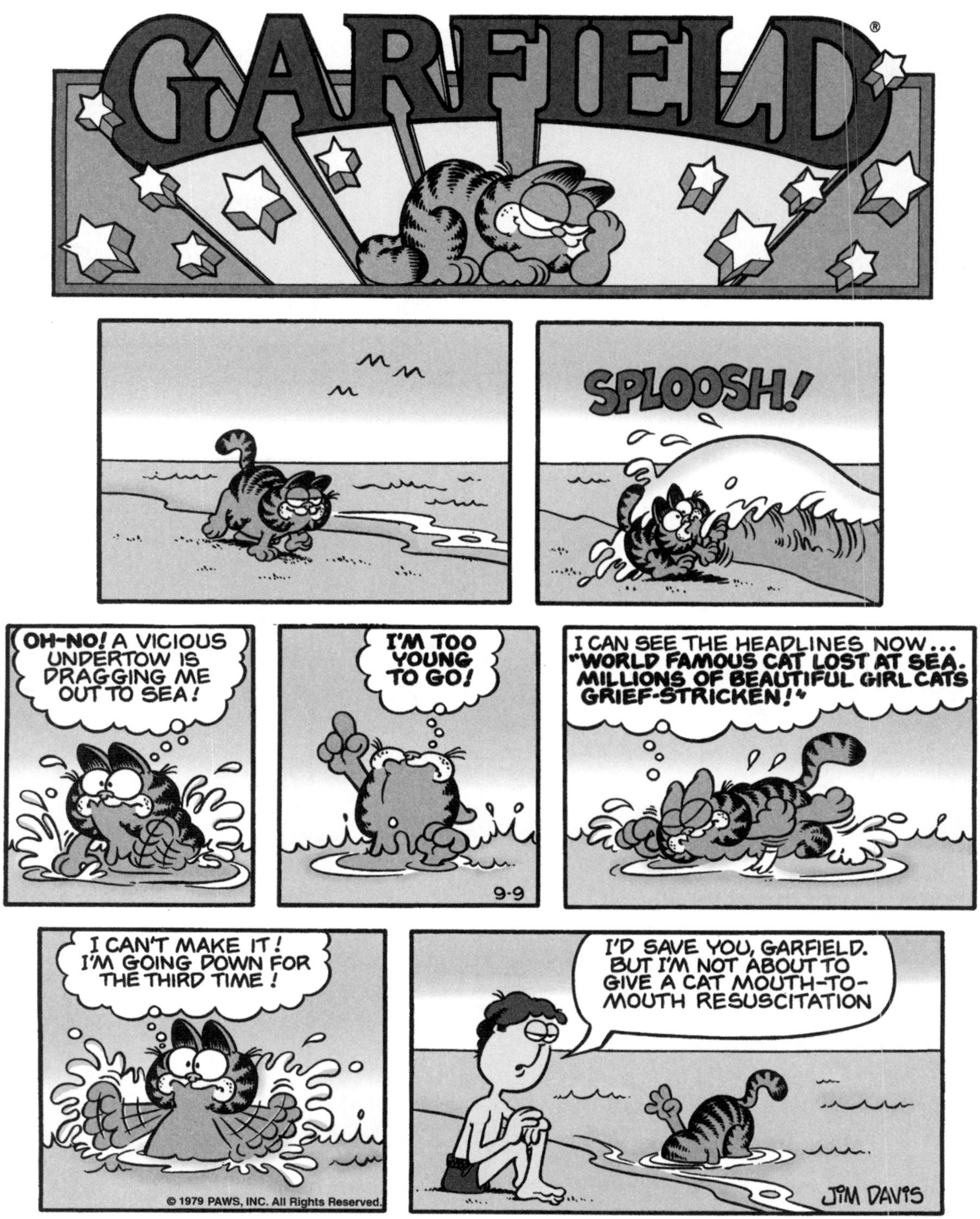
GARFIELD
SPLOOSH!
OH-NO! A VICIOUS UNDERTOW IS DRAGGING ME OUT TO SEA!
I'M TOO YOUNG TO GO!
9-9
I CAN SEE THE HEADLINES NOW... "WORLD FAMOUS CAT LOST AT SEA. MILLIONS OF BEAUTIFUL GIRL CATS GRIEF-STRICKEN!"
I CAN'T MAKE IT! I'M GOING DOWN FOR THE THIRD TIME!
© 1979 PAWS, INC. All Rights Reserved.
I'D SAVE YOU, GARFIELD. BUT I'M NOT ABOUT TO GIVE A CAT MOUTH-TO-MOUTH RESUSCITATION
JIM DAVIS

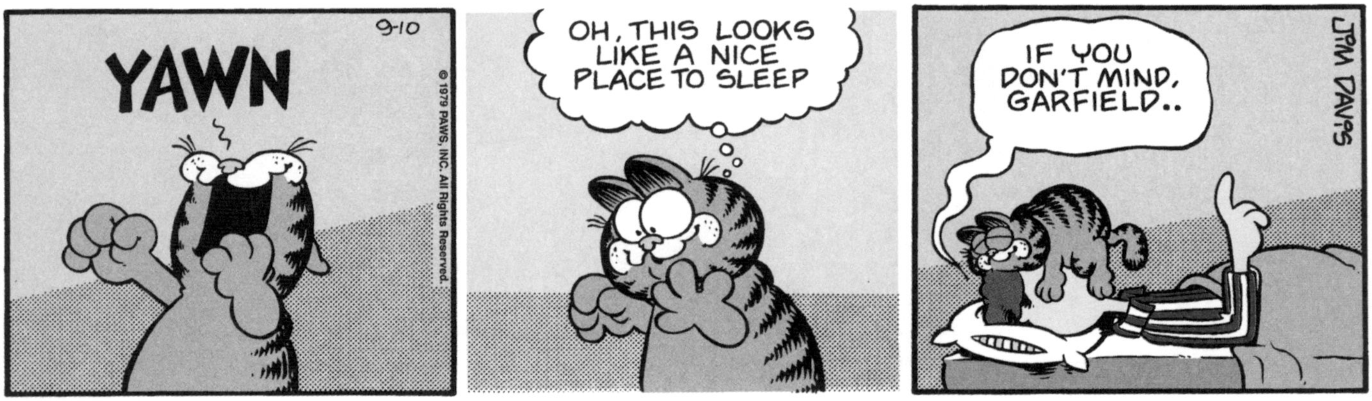
9-10
© 1979 PAWS, INC. All Rights Reserved.
YAWN
OH, THIS LOOKS LIKE A NICE PLACE TO SLEEP
IF YOU DON'T MIND, GARFIELD..
JIM DAVIS

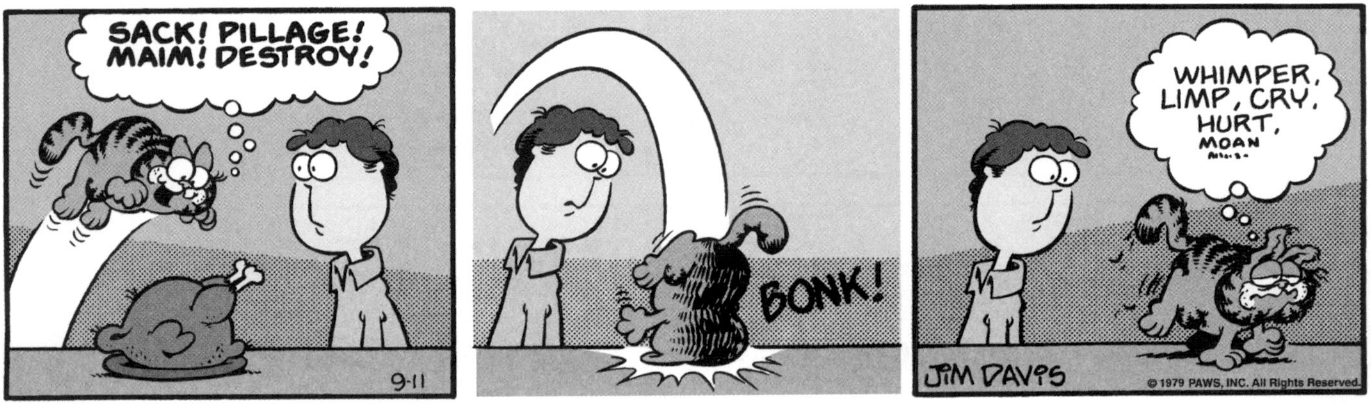
SACK! PILLAGE! MAIM! DESTROY!
9-11
BONK!
WHIMPER, LIMP, CRY, HURT,
MOAN
JIM DAVIS
© 1979 PAWS, INC. All Rights Reserved.

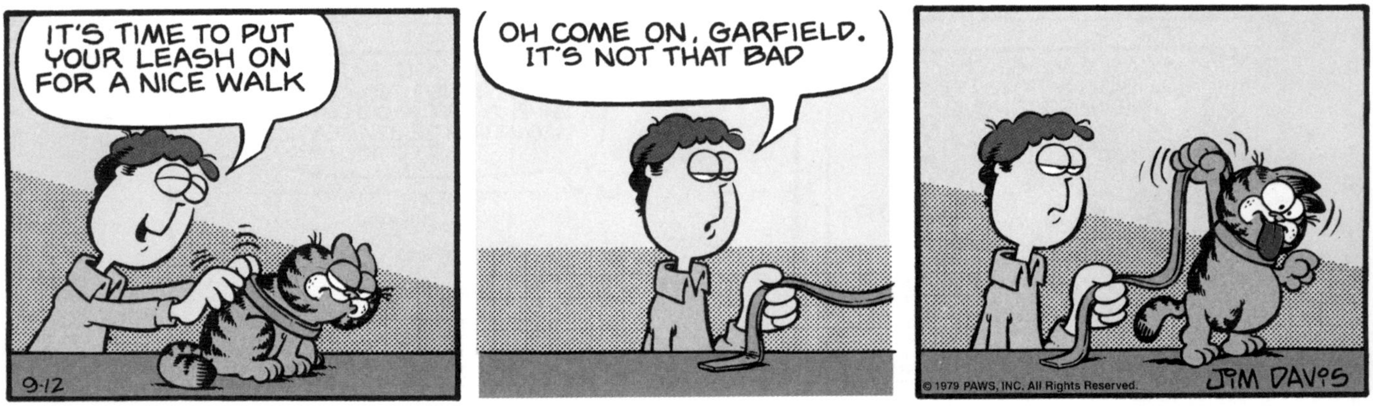
IT'S TIME TO PUT YOUR LEASH ON FOR A NICE WALK
9-12
OH COME ON, GARFIELD. IT'S NOT THAT BAD
© 1979 PAWS, INC. All Rights Reserved.
JIM DAVIS

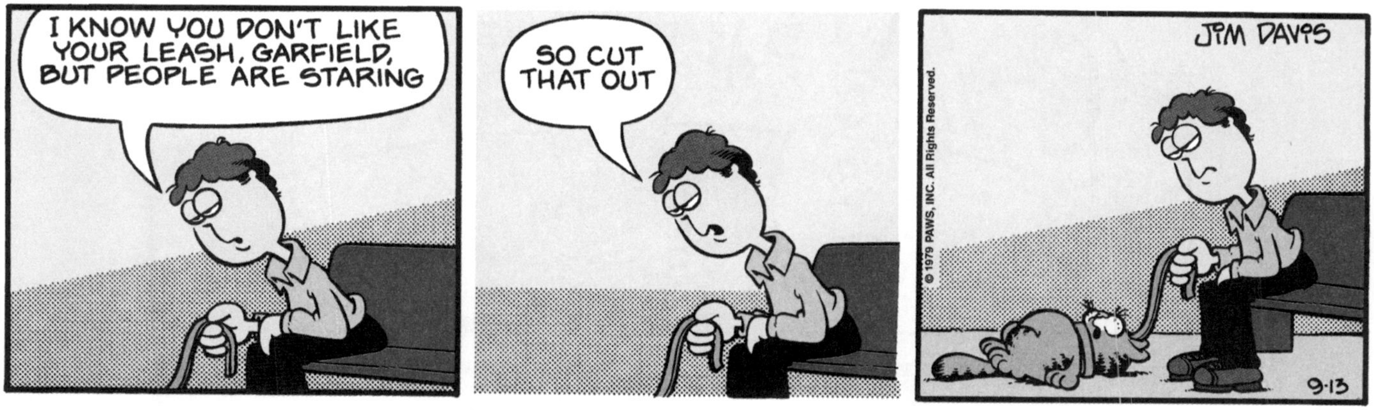
I KNOW YOU DON'T LIKE YOUR LEASH, GARFIELD, BUT PEOPLE ARE STARING
SO CUT THAT OUT
JIM DAVIS
© 1979 PAWS, INC. All Rights Reserved.
9-13

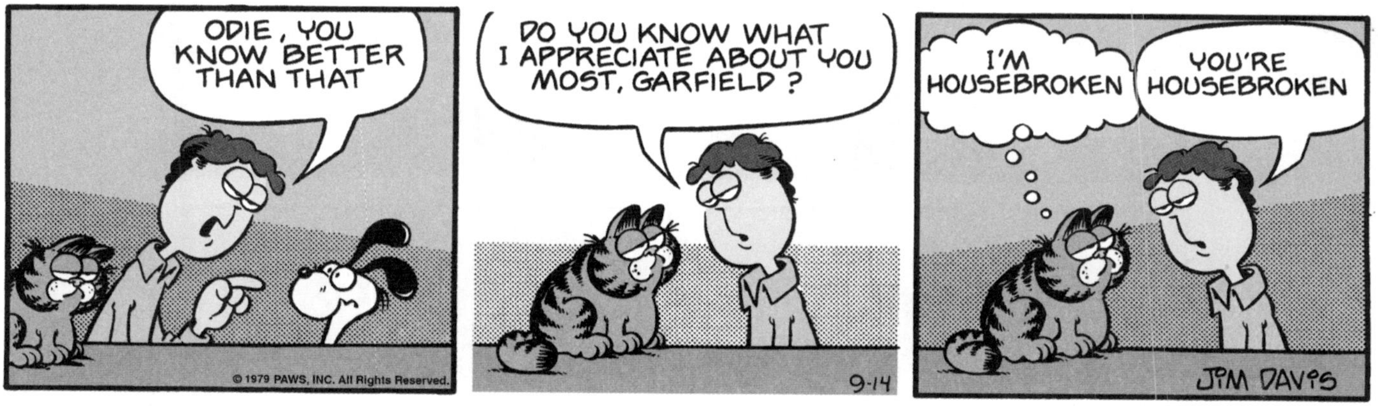
ODIE, YOU KNOW BETTER THAN THAT
© 1979 PAWS, INC. All Rights Reserved.
DO YOU KNOW WHAT I APPRECIATE ABOUT YOU MOST, GARFIELD ?
9-14
I'M HOUSEBROKEN
YOU'RE HOUSEBROKEN
JIM DAVIS

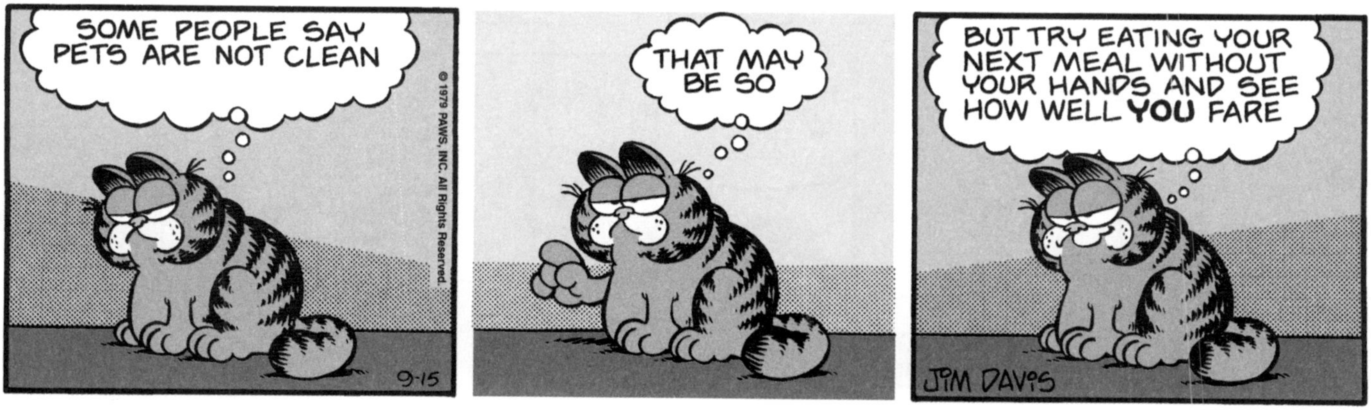
SOME PEOPLE SAY PETS ARE NOT CLEAN
© 1979 PAWS, INC. All Rights Reserved.
9-15
THAT MAY BE SO
BUT TRY EATING YOUR NEXT MEAL WITHOUT YOUR HANDS AND SEE HOW WELL **YOU** FARE
JIM DAVIS

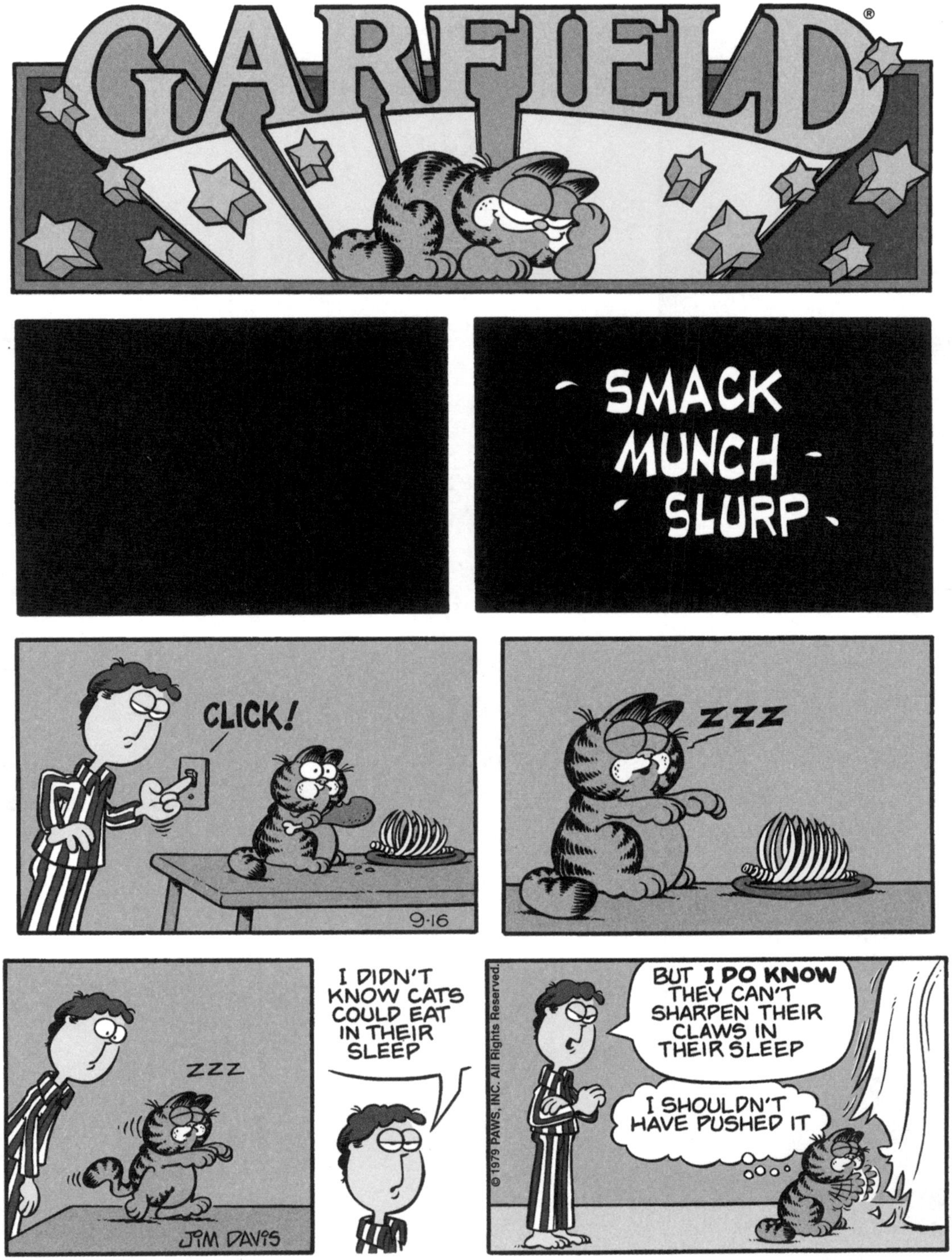
GARFIELD®
SMACK
MUNCH
SLURP
CLICK!
9·16
ZZZ
ZZZ
JIM DAVIS
I DIDN'T KNOW CATS COULD EAT IN THEIR SLEEP
© 1979 PAWS, INC. All Rights Reserved.
BUT I DO KNOW THEY CAN'T SHARPEN THEIR CLAWS IN THEIR SLEEP
I SHOULDN'T HAVE PUSHED IT

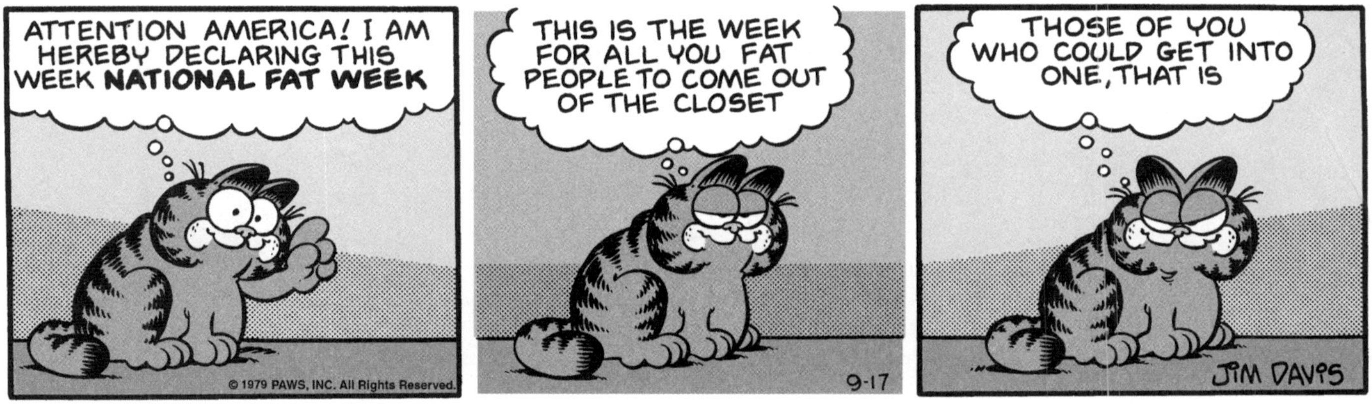
ATTENTION AMERICA! I AM HEREBY DECLARING THIS WEEK **NATIONAL FAT WEEK**
© 1979 PAWS, INC. All Rights Reserved.
THIS IS THE WEEK FOR ALL YOU FAT PEOPLE TO COME OUT OF THE CLOSET
9-17
THOSE OF YOU WHO COULD GET INTO ONE, THAT IS
JIM DAVIS

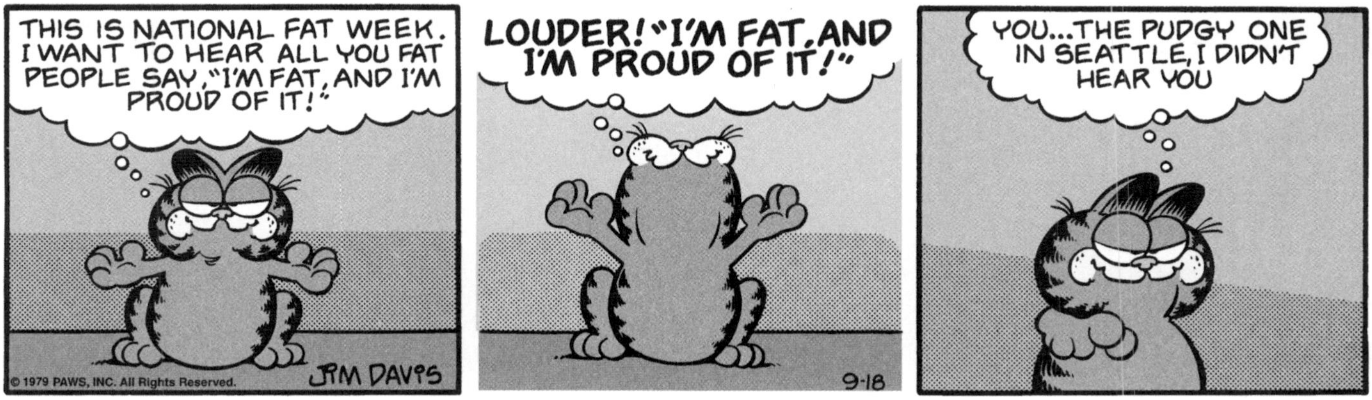
THIS IS NATIONAL FAT WEEK. I WANT TO HEAR ALL YOU FAT PEOPLE SAY, "I'M FAT, AND I'M PROUD OF IT!"
© 1979 PAWS, INC. All Rights Reserved.
JIM DAVIS
LOUDER! "I'M FAT, AND I'M PROUD OF IT!"
9-18
YOU...THE PUDGY ONE IN SEATTLE, I DIDN'T HEAR YOU

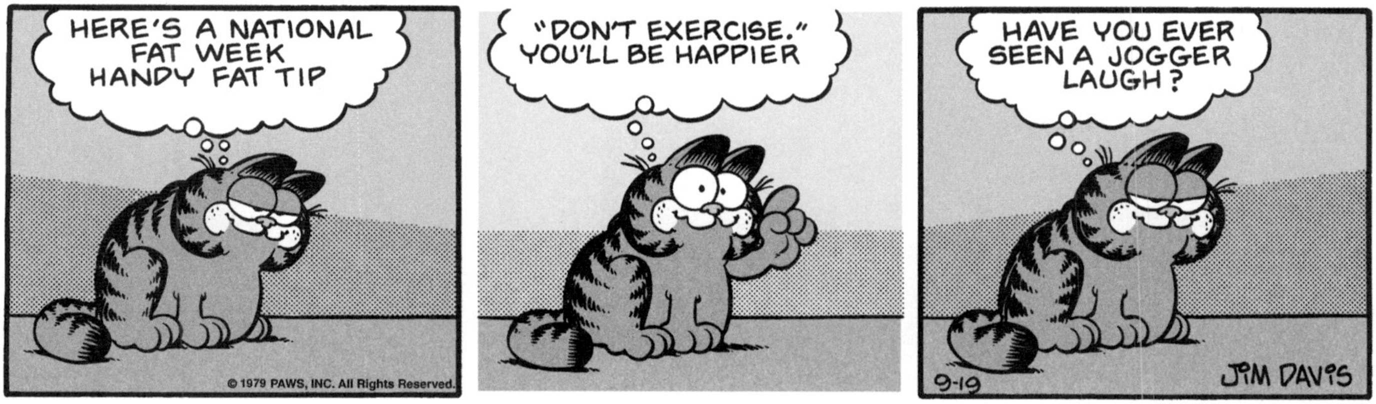
HERE'S A NATIONAL FAT WEEK HANDY FAT TIP
© 1979 PAWS, INC. All Rights Reserved.
"DON'T EXERCISE." YOU'LL BE HAPPIER
HAVE YOU EVER SEEN A JOGGER LAUGH?
9-19
JIM DAVIS

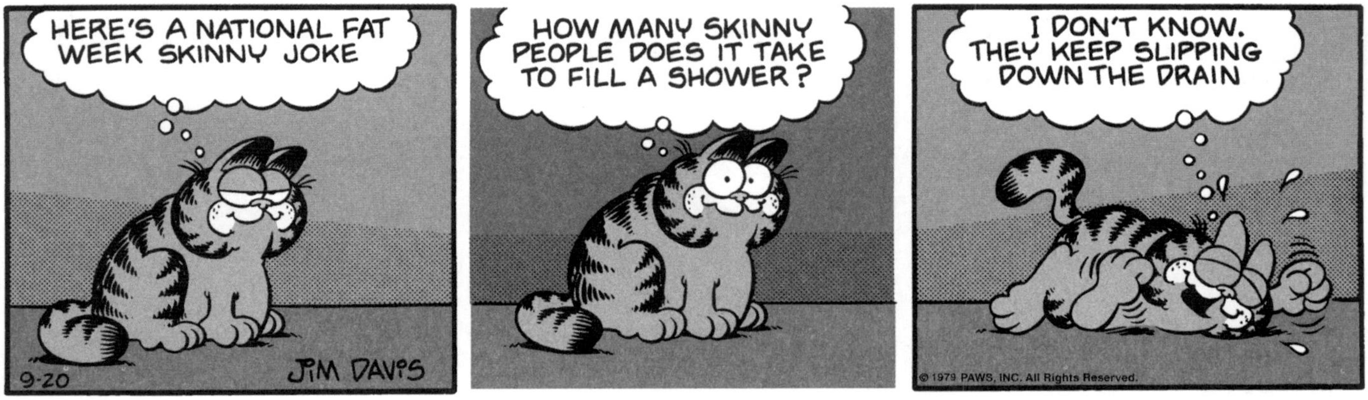
HERE'S A NATIONAL FAT WEEK SKINNY JOKE
9-20
JIM DAVIS
HOW MANY SKINNY PEOPLE DOES IT TAKE TO FILL A SHOWER?
I DON'T KNOW. THEY KEEP SLIPPING DOWN THE DRAIN
© 1979 PAWS, INC. All Rights Reserved.

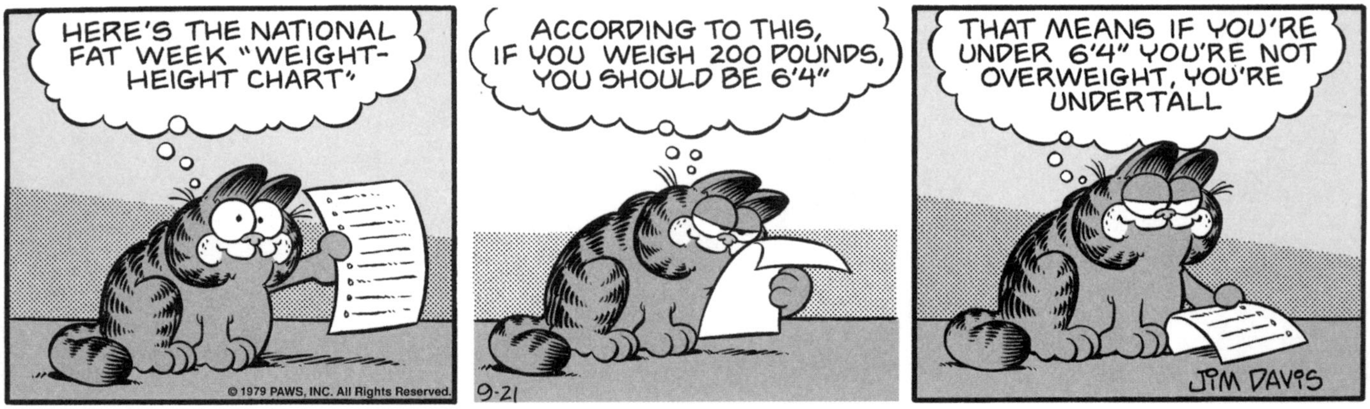
HERE'S THE NATIONAL FAT WEEK "WEIGHT-HEIGHT CHART"
© 1979 PAWS, INC. All Rights Reserved.
ACCORDING TO THIS, IF YOU WEIGH 200 POUNDS, YOU SHOULD BE 6'4"
9-21
THAT MEANS IF YOU'RE UNDER 6'4" YOU'RE NOT OVERWEIGHT, YOU'RE UNDERTALL
JIM DAVIS

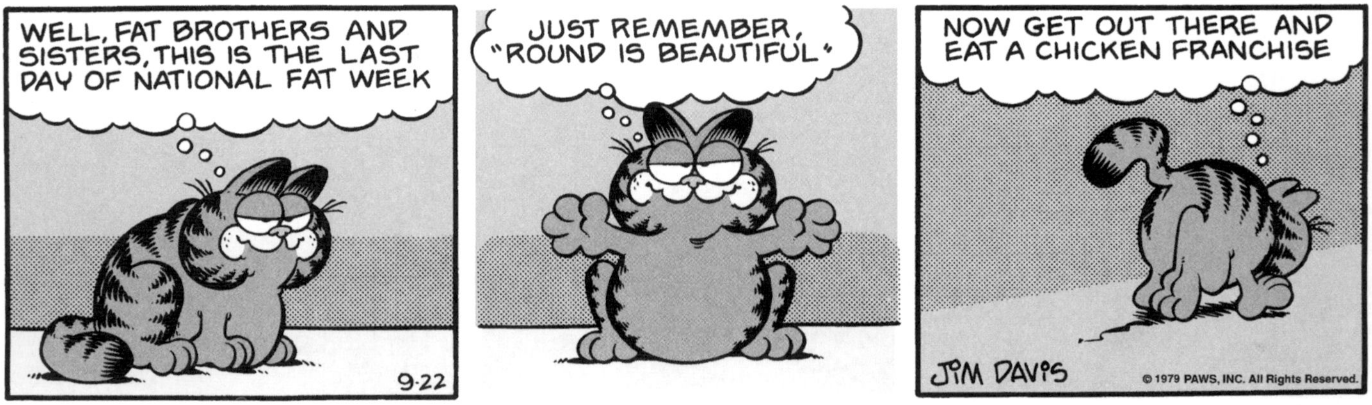
WELL, FAT BROTHERS AND SISTERS, THIS IS THE LAST DAY OF NATIONAL FAT WEEK
9-22
JUST REMEMBER, "ROUND IS BEAUTIFUL"
NOW GET OUT THERE AND EAT A CHICKEN FRANCHISE
JIM DAVIS
© 1979 PAWS, INC. All Rights Reserved.

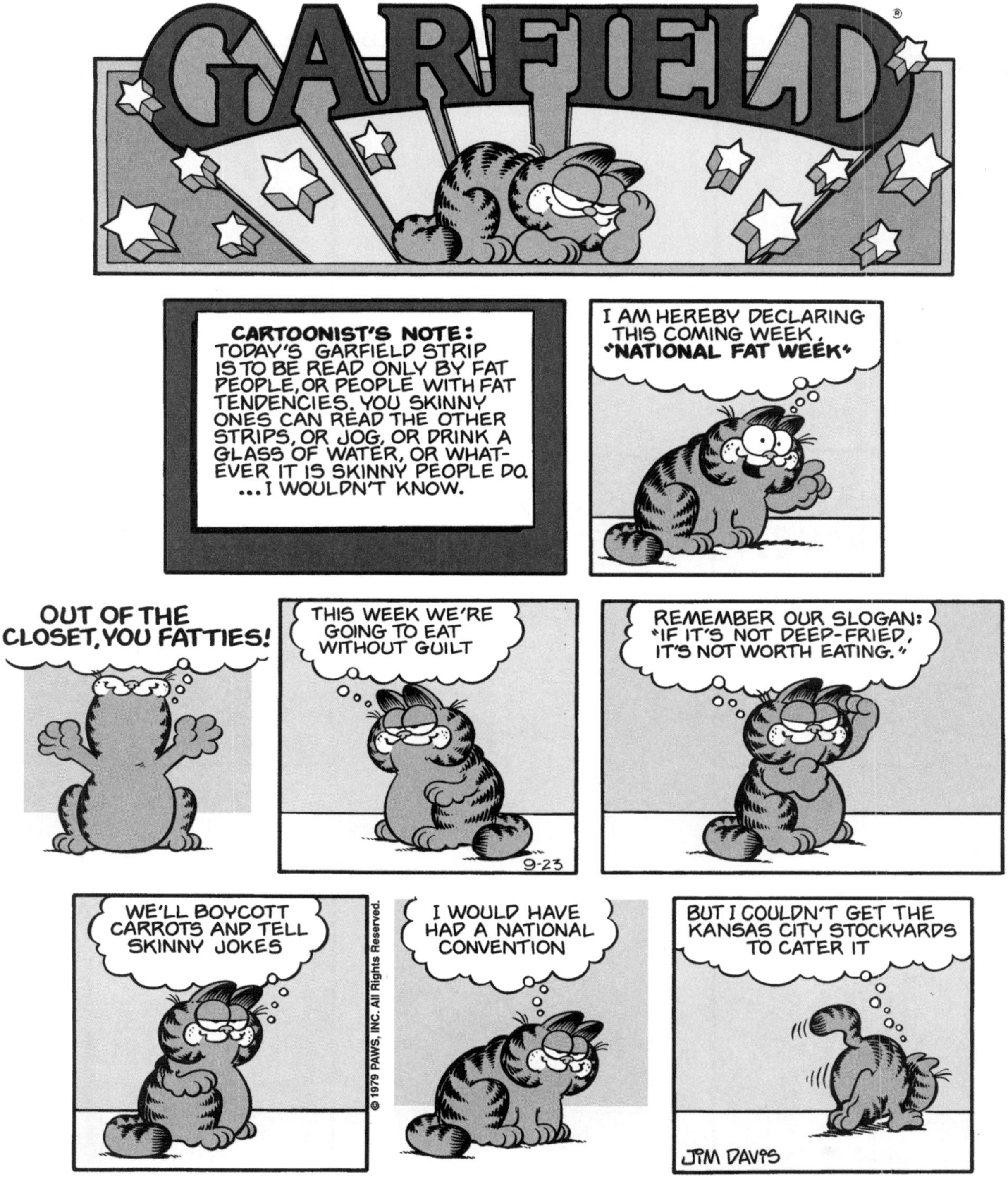
GARFIELD
CARTOONIST'S NOTE: TODAY'S GARFIELD STRIP IS TO BE READ ONLY BY FAT PEOPLE, OR PEOPLE WITH FAT TENDENCIES. YOU SKINNY ONES CAN READ THE OTHER STRIPS, OR JOG, OR DRINK A GLASS OF WATER, OR WHATEVER IT IS SKINNY PEOPLE DO. ...I WOULDN'T KNOW.
I AM HEREBY DECLARING THIS COMING WEEK, "NATIONAL FAT WEEK"
OUT OF THE CLOSET, YOU FATTIES!
THIS WEEK WE'RE GOING TO EAT WITHOUT GUILT
9-23
REMEMBER OUR SLOGAN: "IF IT'S NOT DEEP-FRIED, IT'S NOT WORTH EATING."
WE'LL BOYCOTT CARROTS AND TELL SKINNY JOKES
© 1979 PAWS, INC. All Rights Reserved.
I WOULD HAVE HAD A NATIONAL CONVENTION
BUT I COULDN'T GET THE KANSAS CITY STOCKYARDS TO CATER IT
JIM DAVIS

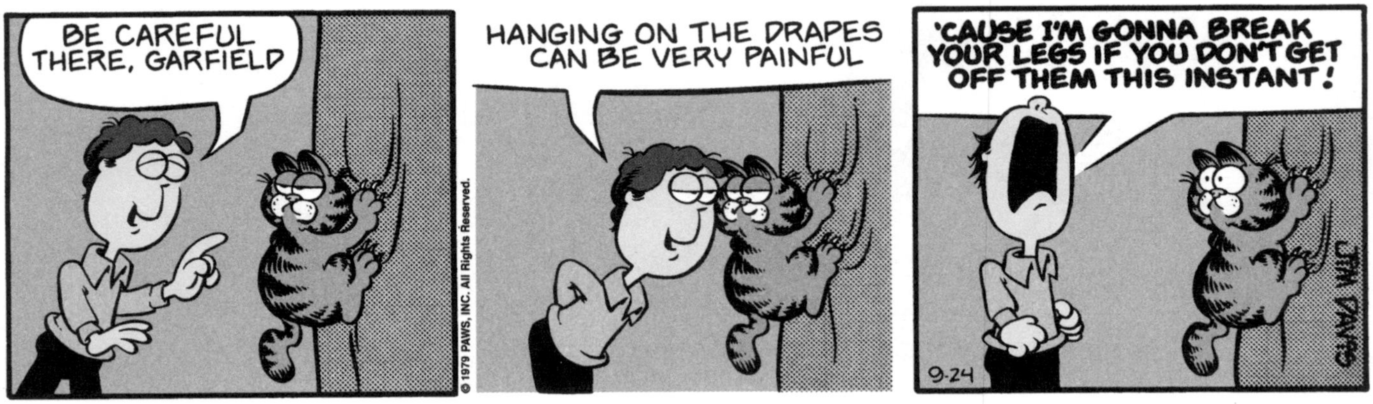
BE CAREFUL THERE, GARFIELD
HANGING ON THE DRAPES CAN BE VERY PAINFUL
© 1979 PAWS, INC. All Rights Reserved.
'CAUSE I'M GONNA BREAK YOUR LEGS IF YOU DON'T GET OFF THEM THIS INSTANT!
JIM DAVIS
9-24

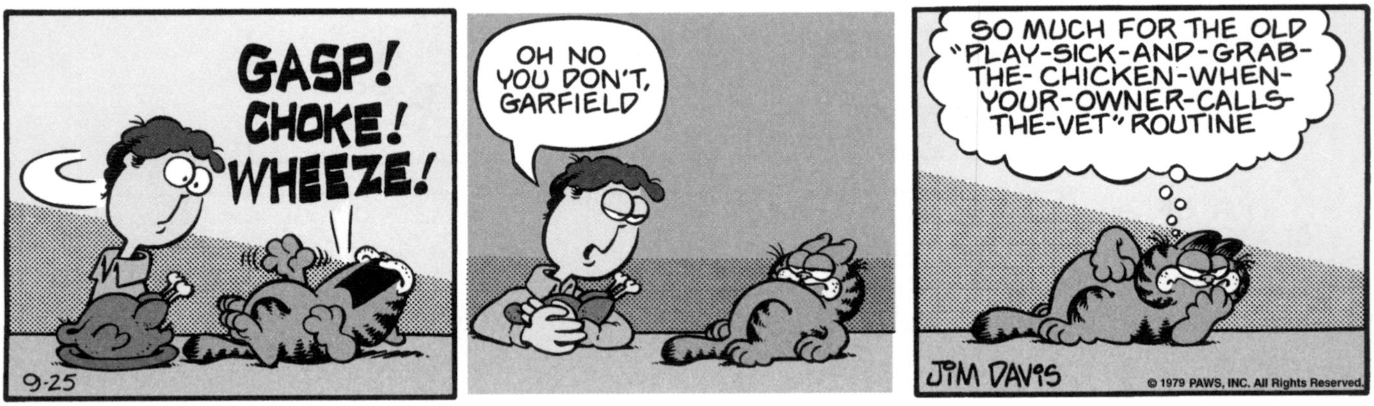
GASP! CHOKE! WHEEZE!
9-25
OH NO YOU DON'T, GARFIELD
SO MUCH FOR THE OLD "PLAY-SICK-AND-GRAB-THE-CHICKEN-WHEN-YOUR-OWNER-CALLS-THE-VET" ROUTINE
JIM DAVIS
© 1979 PAWS, INC. All Rights Reserved.

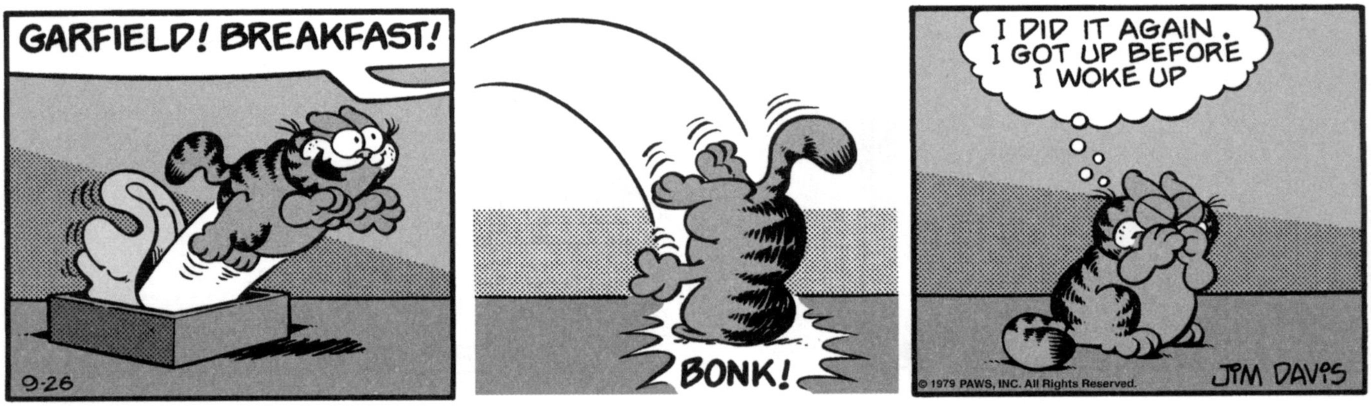
GARFIELD! BREAKFAST!
9-26
BONK!
I DID IT AGAIN. I GOT UP BEFORE I WOKE UP
© 1979 PAWS, INC. All Rights Reserved.
JIM DAVIS

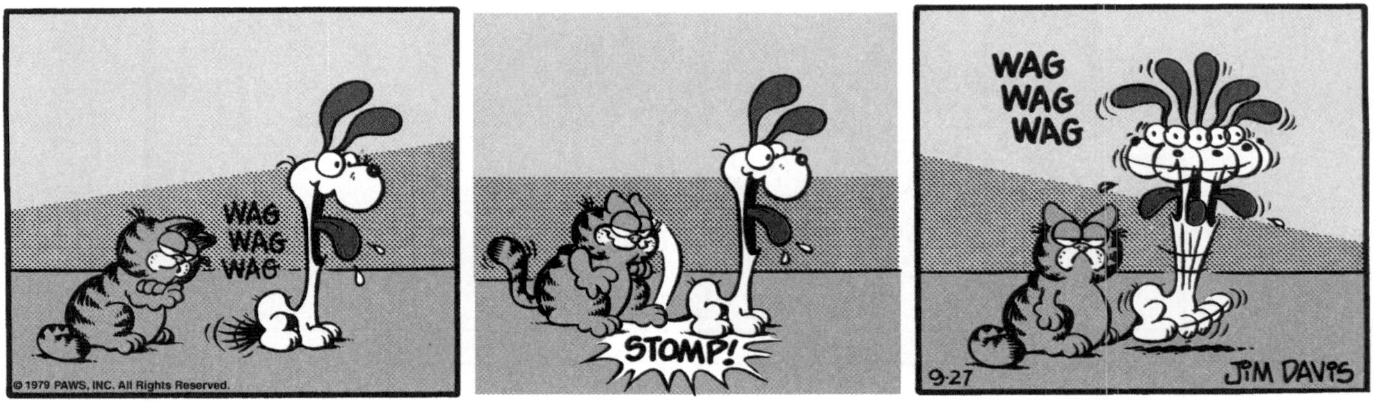

WAG
WAG
WAG
STOMP!
WAG
WAG
WAG
© 1979 PAWS, INC. All Rights Reserved.
9-27
JIM DAVIS

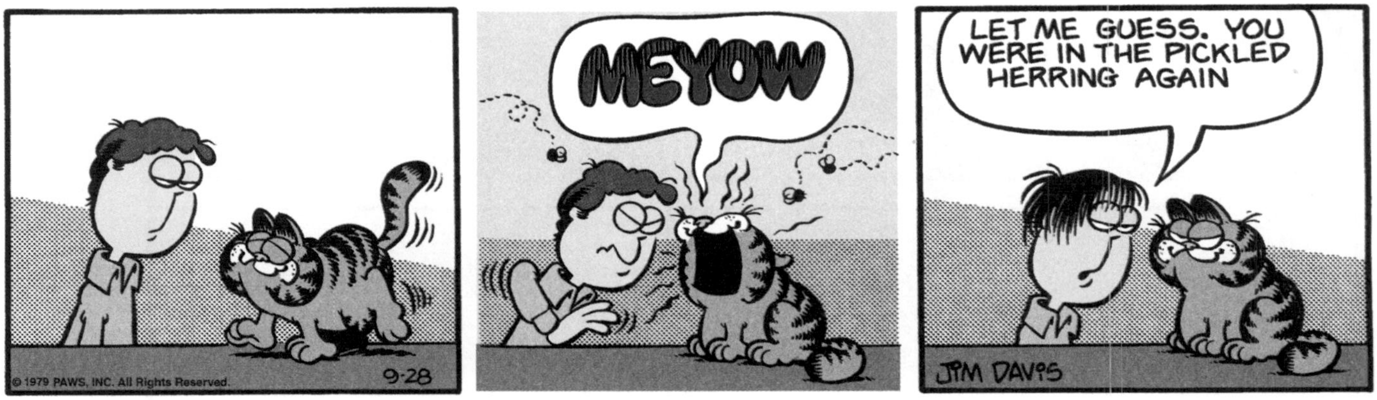

MEYOW
LET ME GUESS. YOU WERE IN THE PICKLED HERRING AGAIN
© 1979 PAWS, INC. All Rights Reserved.
9-28
JIM DAVIS

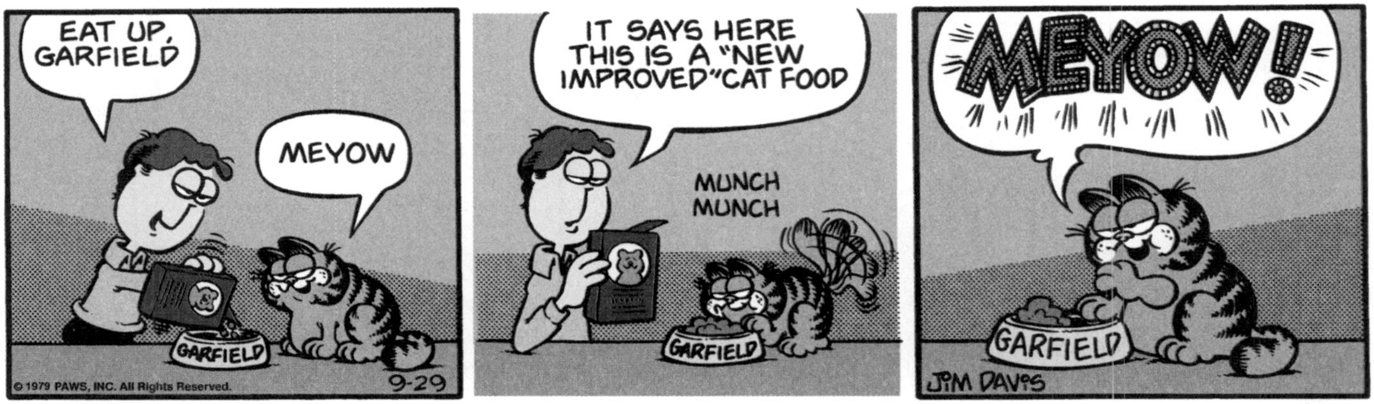

EAT UP, GARFIELD
MEYOW
GARFIELD
IT SAYS HERE THIS IS A "NEW IMPROVED" CAT FOOD
MUNCH
MUNCH
GARFIELD
MEYOW!
GARFIELD
© 1979 PAWS, INC. All Rights Reserved.
9-29
JIM DAVIS

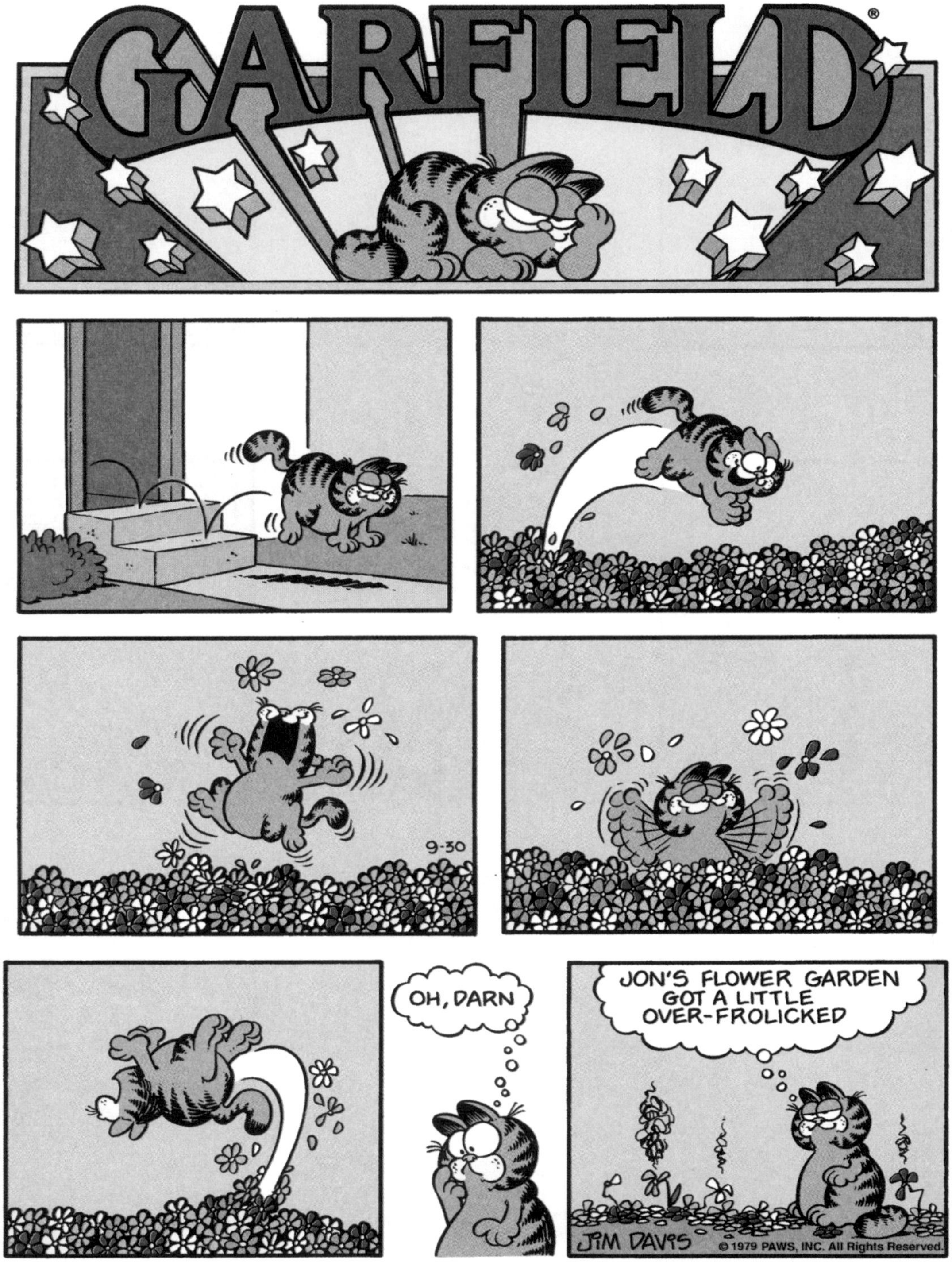
GARFIELD®
9-30
OH, DARN
JON'S FLOWER GARDEN GOT A LITTLE OVER-FROLICKED
JIM DAVIS
© 1979 PAWS, INC. All Rights Reserved.

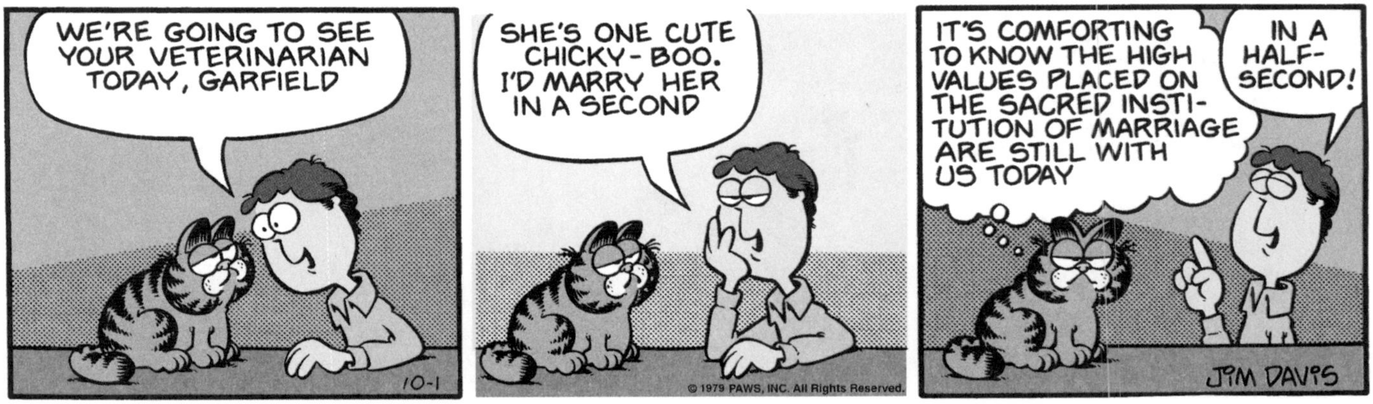
WE'RE GOING TO SEE YOUR VETERINARIAN TODAY, GARFIELD
10-1
SHE'S ONE CUTE CHICKY-BOO. I'D MARRY HER IN A SECOND
© 1979 PAWS, INC. All Rights Reserved.
IT'S COMFORTING TO KNOW THE HIGH VALUES PLACED ON THE SACRED INSTITUTION OF MARRIAGE ARE STILL WITH US TODAY
IN A HALF-SECOND!
JIM DAVIS

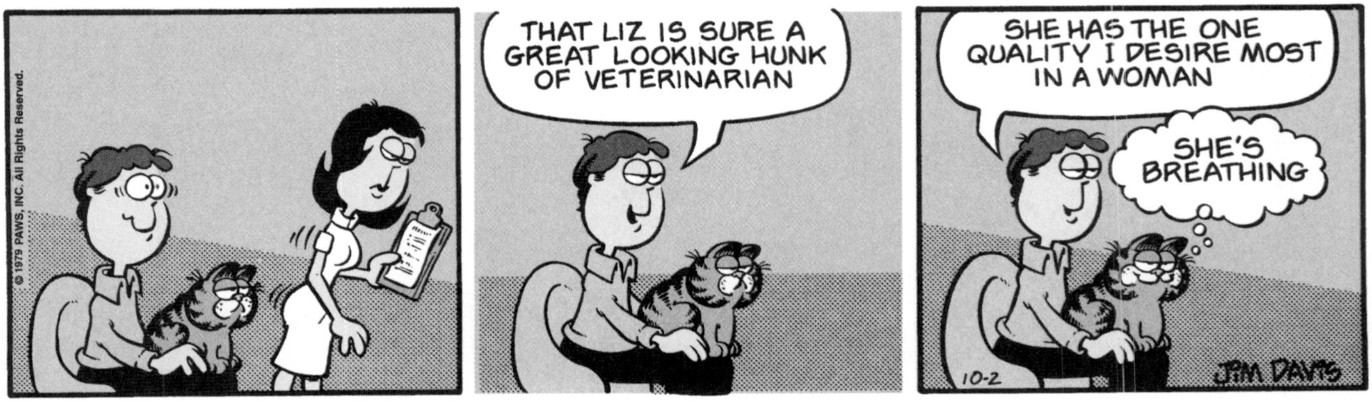
© 1979 PAWS, INC. All Rights Reserved.
THAT LIZ IS SURE A GREAT LOOKING HUNK OF VETERINARIAN
SHE HAS THE ONE QUALITY I DESIRE MOST IN A WOMAN
SHE'S BREATHING
10-2
JIM DAVIS

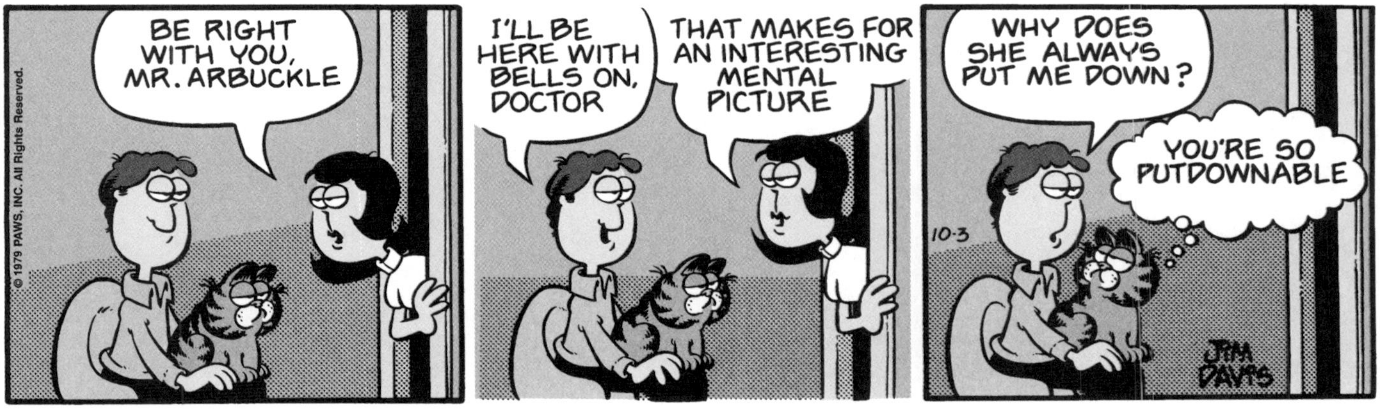
© 1979 PAWS, INC. All Rights Reserved.
BE RIGHT WITH YOU, MR. ARBUCKLE
I'LL BE HERE WITH BELLS ON, DOCTOR
THAT MAKES FOR AN INTERESTING MENTAL PICTURE
WHY DOES SHE ALWAYS PUT ME DOWN?
YOU'RE SO PUTDOWNABLE
10-3
JIM DAVIS

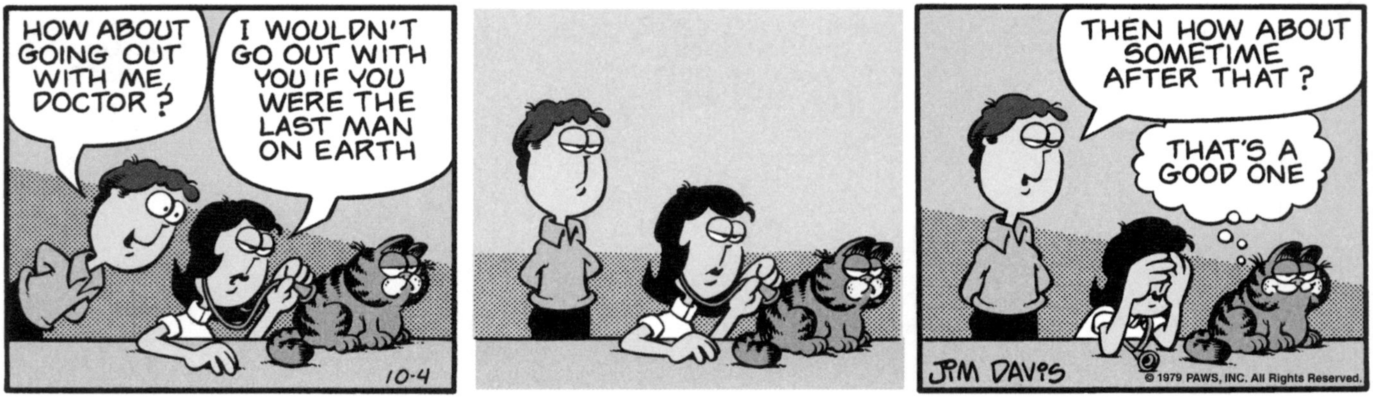
HOW ABOUT GOING OUT WITH ME, DOCTOR ?
I WOULDN'T GO OUT WITH YOU IF YOU WERE THE LAST MAN ON EARTH
10-4
THEN HOW ABOUT SOMETIME AFTER THAT ?
THAT'S A GOOD ONE
JIM DAVIS
© 1979 PAWS, INC. All Rights Reserved.

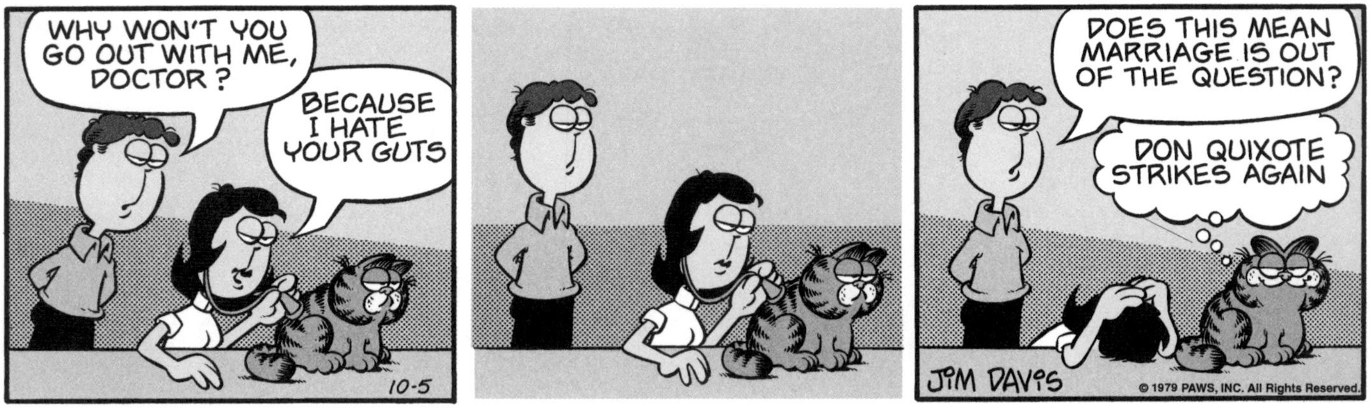
WHY WON'T YOU GO OUT WITH ME, DOCTOR ?
BECAUSE I HATE YOUR GUTS
10-5
DOES THIS MEAN MARRIAGE IS OUT OF THE QUESTION?
DON QUIXOTE STRIKES AGAIN
JIM DAVIS
© 1979 PAWS, INC. All Rights Reserved.

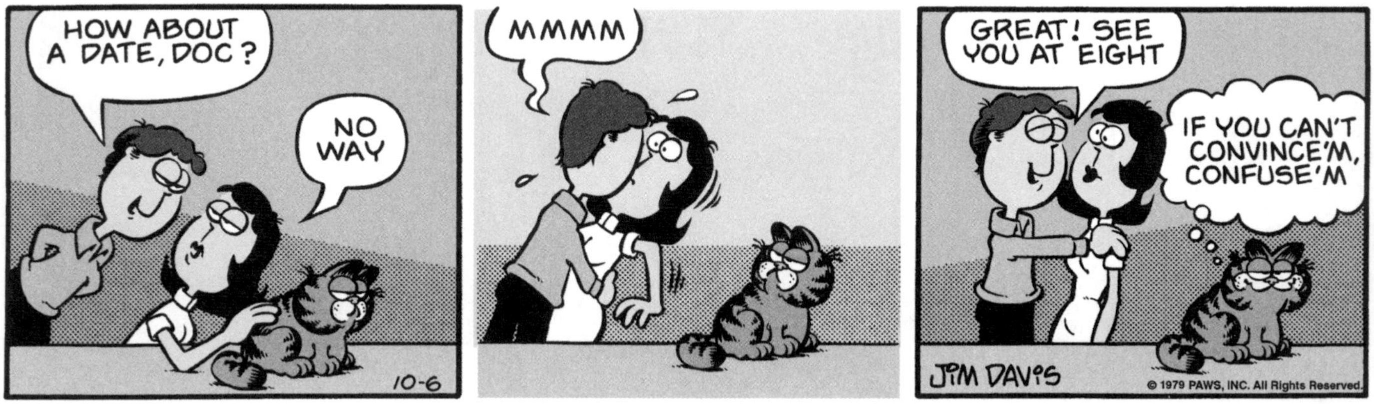
HOW ABOUT A DATE, DOC ?
NO WAY
10-6
MMMM
GREAT! SEE YOU AT EIGHT
IF YOU CAN'T CONVINCE'M, CONFUSE'M
JIM DAVIS
© 1979 PAWS, INC. All Rights Reserved.

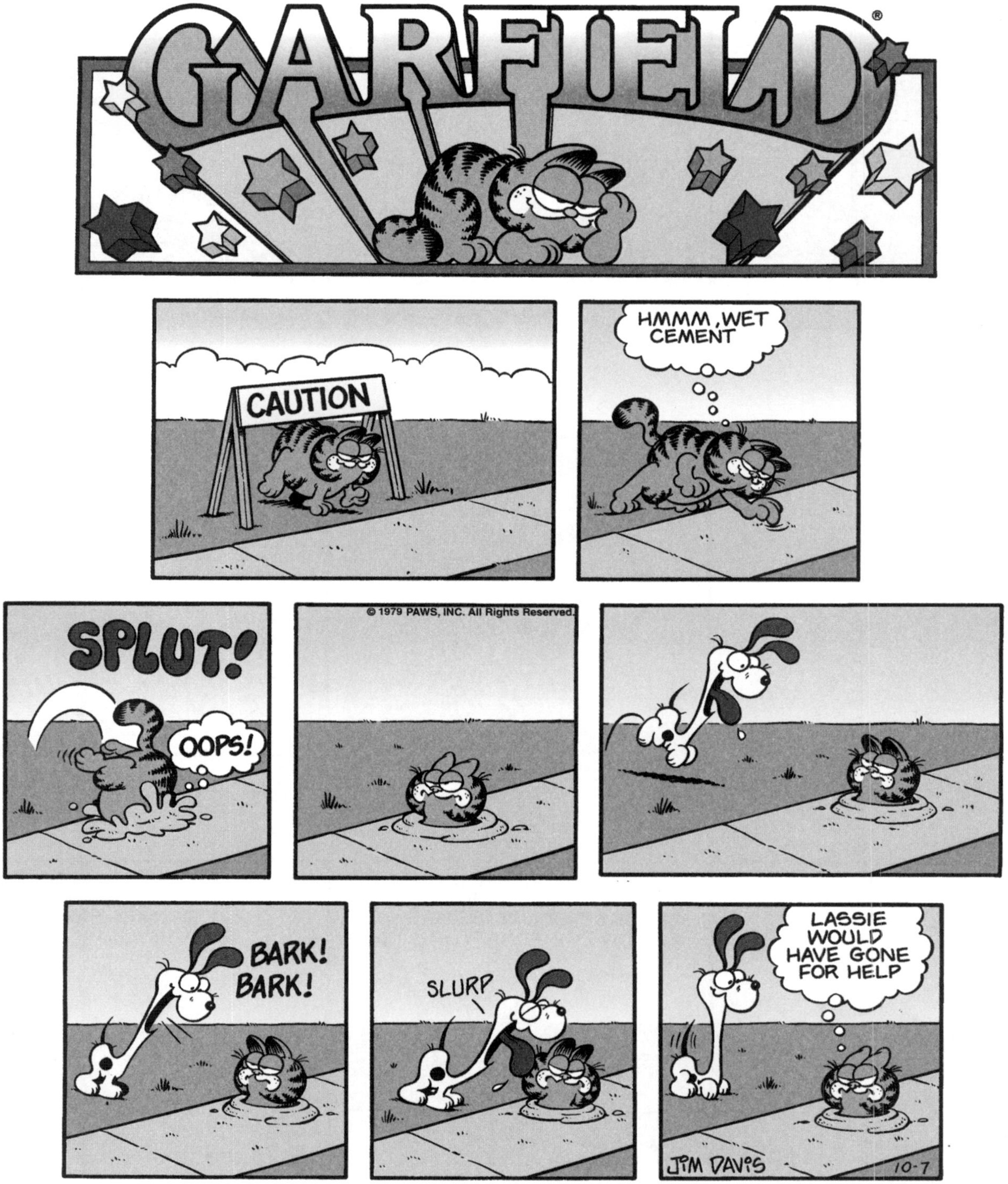
GARFIELD®
CAUTION
HMMM, WET CEMENT
SPLUT!
OOPS!
© 1979 PAWS, INC. All Rights Reserved.
BARK! BARK!
SLURP
LASSIE WOULD HAVE GONE FOR HELP
JIM DAVIS
10-7

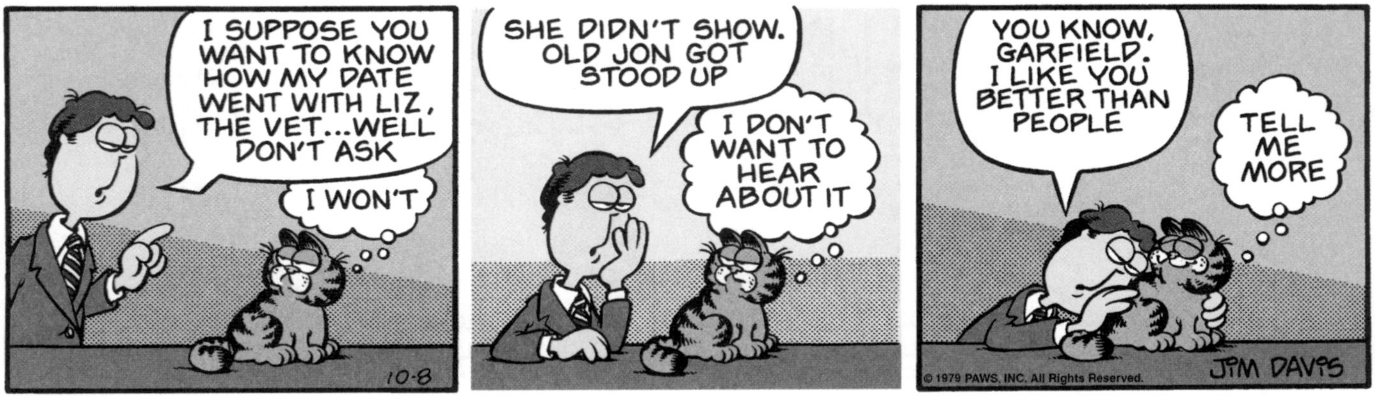
I SUPPOSE YOU WANT TO KNOW HOW MY DATE WENT WITH LIZ, THE VET...WELL DON'T ASK
I WON'T
10-8
SHE DIDN'T SHOW. OLD JON GOT STOOD UP
I DON'T WANT TO HEAR ABOUT IT
YOU KNOW, GARFIELD. I LIKE YOU BETTER THAN PEOPLE
TELL ME MORE
© 1979 PAWS, INC. All Rights Reserved.
JIM DAVIS

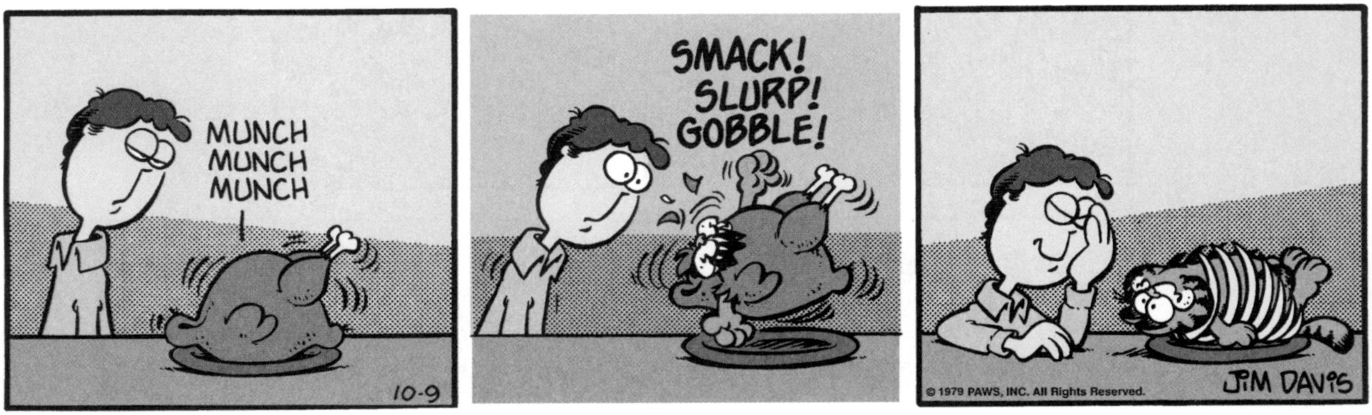
MUNCH MUNCH MUNCH
10-9
SMACK! SLURP! GOBBLE!
© 1979 PAWS, INC. All Rights Reserved.
JIM DAVIS

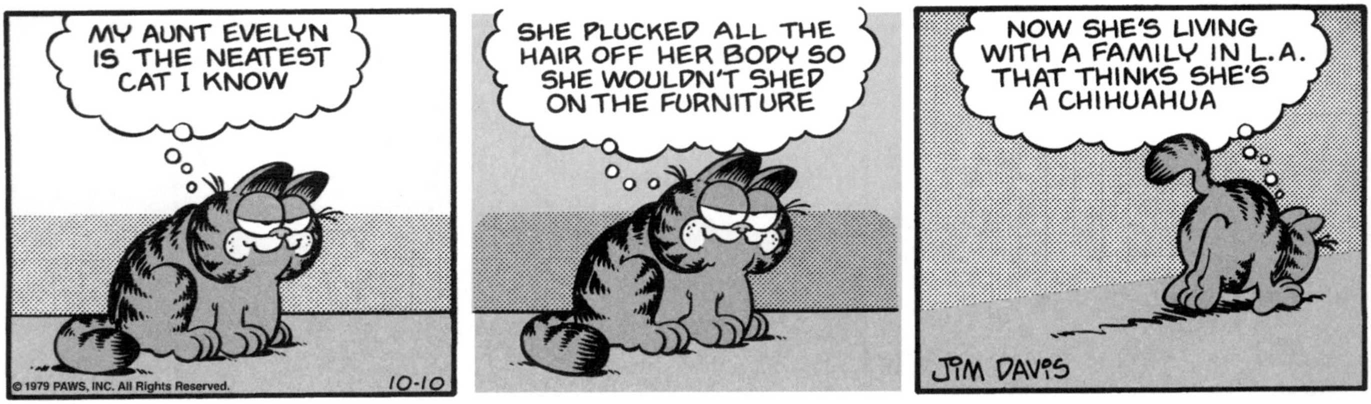
MY AUNT EVELYN IS THE NEATEST CAT I KNOW
© 1979 PAWS, INC. All Rights Reserved.
10-10
SHE PLUCKED ALL THE HAIR OFF HER BODY SO SHE WOULDN'T SHED ON THE FURNITURE
NOW SHE'S LIVING WITH A FAMILY IN L.A. THAT THINKS SHE'S A CHIHUAHUA
JIM DAVIS

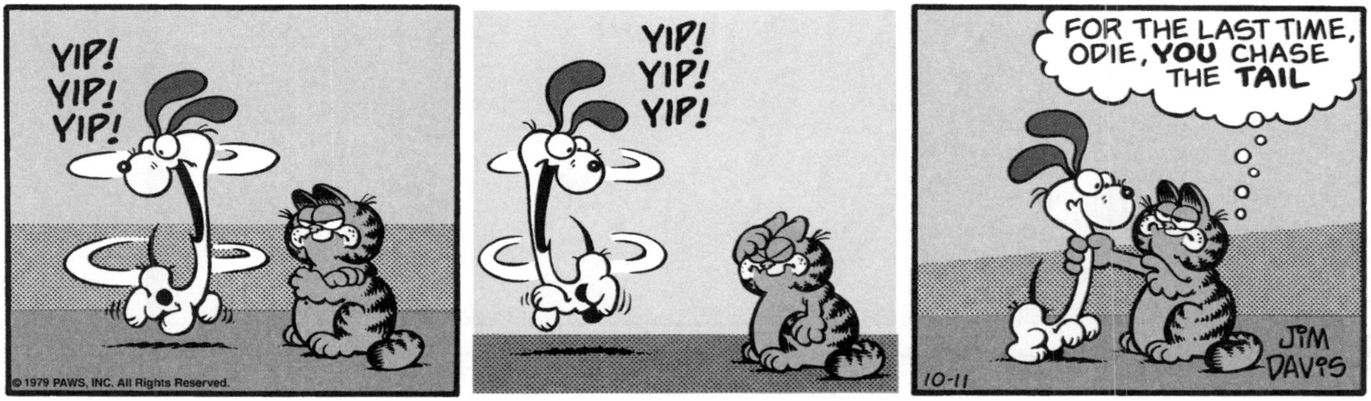
YIP! YIP! YIP!
© 1979 PAWS, INC. All Rights Reserved.
YIP! YIP! YIP!
FOR THE LAST TIME, ODIE, **YOU** CHASE THE **TAIL**
10-11
JIM DAVIS

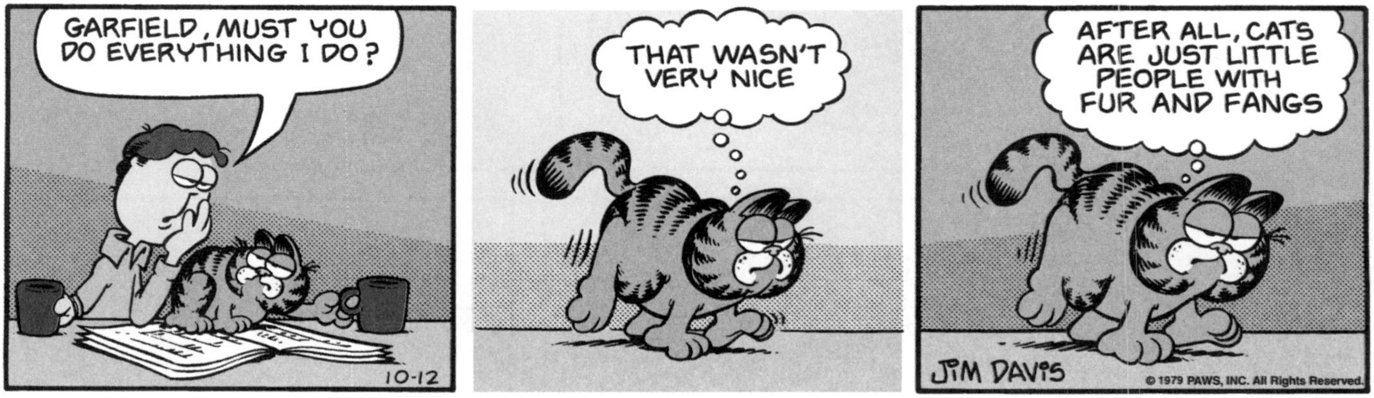
GARFIELD, MUST YOU DO EVERYTHING I DO?
10-12
THAT WASN'T VERY NICE
AFTER ALL, CATS ARE JUST LITTLE PEOPLE WITH FUR AND FANGS
JIM DAVIS
© 1979 PAWS, INC. All Rights Reserved.

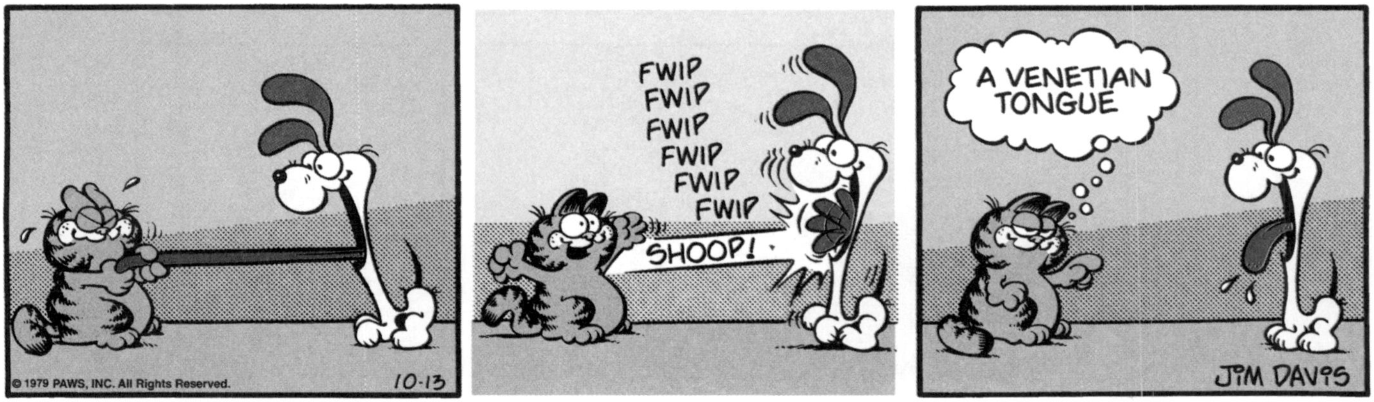
© 1979 PAWS, INC. All Rights Reserved.
10-13
FWIP FWIP FWIP FWIP FWIP FWIP
SHOOP!
A VENETIAN TONGUE
JIM DAVIS

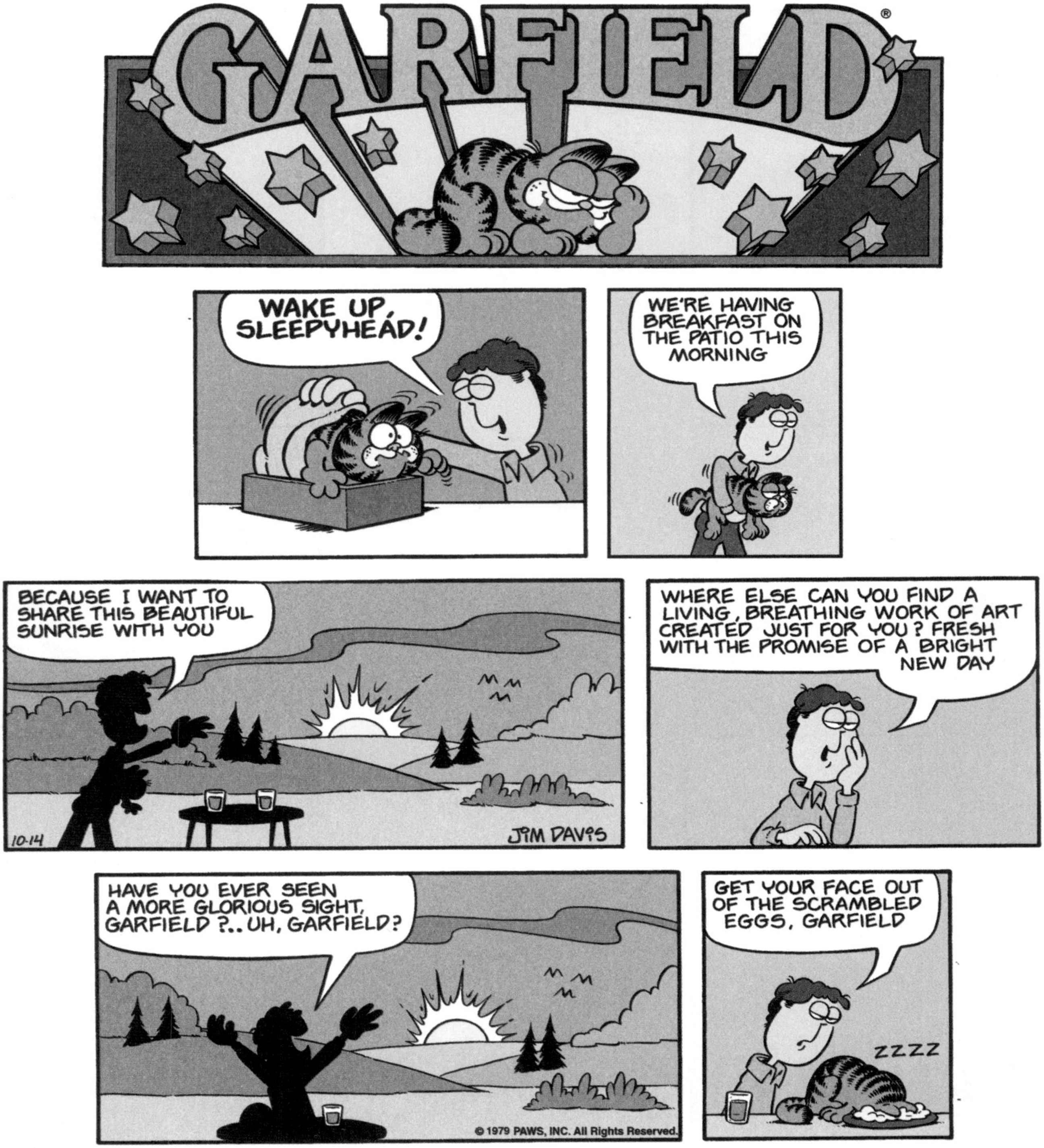
GARFIELD
WAKE UP, SLEEPYHEAD!
WE'RE HAVING BREAKFAST ON THE PATIO THIS MORNING
BECAUSE I WANT TO SHARE THIS BEAUTIFUL SUNRISE WITH YOU
10-14
JIM DAVIS
WHERE ELSE CAN YOU FIND A LIVING, BREATHING WORK OF ART CREATED JUST FOR YOU? FRESH WITH THE PROMISE OF A BRIGHT NEW DAY
HAVE YOU EVER SEEN A MORE GLORIOUS SIGHT, GARFIELD?.. UH, GARFIELD?
© 1979 PAWS, INC. All Rights Reserved.
GET YOUR FACE OUT OF THE SCRAMBLED EGGS, GARFIELD
ZZZZ

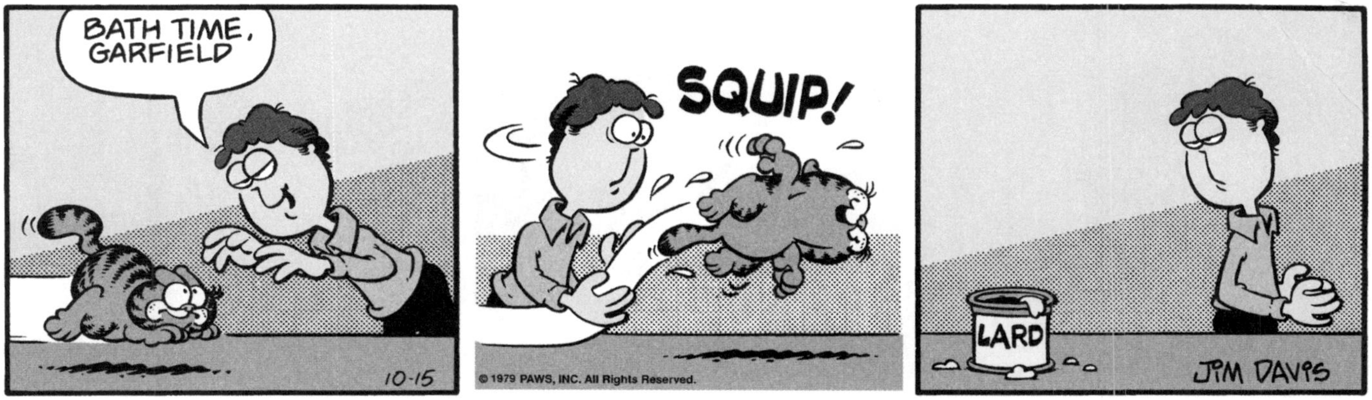
BATH TIME, GARFIELD
10-15
SQUIP!
© 1979 PAWS, INC. All Rights Reserved.
LARD
JIM DAVIS

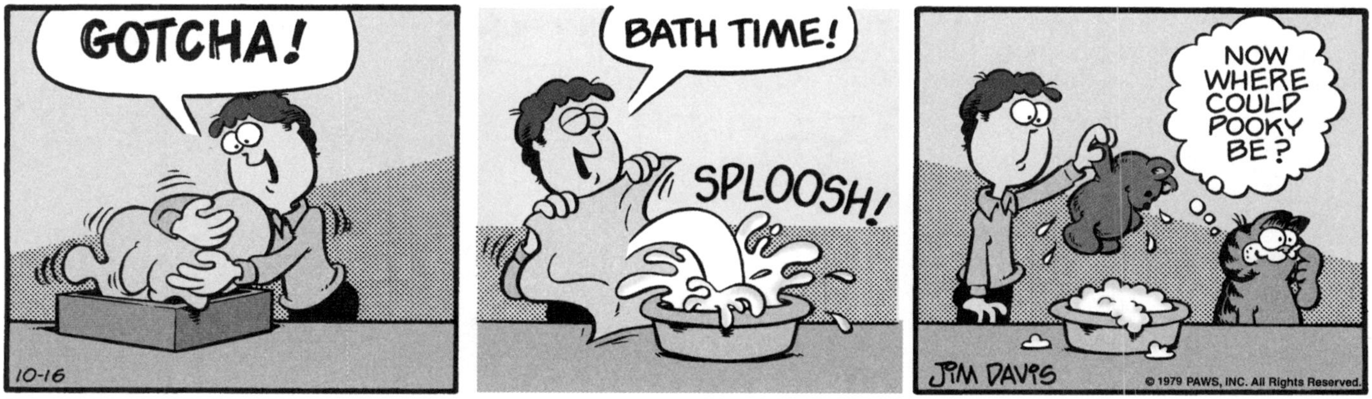
GOTCHA!
10-16
BATH TIME!
SPLOOSH!
NOW WHERE COULD POOKY BE?
JIM DAVIS
© 1979 PAWS, INC. All Rights Reserved.

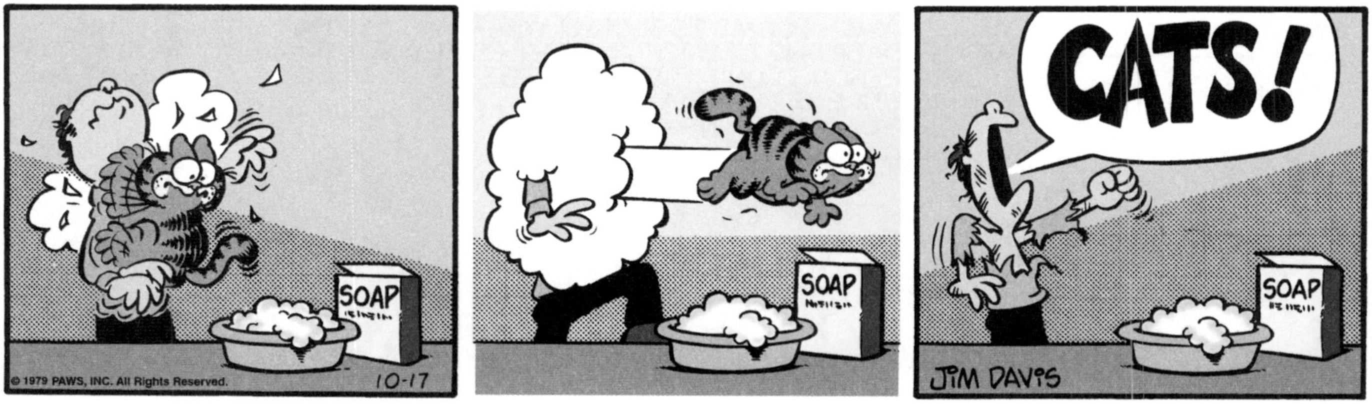
SOAP
© 1979 PAWS, INC. All Rights Reserved.
10-17
SOAP
CATS!
SOAP
JIM DAVIS

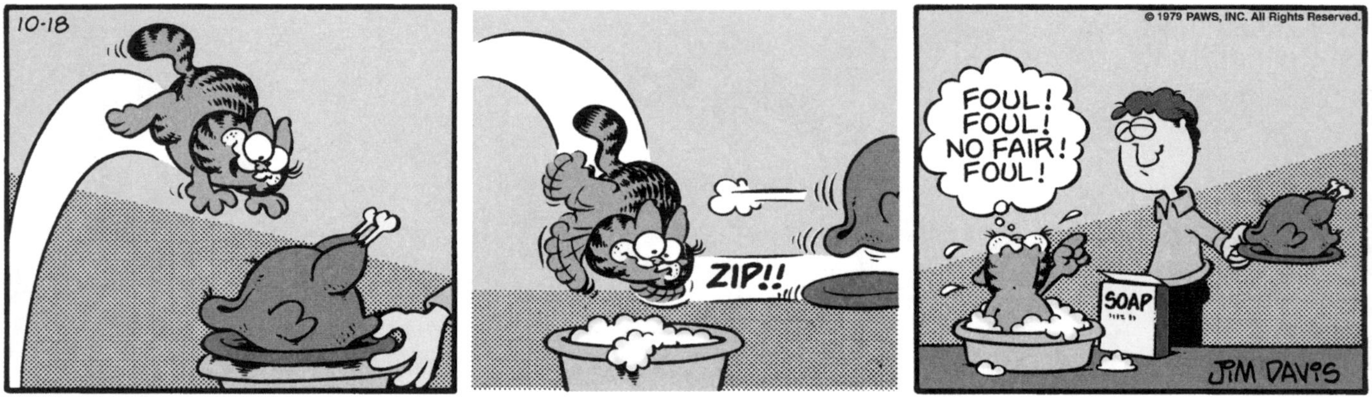
10-18
© 1979 PAWS, INC. All Rights Reserved.
ZIP!!
FOUL! FOUL! NO FAIR! FOUL!
SOAP
JIM DAVIS

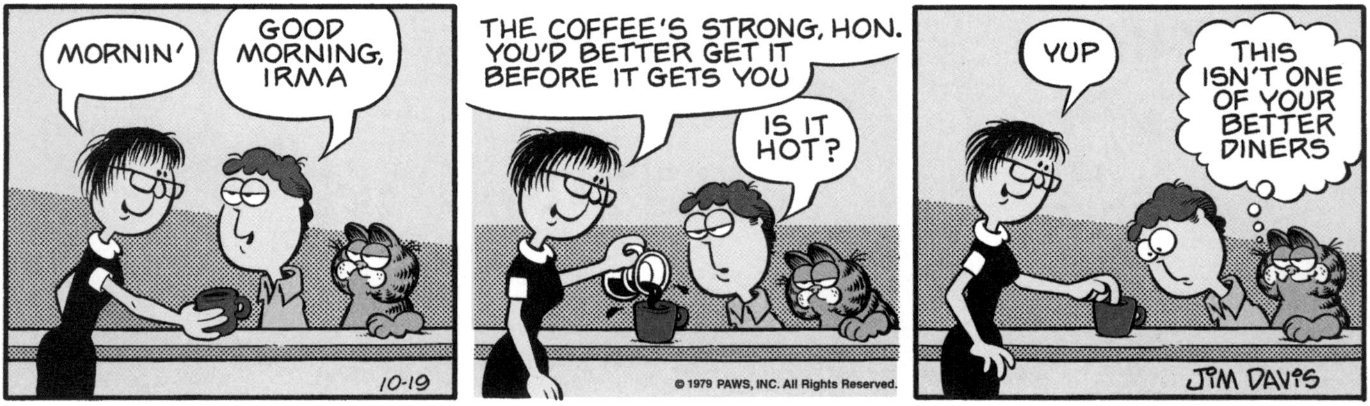
MORNIN'
GOOD MORNING, IRMA
10-19
THE COFFEE'S STRONG, HON. YOU'D BETTER GET IT BEFORE IT GETS YOU
IS IT HOT?
© 1979 PAWS, INC. All Rights Reserved.
YUP
THIS ISN'T ONE OF YOUR BETTER DINERS
JIM DAVIS

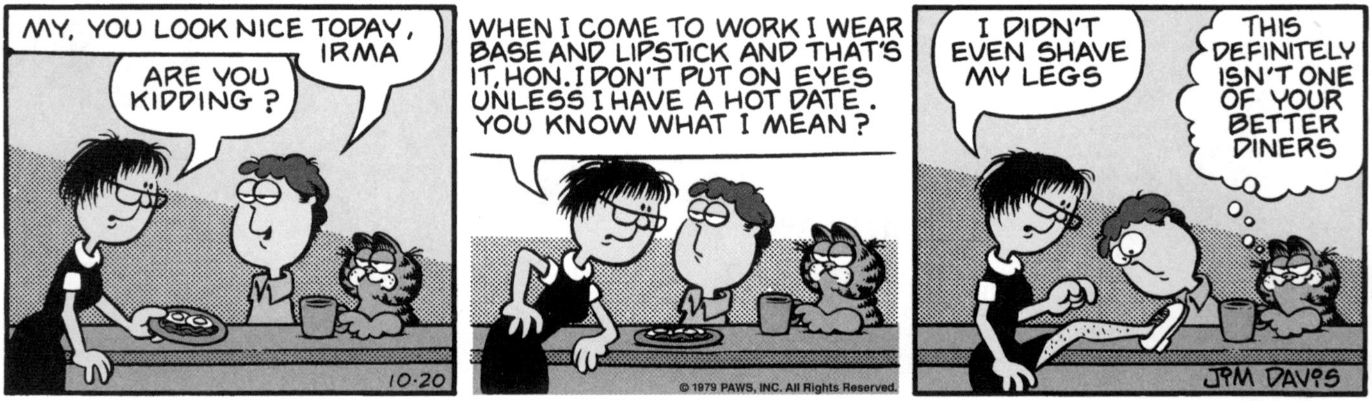
MY, YOU LOOK NICE TODAY, IRMA
ARE YOU KIDDING?
10-20
WHEN I COME TO WORK I WEAR BASE AND LIPSTICK AND THAT'S IT, HON. I DON'T PUT ON EYES UNLESS I HAVE A HOT DATE. YOU KNOW WHAT I MEAN?
© 1979 PAWS, INC. All Rights Reserved.
I DIDN'T EVEN SHAVE MY LEGS
THIS DEFINITELY ISN'T ONE OF YOUR BETTER DINERS
JIM DAVIS

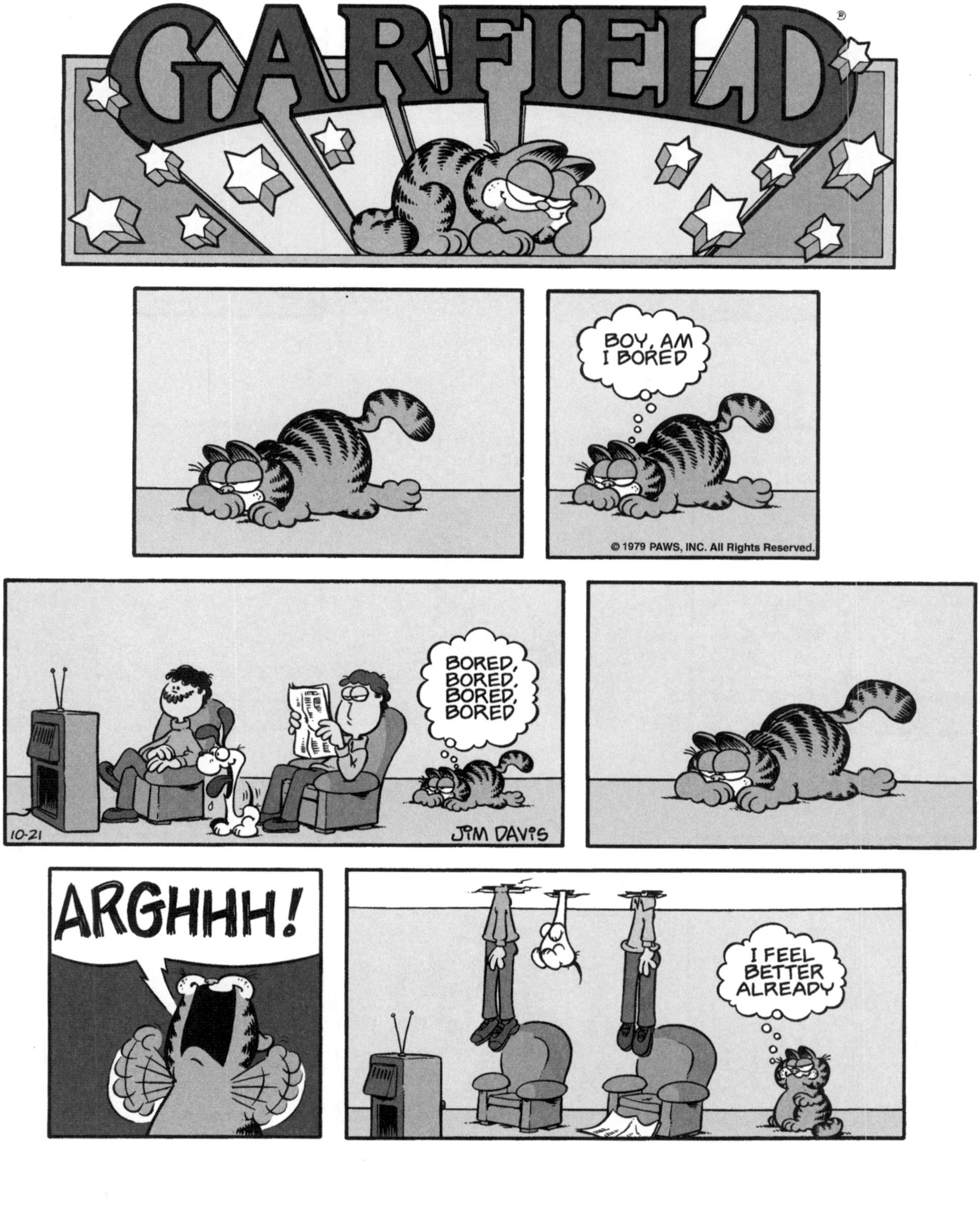
GARFIELD®
BOY, AM I BORED
© 1979 PAWS, INC. All Rights Reserved.
BORED, BORED, BORED, BORED
10-21
JIM DAVIS
ARGHHH!
I FEEL BETTER ALREADY

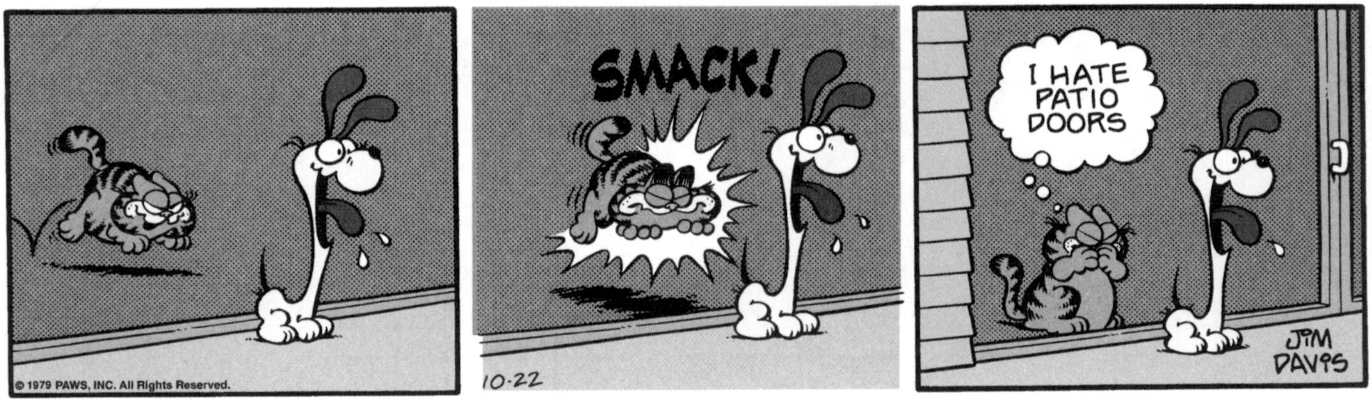
© 1979 PAWS, INC. All Rights Reserved.
SMACK!
10-22
I HATE PATIO DOORS
JIM DAVIS

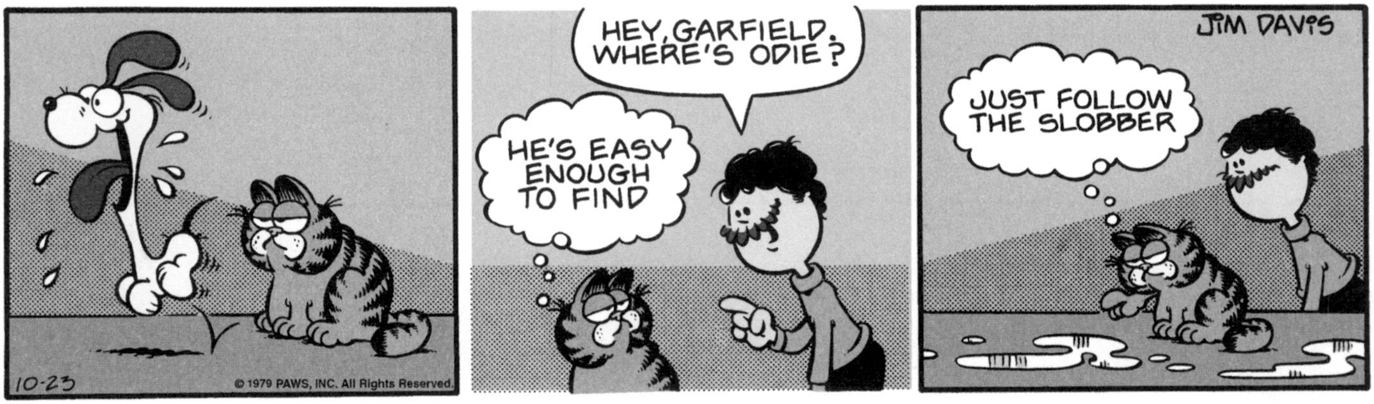
10-23
© 1979 PAWS, INC. All Rights Reserved.
HEY, GARFIELD, WHERE'S ODIE?
HE'S EASY ENOUGH TO FIND
JIM DAVIS
JUST FOLLOW THE SLOBBER

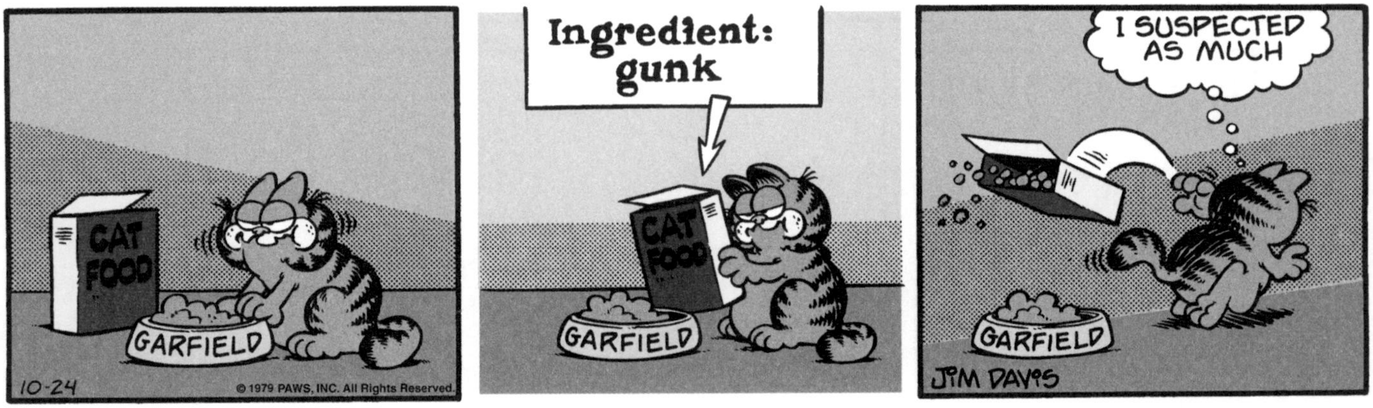
CAT FOOD
GARFIELD
10-24
© 1979 PAWS, INC. All Rights Reserved.
Ingredient: gunk
I SUSPECTED AS MUCH
JIM DAVIS

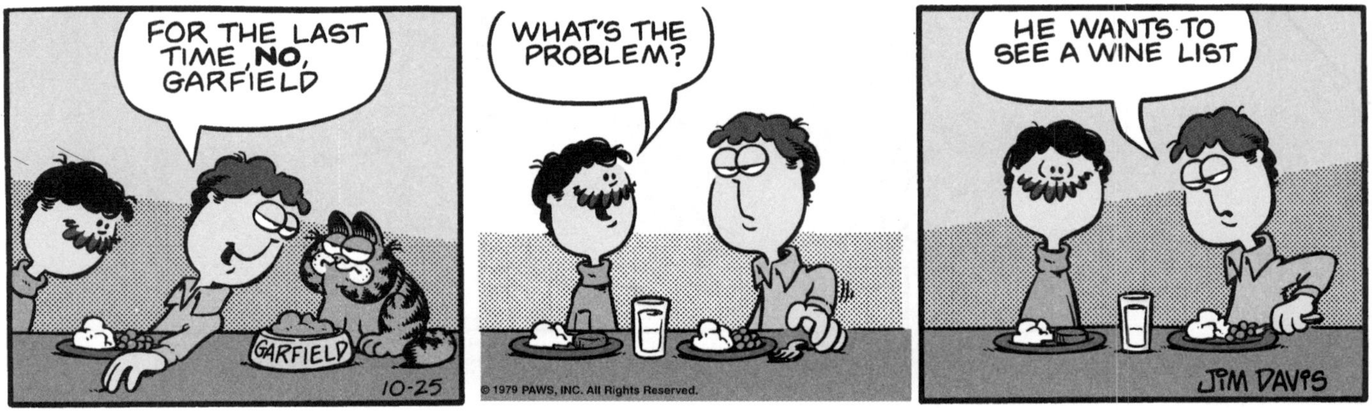
FOR THE LAST TIME, NO, GARFIELD
10-25
WHAT'S THE PROBLEM?
© 1979 PAWS, INC. All Rights Reserved.
HE WANTS TO SEE A WINE LIST
JIM DAVIS

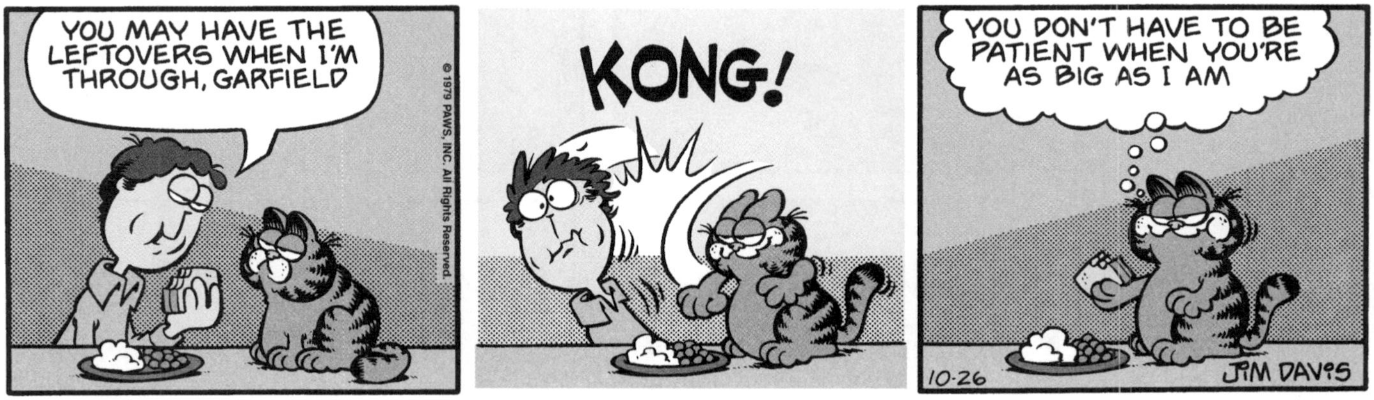
YOU MAY HAVE THE LEFTOVERS WHEN I'M THROUGH, GARFIELD
© 1979 PAWS, INC. All Rights Reserved.
KONG!
YOU DON'T HAVE TO BE PATIENT WHEN YOU'RE AS BIG AS I AM
10-26
JIM DAVIS

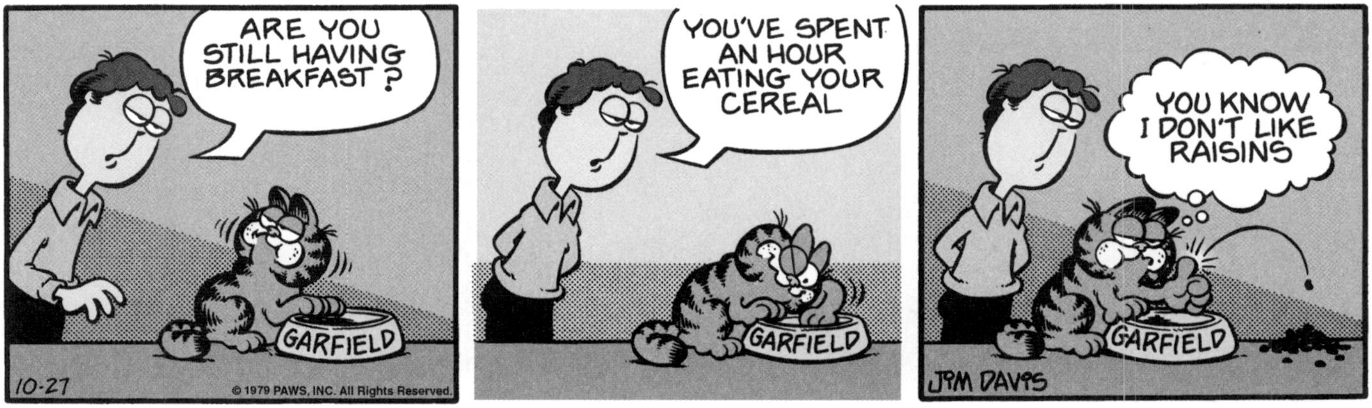
ARE YOU STILL HAVING BREAKFAST ?
GARFIELD
10-27
© 1979 PAWS, INC. All Rights Reserved.
YOU'VE SPENT AN HOUR EATING YOUR CEREAL
GARFIELD
YOU KNOW I DON'T LIKE RAISINS
GARFIELD
JIM DAVIS

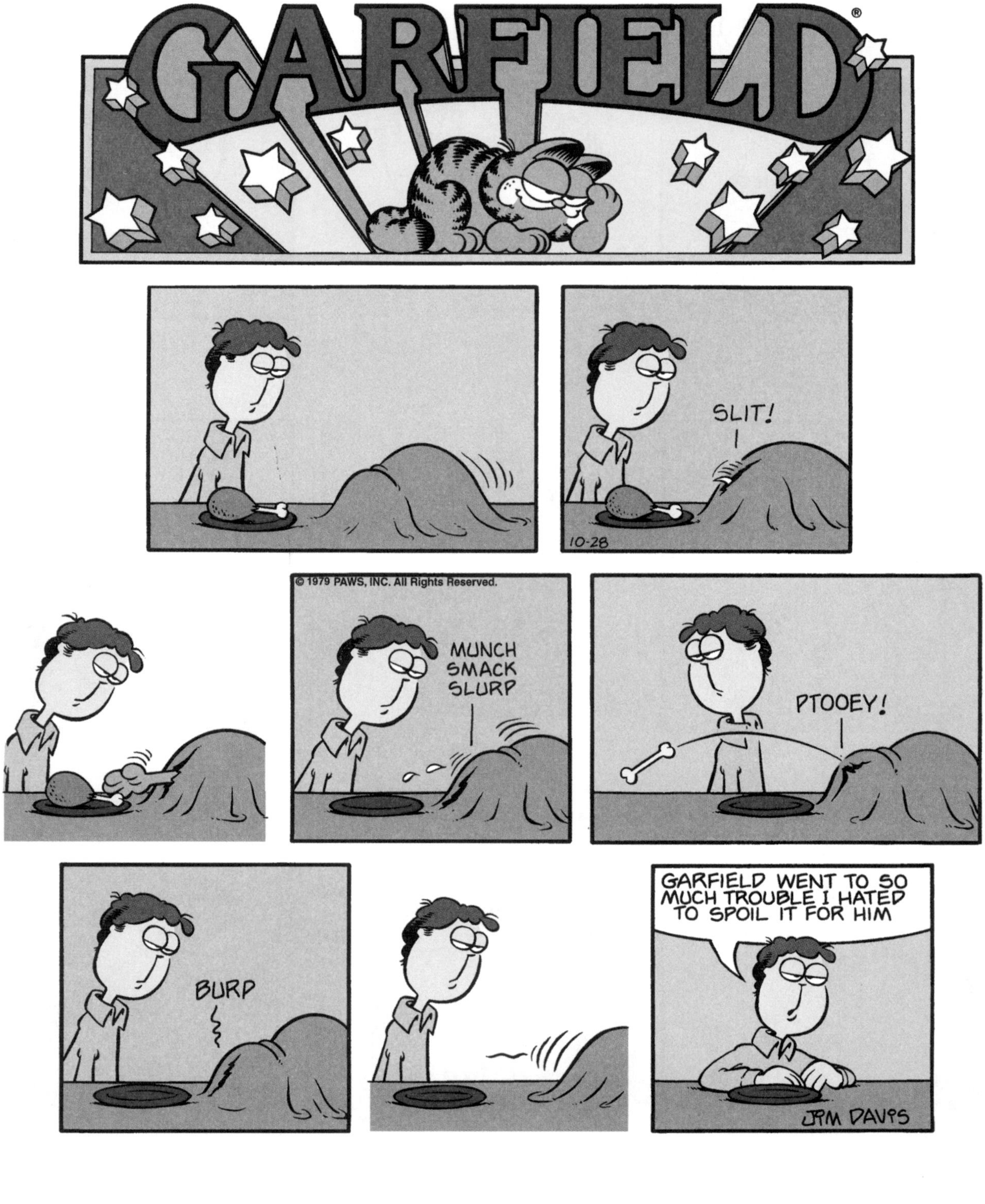
GARFIELD®
SLIT!
10-28
© 1979 PAWS, INC. All Rights Reserved.
MUNCH SMACK SLURP
PTOOEY!
BURP
GARFIELD WENT TO SO MUCH TROUBLE I HATED TO SPOIL IT FOR HIM
JIM DAVIS

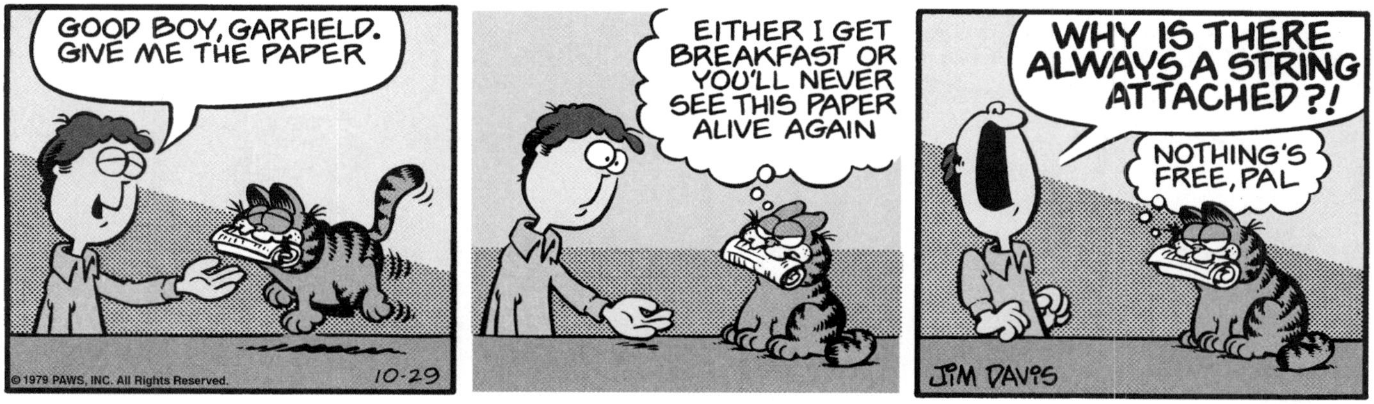
GOOD BOY, GARFIELD. GIVE ME THE PAPER
© 1979 PAWS, INC. All Rights Reserved.
10-29
EITHER I GET BREAKFAST OR YOU'LL NEVER SEE THIS PAPER ALIVE AGAIN
WHY IS THERE ALWAYS A STRING ATTACHED?!
NOTHING'S FREE, PAL
JIM DAVIS

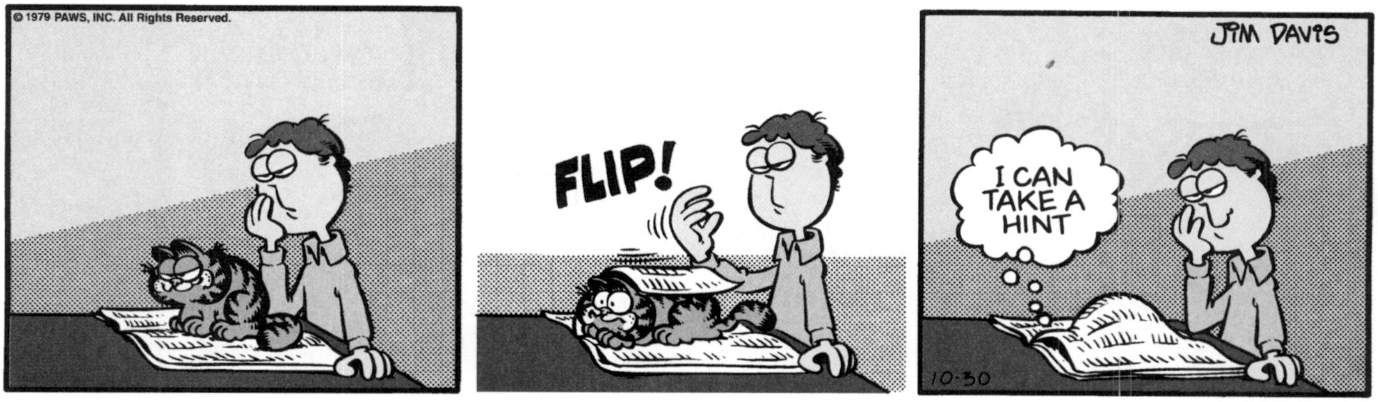
© 1979 PAWS, INC. All Rights Reserved.
FLIP!
JIM DAVIS
I CAN TAKE A HINT
10-30

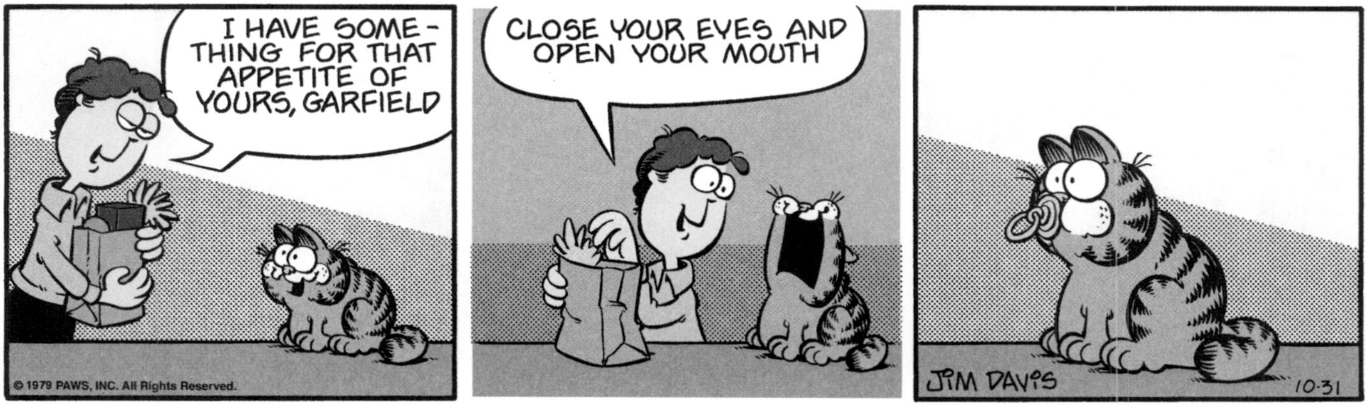
I HAVE SOME-THING FOR THAT APPETITE OF YOURS, GARFIELD
© 1979 PAWS, INC. All Rights Reserved.
CLOSE YOUR EYES AND OPEN YOUR MOUTH
JIM DAVIS
10-31

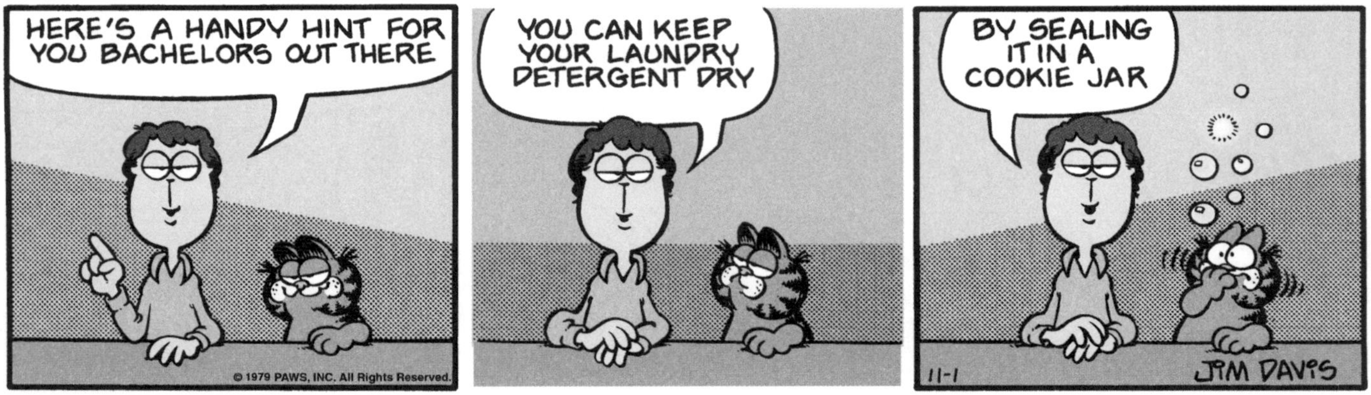
HERE'S A HANDY HINT FOR YOU BACHELORS OUT THERE
© 1979 PAWS, INC. All Rights Reserved.
YOU CAN KEEP YOUR LAUNDRY DETERGENT DRY
BY SEALING IT IN A COOKIE JAR
11-1
JIM DAVIS

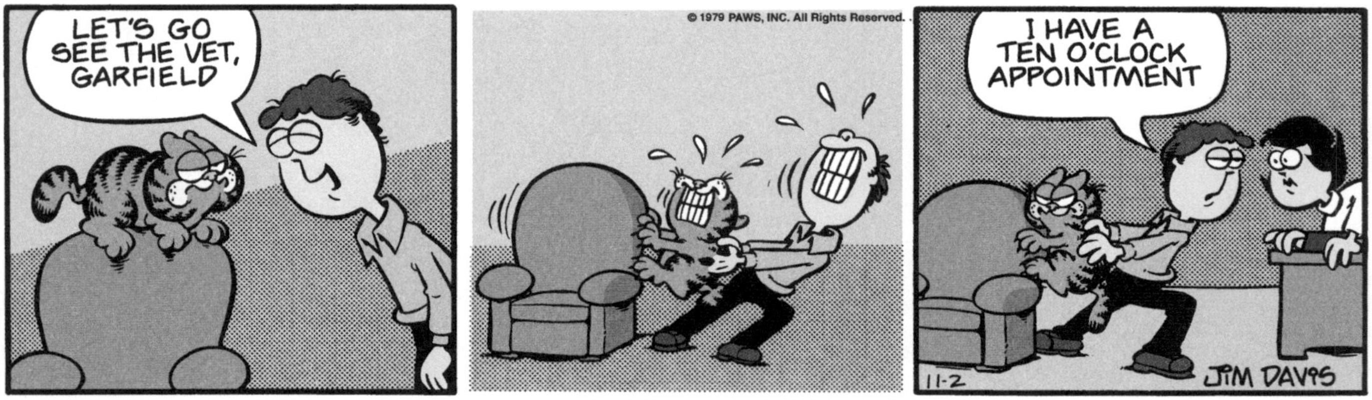
LET'S GO SEE THE VET, GARFIELD
© 1979 PAWS, INC. All Rights Reserved.
I HAVE A TEN O'CLOCK APPOINTMENT
11-2
JIM DAVIS

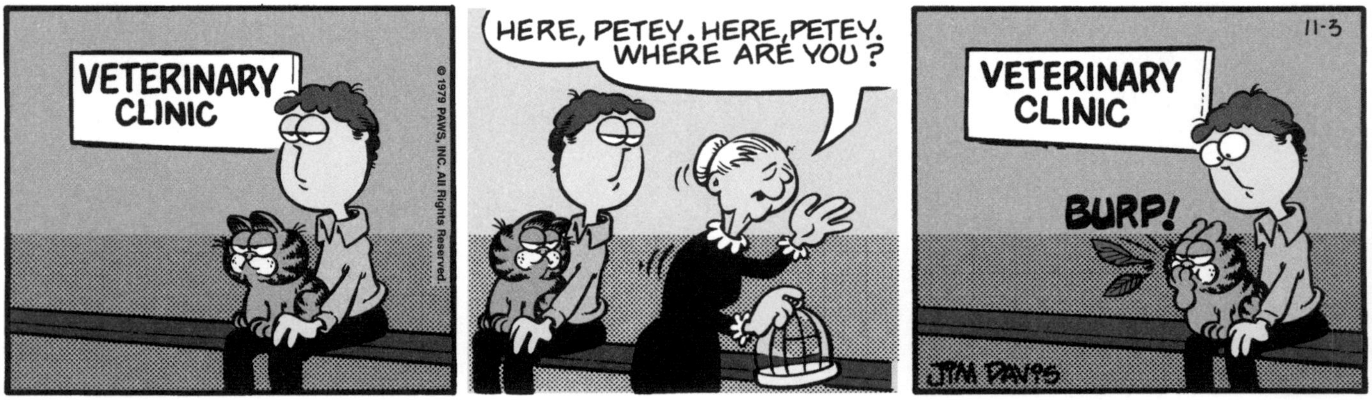
VETERINARY CLINIC
© 1979 PAWS, INC. All Rights Reserved.
HERE, PETEY. HERE, PETEY. WHERE ARE YOU ?
11-3
VETERINARY CLINIC
BURP!
JIM DAVIS

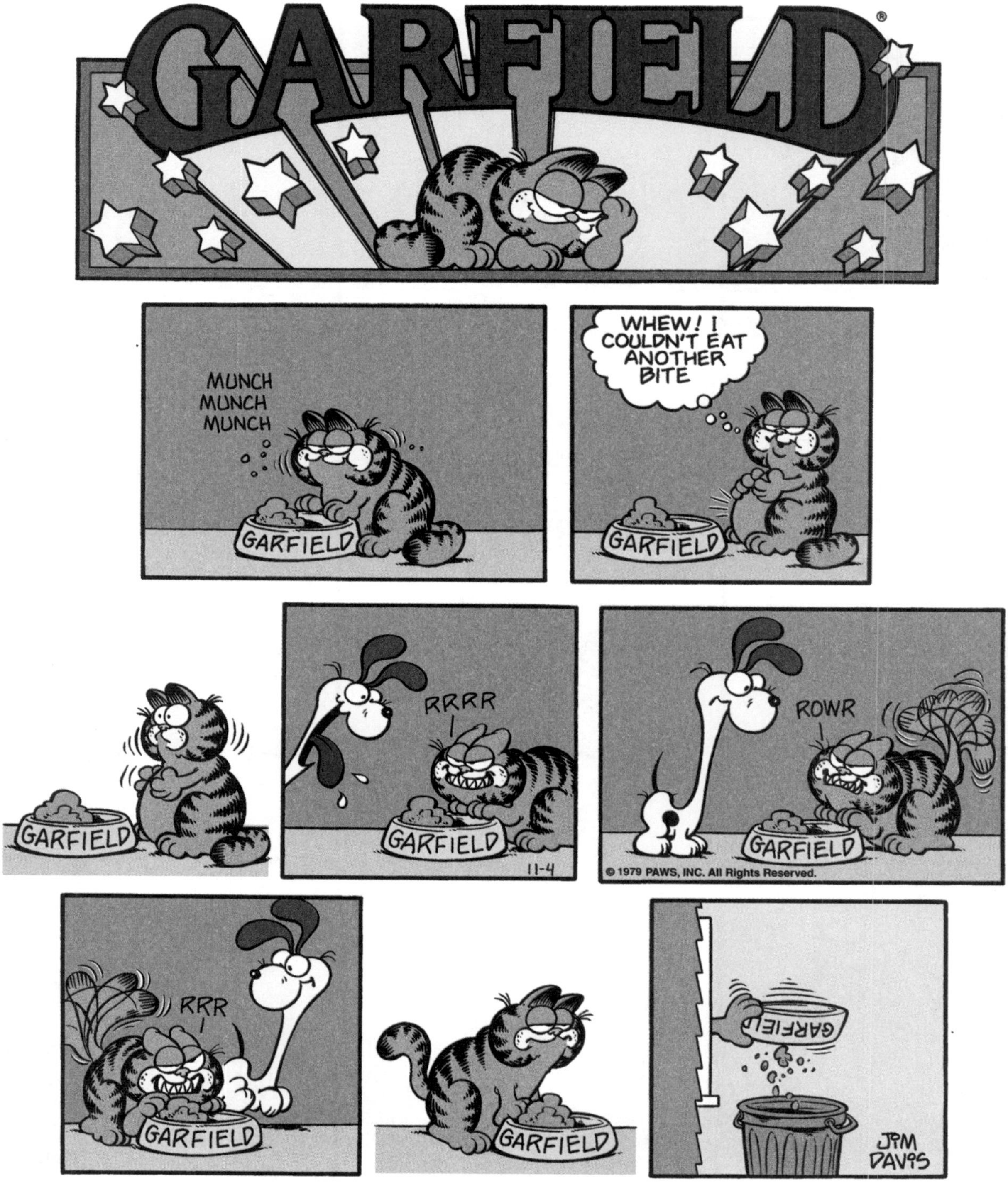
GARFIELD
MUNCH
MUNCH
MUNCH
GARFIELD
WHEW! I COULDN'T EAT ANOTHER BITE
GARFIELD
GARFIELD
RRRR
GARFIELD
11-4
ROWR
GARFIELD
© 1979 PAWS, INC. All Rights Reserved.
RRR
GARFIELD
GARFIELD
GARFIELD
JIM DAVIS

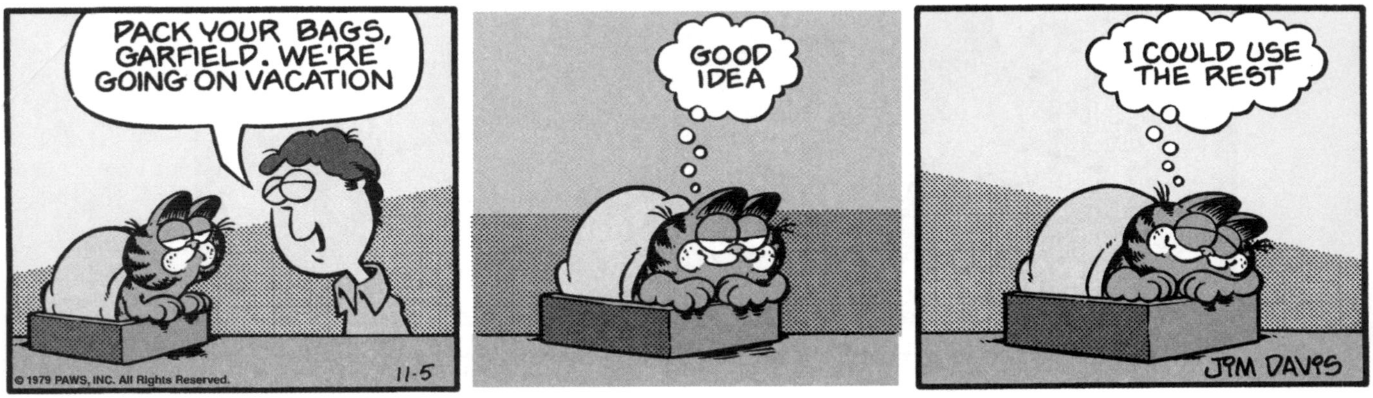
PACK YOUR BAGS, GARFIELD. WE'RE GOING ON VACATION
GOOD IDEA
I COULD USE THE REST
© 1979 PAWS, INC. All Rights Reserved.
11-5
JIM DAVIS

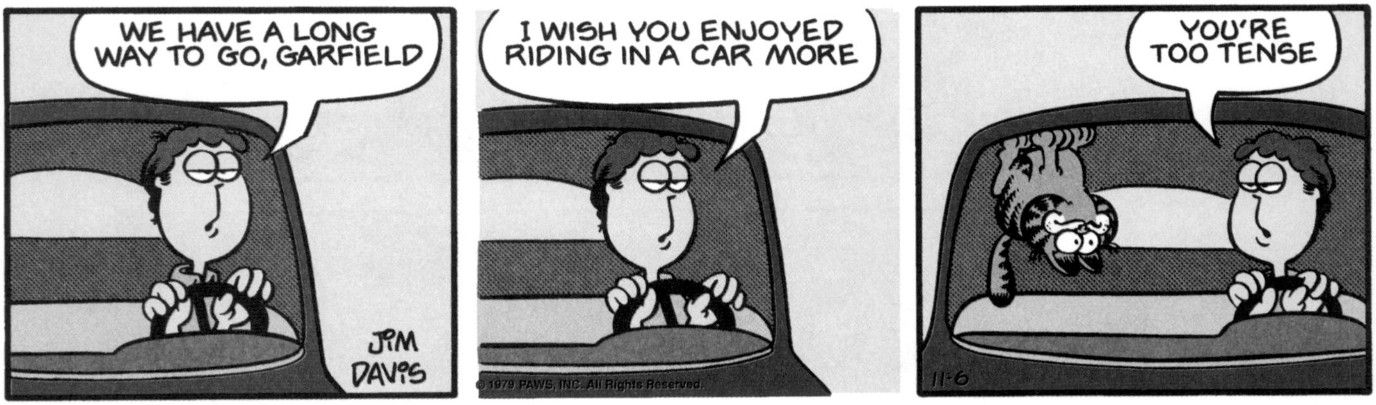
WE HAVE A LONG WAY TO GO, GARFIELD
JIM DAVIS
I WISH YOU ENJOYED RIDING IN A CAR MORE
© 1979 PAWS, INC. All Rights Reserved.
YOU'RE TOO TENSE
11-6

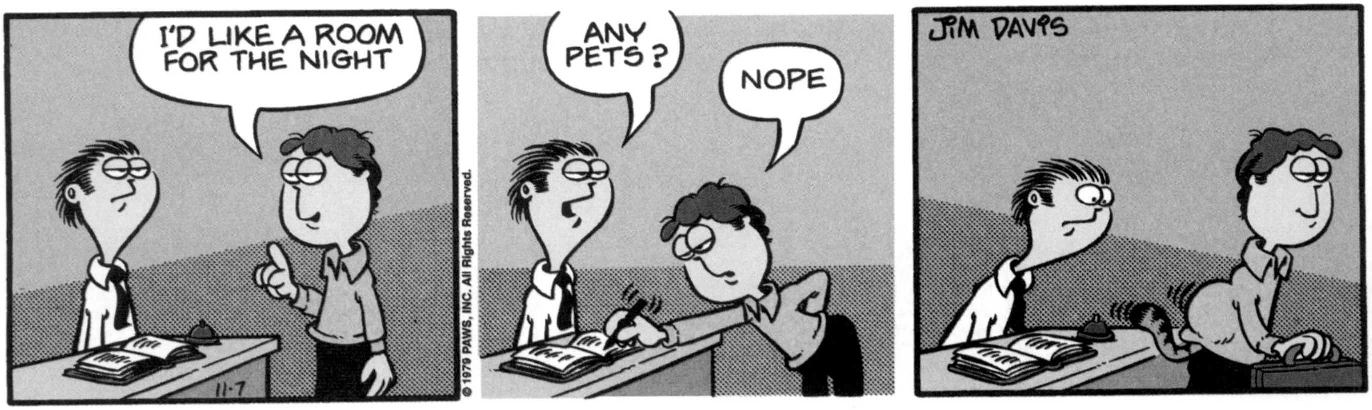
I'D LIKE A ROOM FOR THE NIGHT
11-7
© 1979 PAWS, INC. All Rights Reserved.
ANY PETS?
NOPE
JIM DAVIS

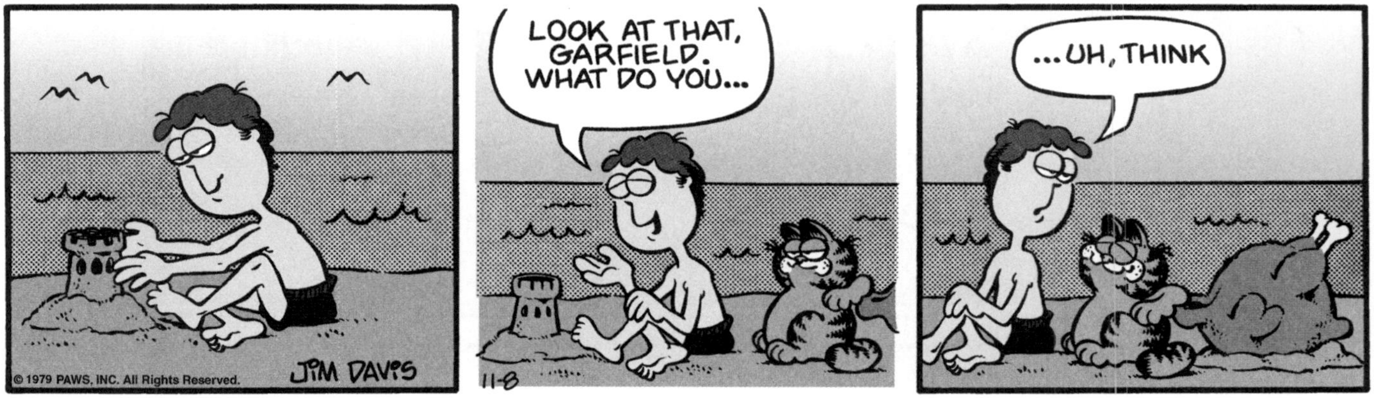
© 1979 PAWS, INC. All Rights Reserved.
JIM DAVIS
LOOK AT THAT, GARFIELD. WHAT DO YOU...
11-8
...UH, THINK

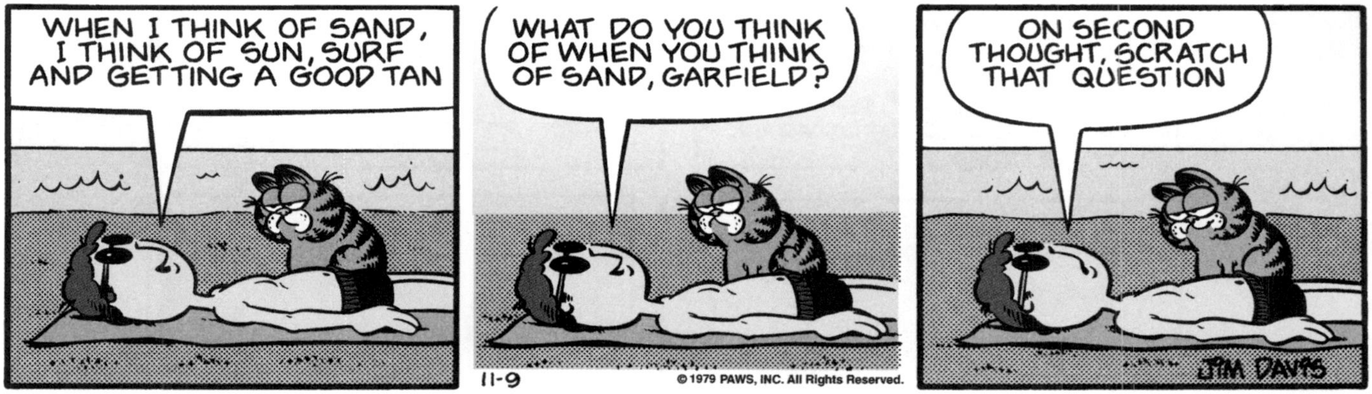
WHEN I THINK OF SAND, I THINK OF SUN, SURF AND GETTING A GOOD TAN
WHAT DO YOU THINK OF WHEN YOU THINK OF SAND, GARFIELD?
11-9
© 1979 PAWS, INC. All Rights Reserved.
ON SECOND THOUGHT, SCRATCH THAT QUESTION
JIM DAVIS

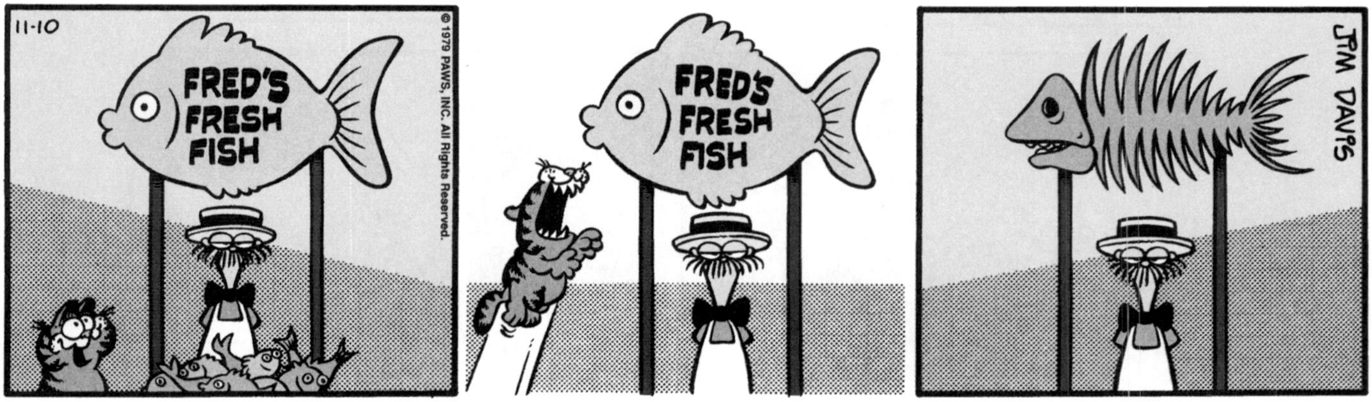
11-10
© 1979 PAWS, INC. All Rights Reserved.
FRED'S FRESH FISH
FRED'S FRESH FISH
JIM DAVIS

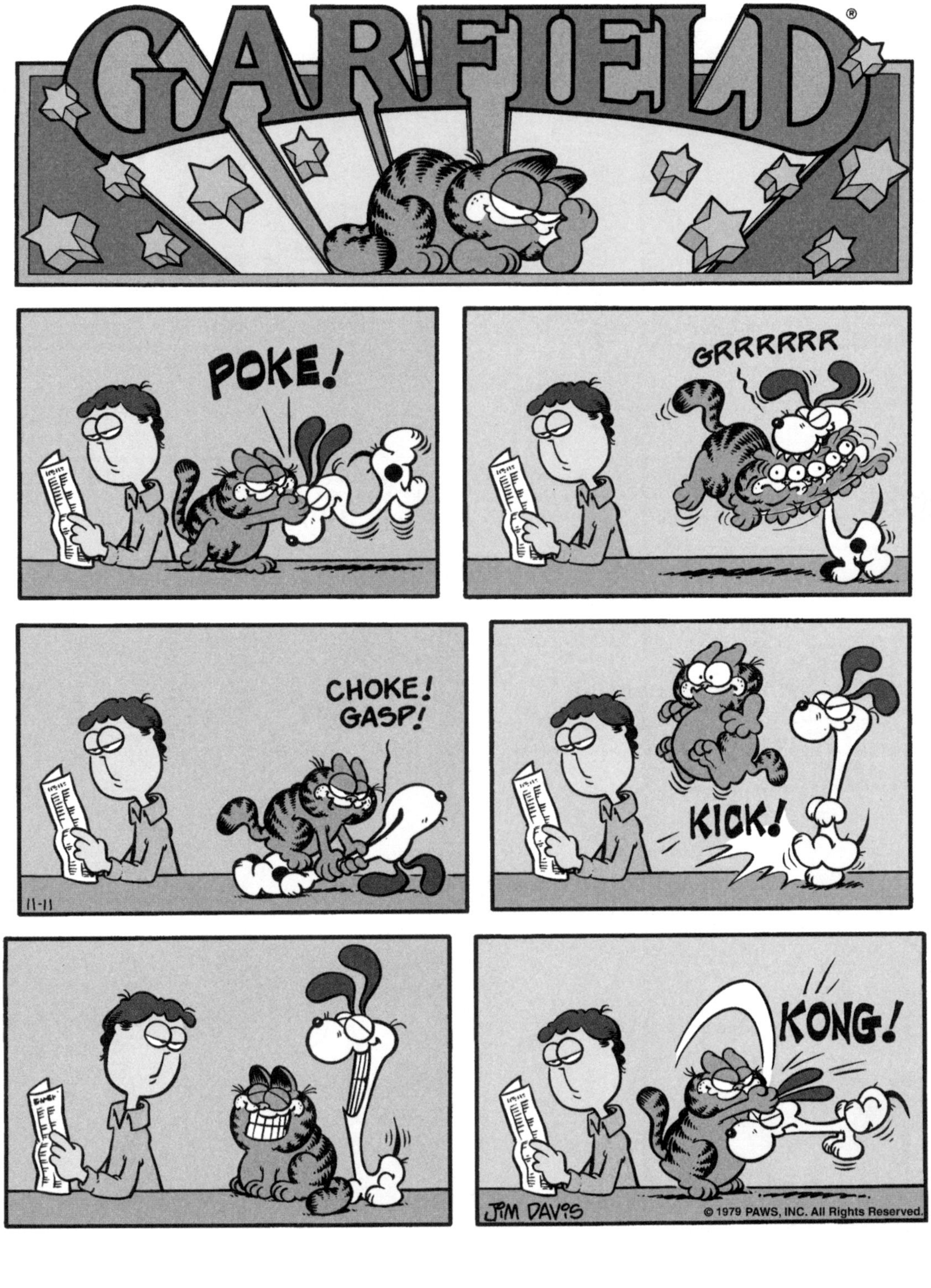
GARFIELD®
POKE!
GRRRRRR
CHOKE! GASP!
11-11
KICK!
KONG!
JIM DAVIS
© 1979 PAWS, INC. All Rights Reserved.

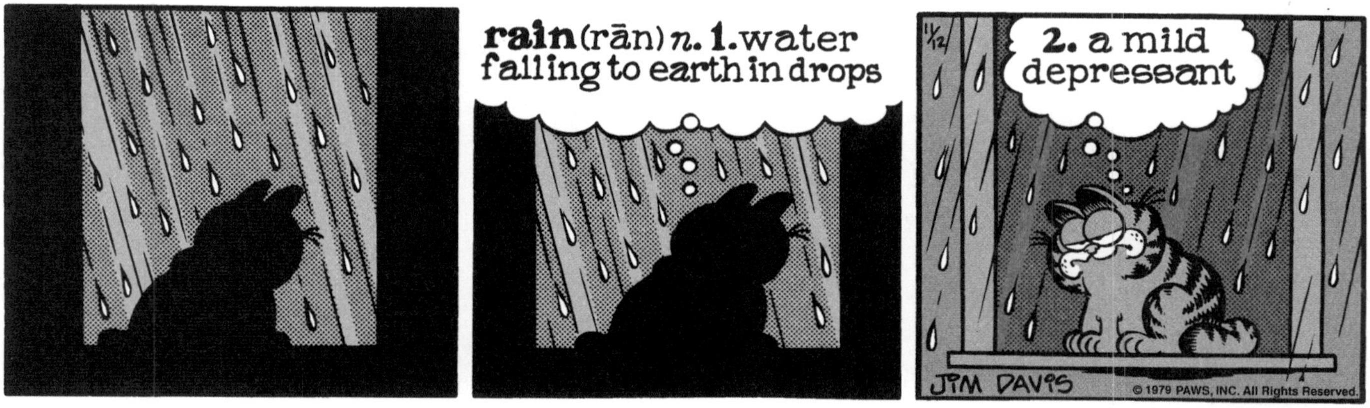
rain (rān) n. 1. water falling to earth in drops
11/12
2. a mild depressant
JIM DAVIS
© 1979 PAWS, INC. All Rights Reserved.

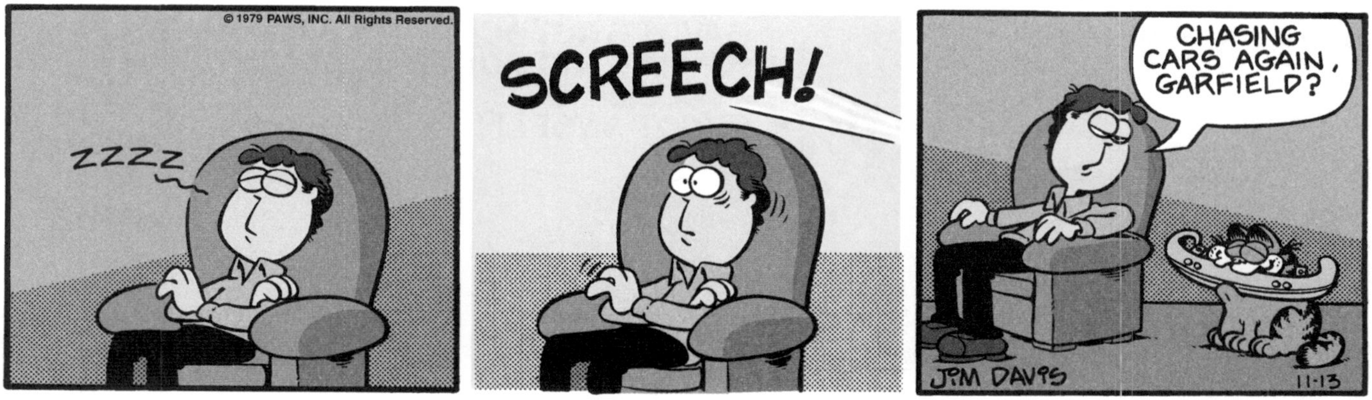
© 1979 PAWS, INC. All Rights Reserved.
ZZZZ
SCREECH!
CHASING CARS AGAIN, GARFIELD?
JIM DAVIS
11-13

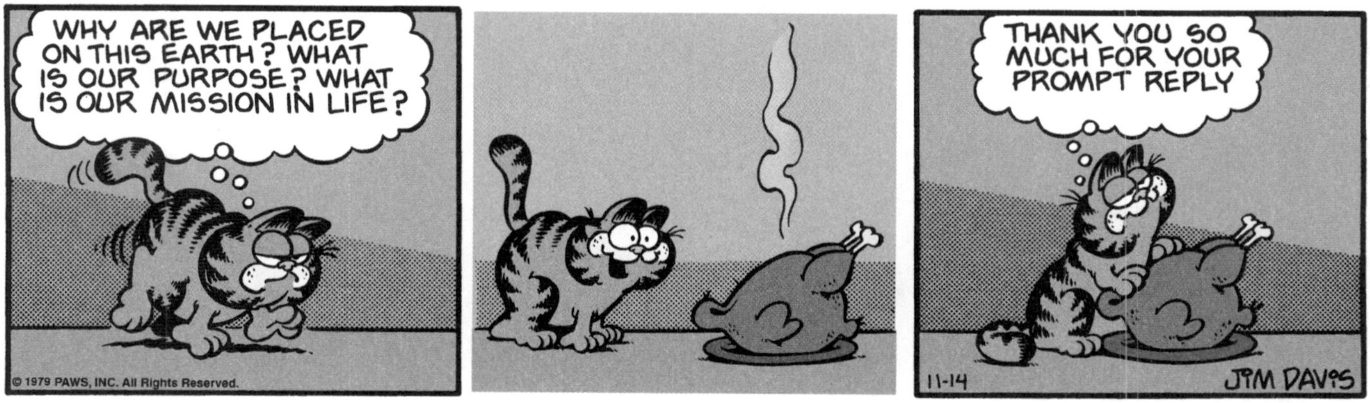
WHY ARE WE PLACED ON THIS EARTH? WHAT IS OUR PURPOSE? WHAT IS OUR MISSION IN LIFE?
© 1979 PAWS, INC. All Rights Reserved.
THANK YOU SO MUCH FOR YOUR PROMPT REPLY
11-14
JIM DAVIS

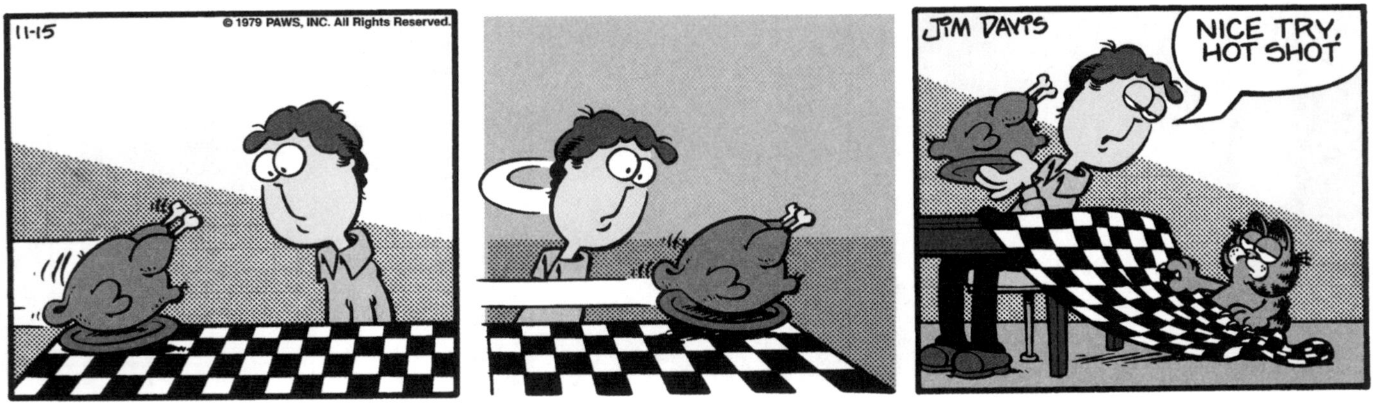
11-15
© 1979 PAWS, INC. All Rights Reserved.
JIM DAVIS
NICE TRY, HOT SHOT

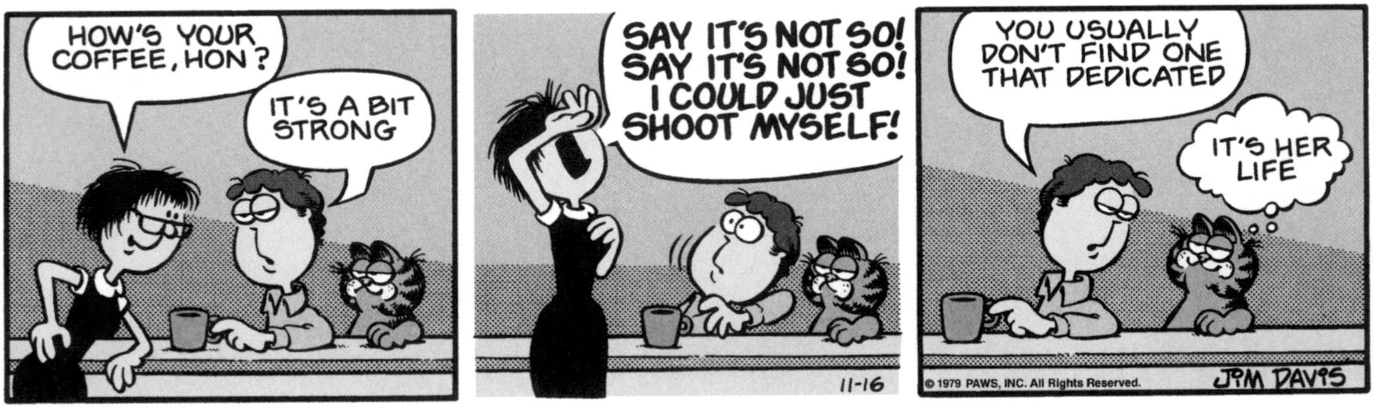
HOW'S YOUR COFFEE, HON?
IT'S A BIT STRONG
SAY IT'S NOT SO! SAY IT'S NOT SO! I COULD JUST SHOOT MYSELF!
11-16
YOU USUALLY DON'T FIND ONE THAT DEDICATED
IT'S HER LIFE
© 1979 PAWS, INC. All Rights Reserved.
JIM DAVIS

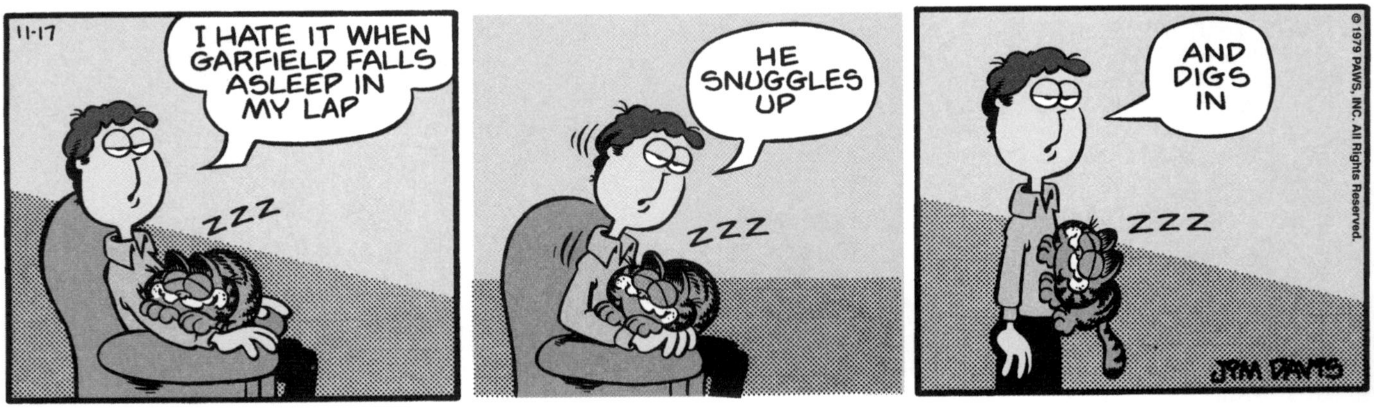
11-17
I HATE IT WHEN GARFIELD FALLS ASLEEP IN MY LAP
ZZZ
HE SNUGGLES UP
ZZZ
AND DIGS IN
ZZZ
© 1979 PAWS, INC. All Rights Reserved.
JIM DAVIS

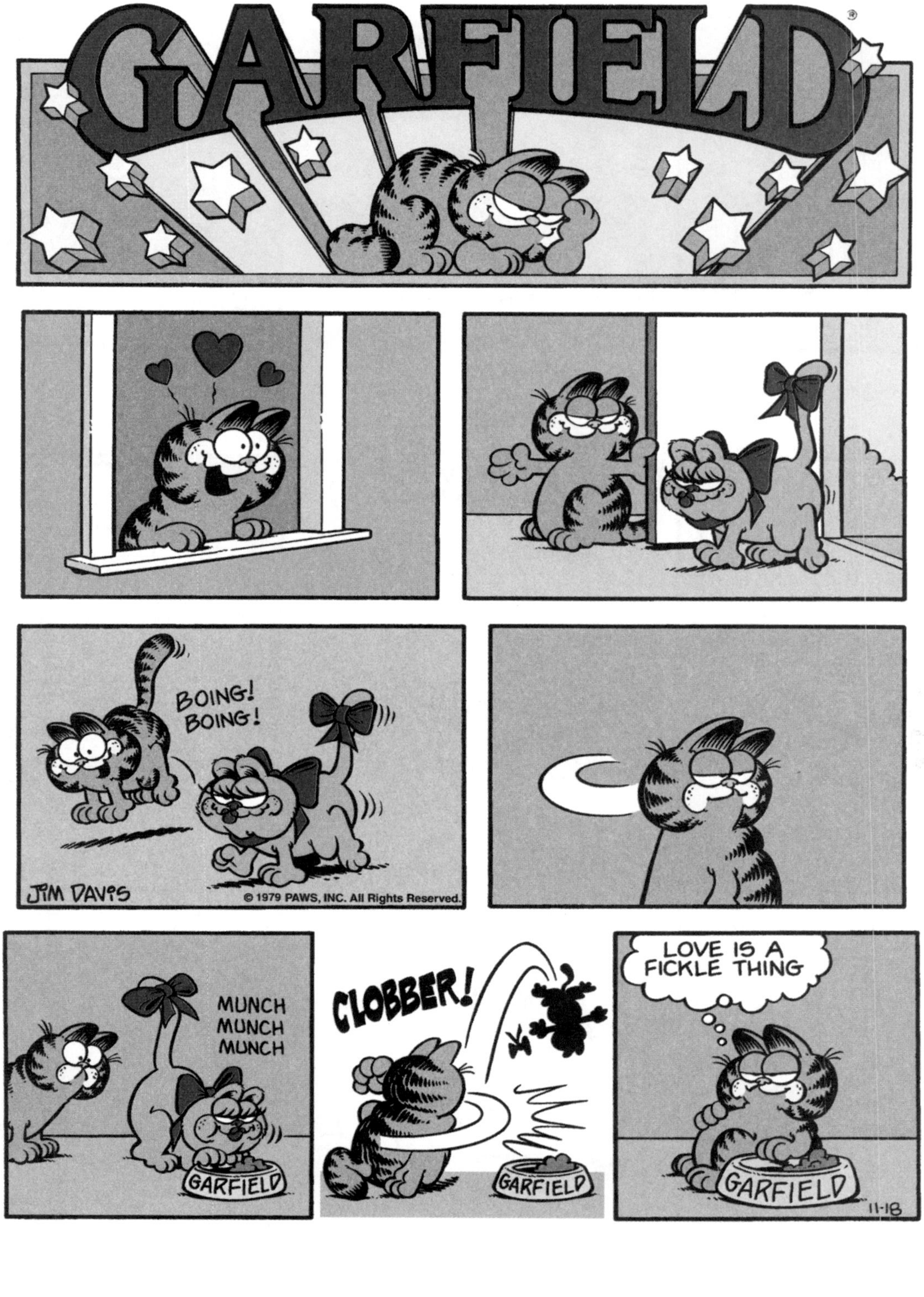
GARFIELD
BOING! BOING!
JIM DAVIS
© 1979 PAWS, INC. All Rights Reserved.
MUNCH MUNCH MUNCH
GARFIELD
CLOBBER!
GARFIELD
LOVE IS A FICKLE THING
GARFIELD
11-18

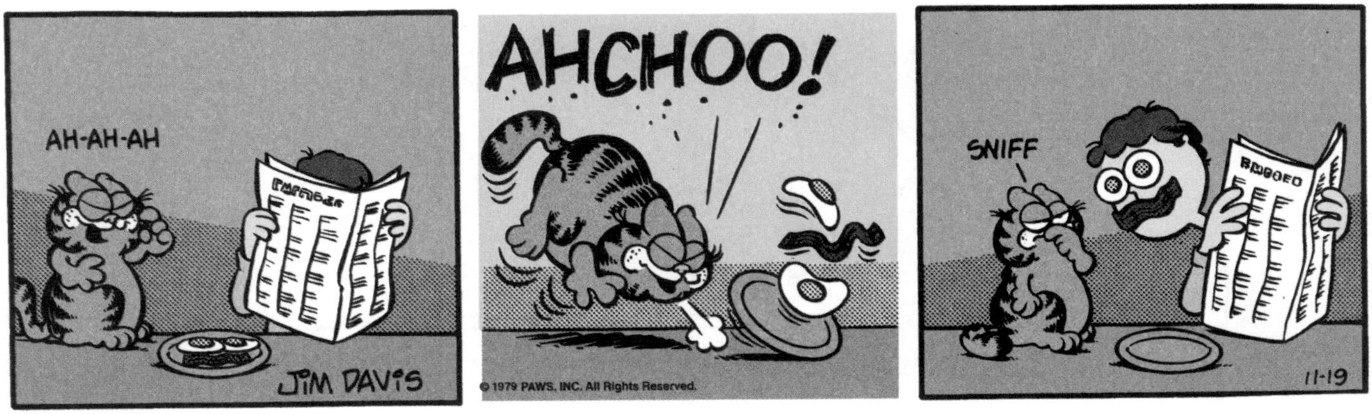
AH-AH-AH
JIM DAVIS
AHCHOO!
© 1979 PAWS, INC. All Rights Reserved.
SNIFF
11-19

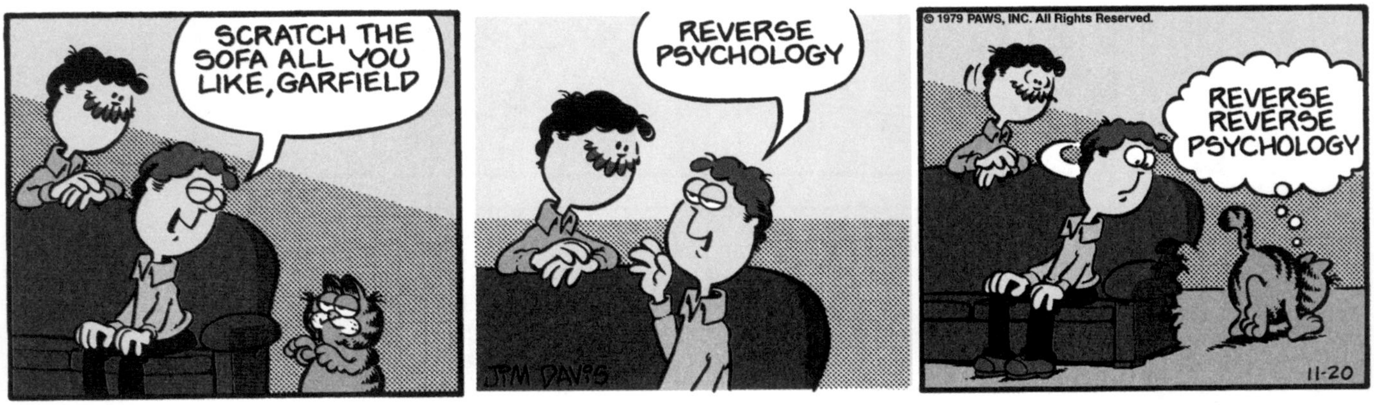
SCRATCH THE SOFA ALL YOU LIKE, GARFIELD
REVERSE PSYCHOLOGY
JIM DAVIS
© 1979 PAWS, INC. All Rights Reserved.
REVERSE REVERSE PSYCHOLOGY
11-20

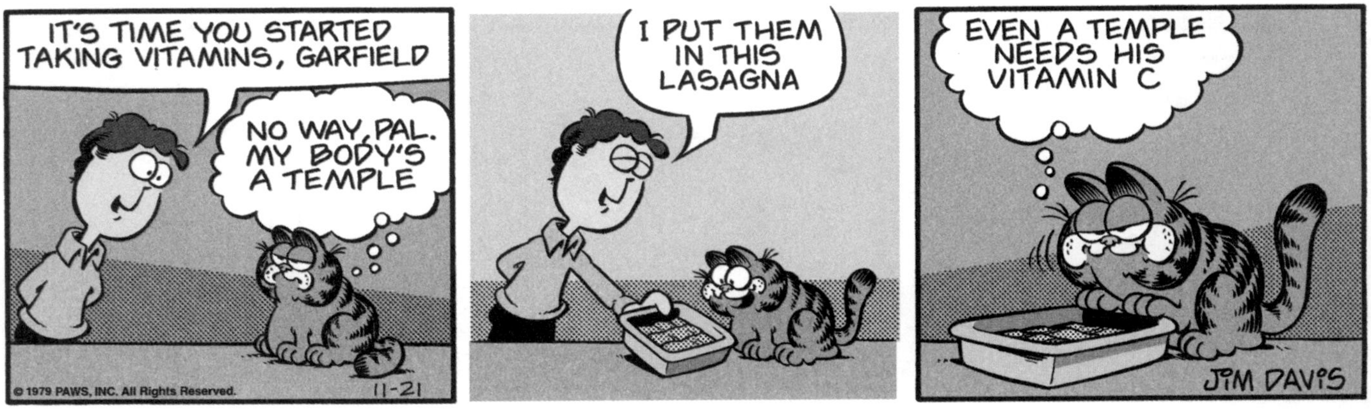
IT'S TIME YOU STARTED TAKING VITAMINS, GARFIELD
NO WAY, PAL. MY BODY'S A TEMPLE
© 1979 PAWS, INC. All Rights Reserved.
11-21
I PUT THEM IN THIS LASAGNA
EVEN A TEMPLE NEEDS HIS VITAMIN C
JIM DAVIS

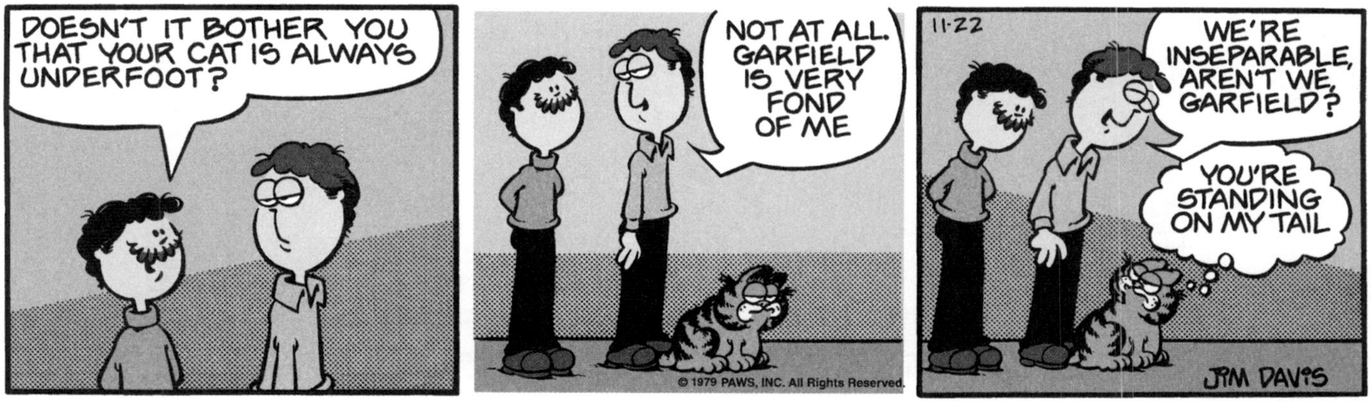
DOESN'T IT BOTHER YOU THAT YOUR CAT IS ALWAYS UNDERFOOT?
NOT AT ALL. GARFIELD IS VERY FOND OF ME
© 1979 PAWS, INC. All Rights Reserved.
11-22
WE'RE INSEPARABLE, AREN'T WE, GARFIELD?
YOU'RE STANDING ON MY TAIL
JIM DAVIS

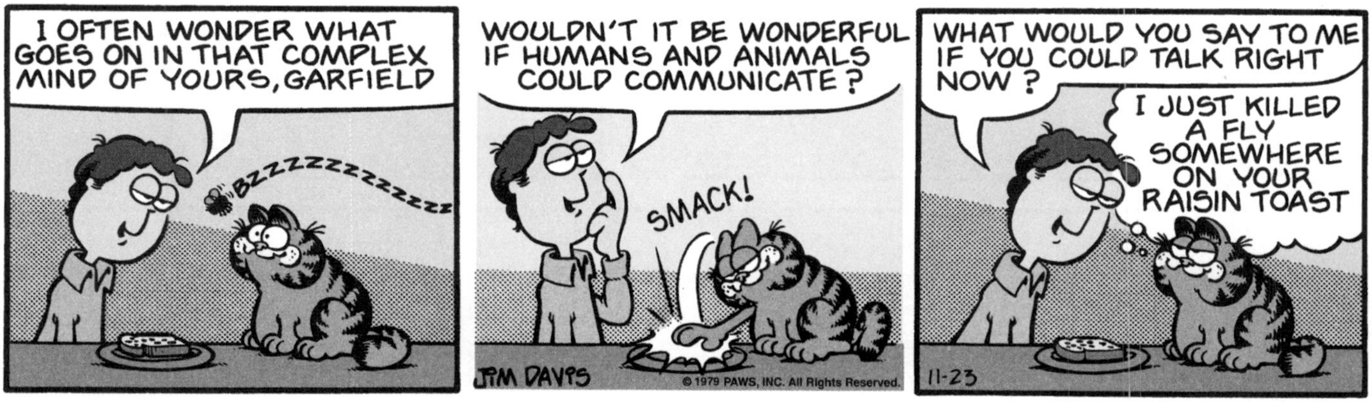
I OFTEN WONDER WHAT GOES ON IN THAT COMPLEX MIND OF YOURS, GARFIELD
BZZZZZZZZZZZZZ
WOULDN'T IT BE WONDERFUL IF HUMANS AND ANIMALS COULD COMMUNICATE?
SMACK!
JIM DAVIS
© 1979 PAWS, INC. All Rights Reserved.
WHAT WOULD YOU SAY TO ME IF YOU COULD TALK RIGHT NOW?
I JUST KILLED A FLY SOMEWHERE ON YOUR RAISIN TOAST
11-23

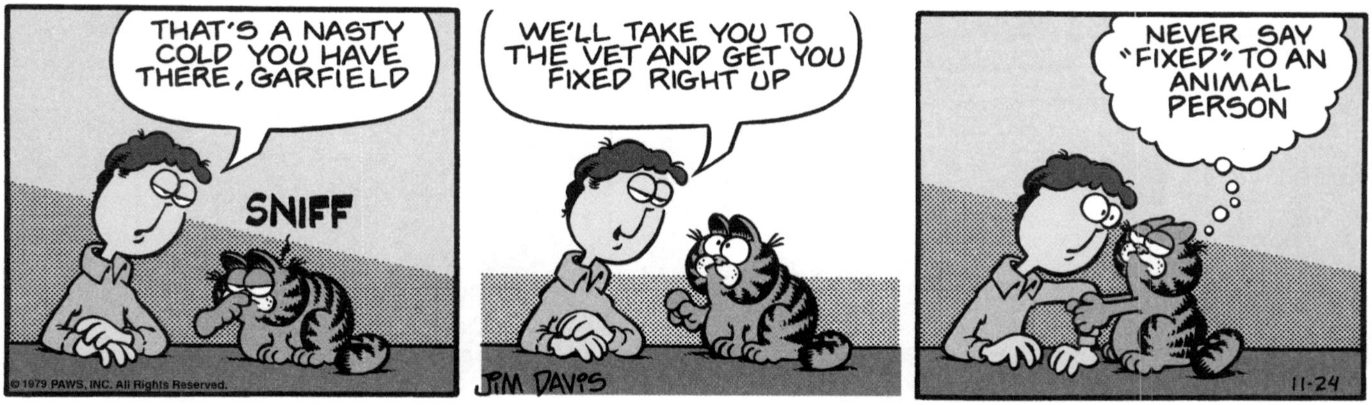
THAT'S A NASTY COLD YOU HAVE THERE, GARFIELD
SNIFF
© 1979 PAWS, INC. All Rights Reserved.
WE'LL TAKE YOU TO THE VET AND GET YOU FIXED RIGHT UP
JIM DAVIS
NEVER SAY "FIXED" TO AN ANIMAL PERSON
11-24

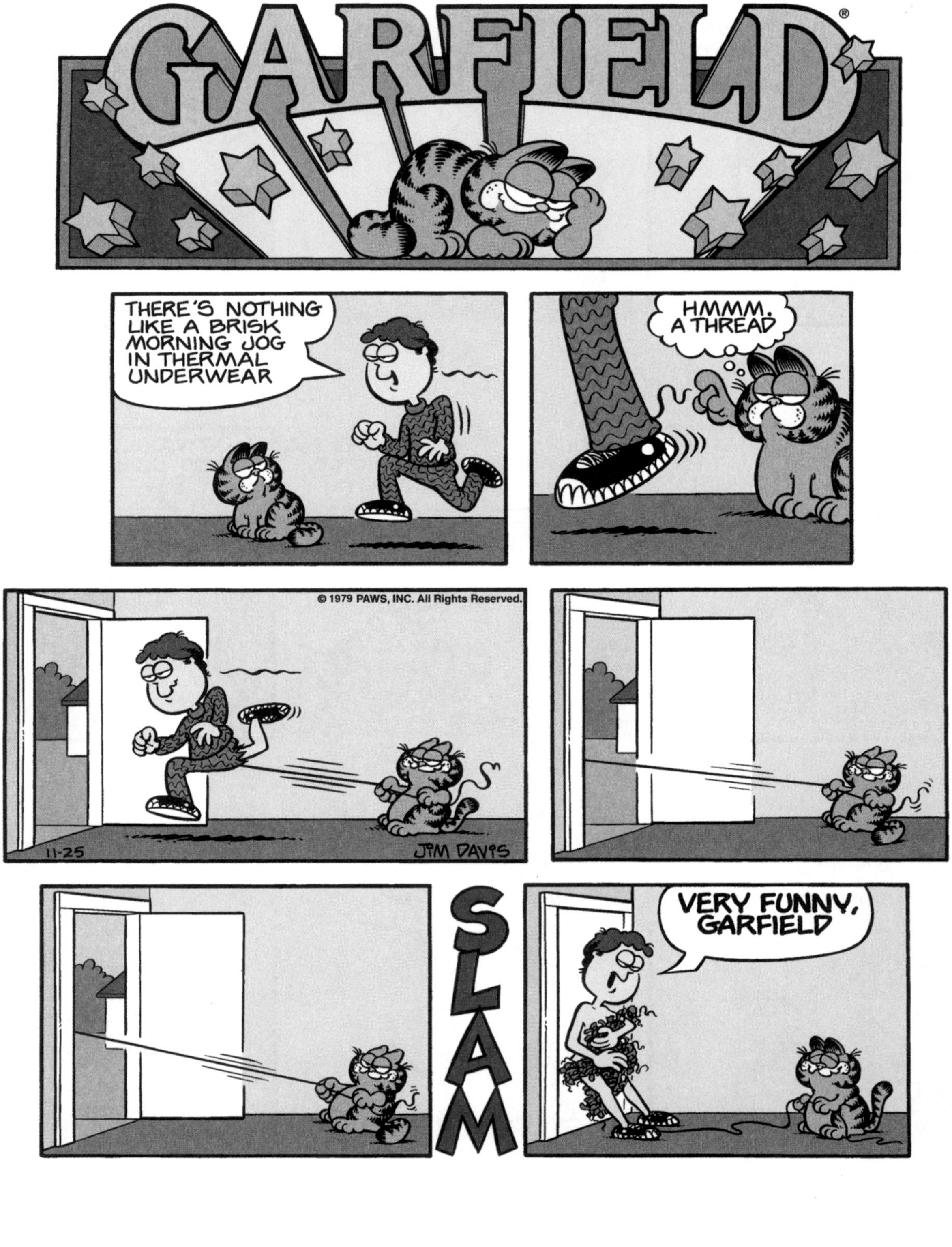
GARFIELD®
THERE'S NOTHING LIKE A BRISK MORNING JOG IN THERMAL UNDERWEAR
HMMM, A THREAD
© 1979 PAWS, INC. All Rights Reserved.
11-25
JIM DAVIS
SLAM
VERY FUNNY, GARFIELD

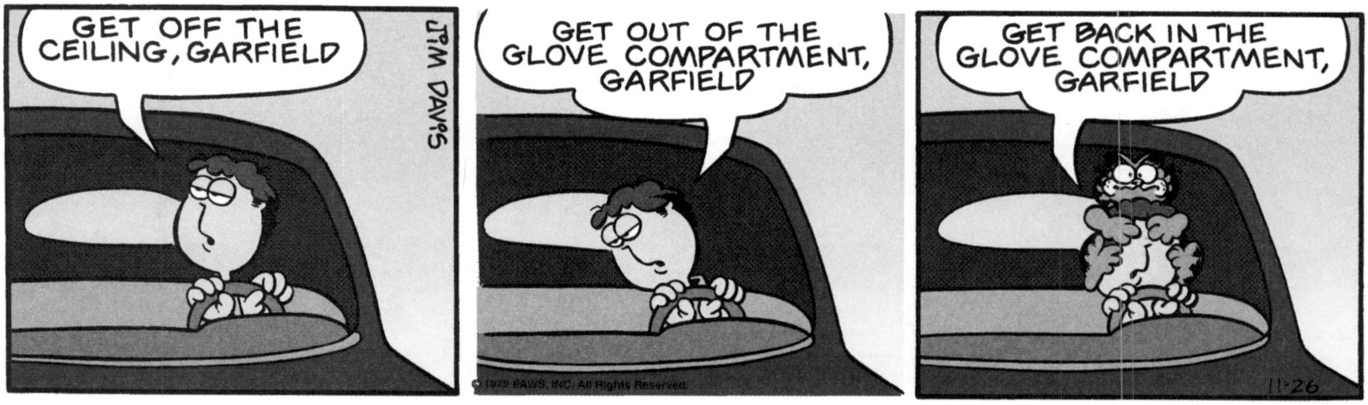
GET OFF THE CEILING, GARFIELD
JIM DAVIS
GET OUT OF THE GLOVE COMPARTMENT, GARFIELD
© 1979 PAWS, INC. All Rights Reserved.
GET BACK IN THE GLOVE COMPARTMENT, GARFIELD
11-26

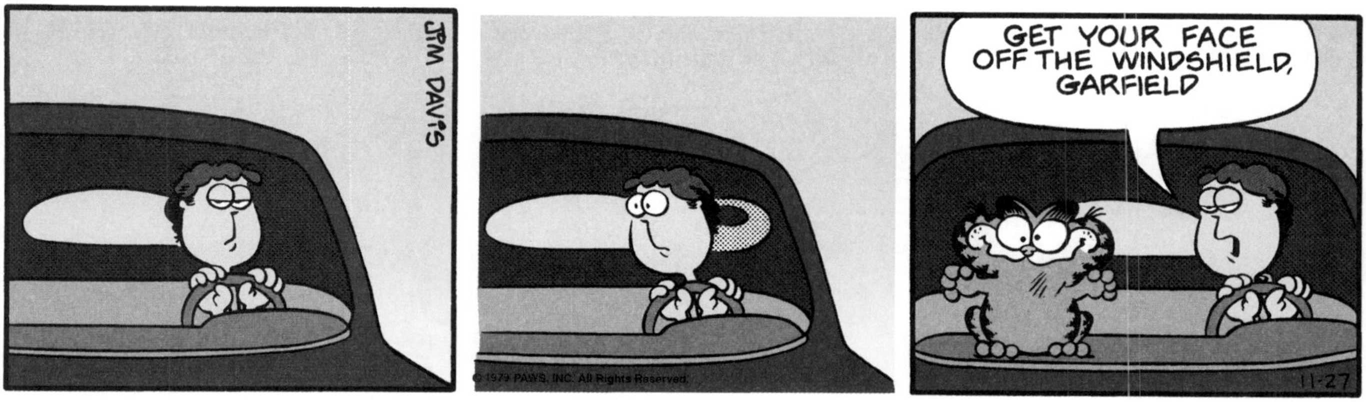
JIM DAVIS
© 1979 PAWS, INC. All Rights Reserved.
GET YOUR FACE OFF THE WINDSHIELD, GARFIELD
11-27

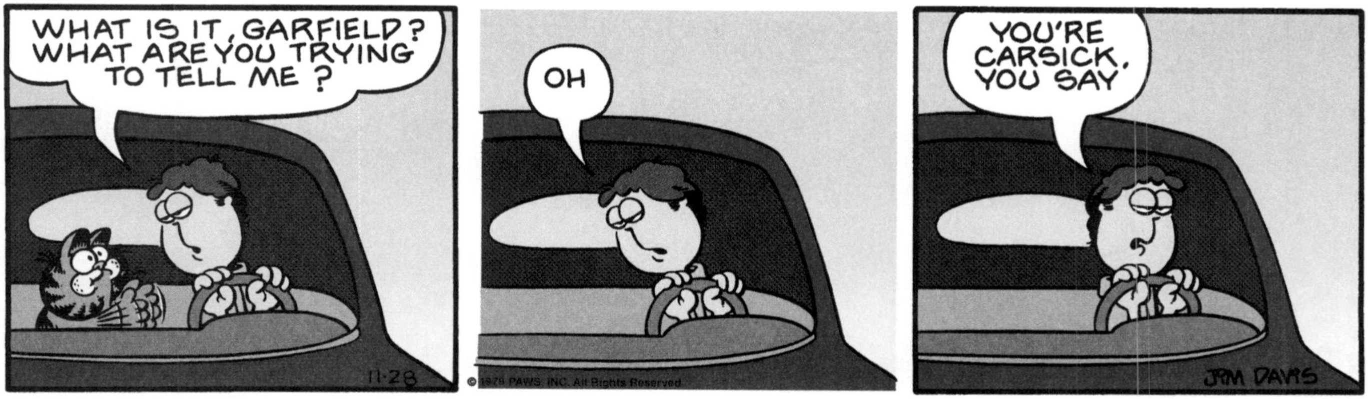
WHAT IS IT, GARFIELD? WHAT ARE YOU TRYING TO TELL ME?
11-28
OH
© 1979 PAWS, INC. All Rights Reserved.
YOU'RE CARSICK, YOU SAY
JIM DAVIS

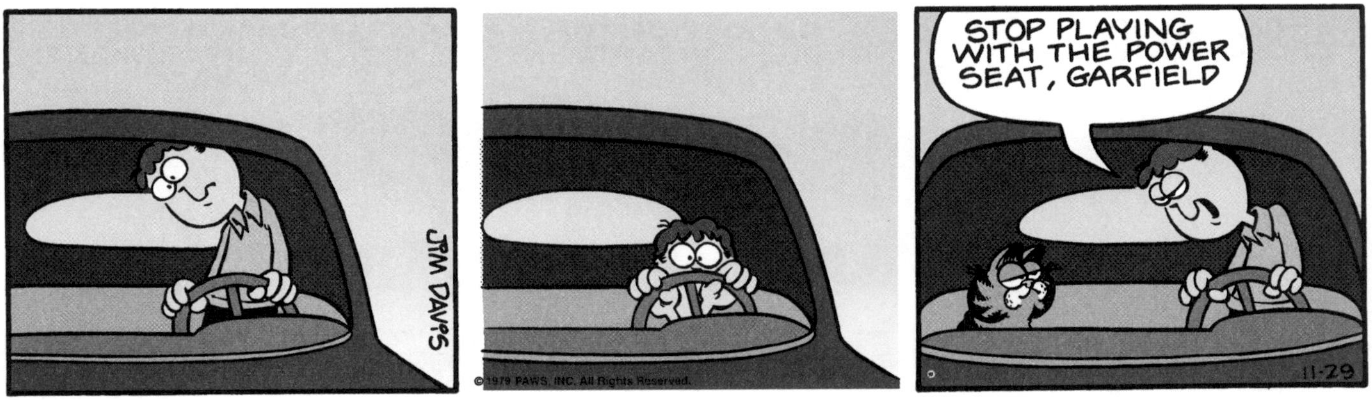
JIM DAVIS
© 1979 PAWS, INC. All Rights Reserved.
STOP PLAYING WITH THE POWER SEAT, GARFIELD
11-29

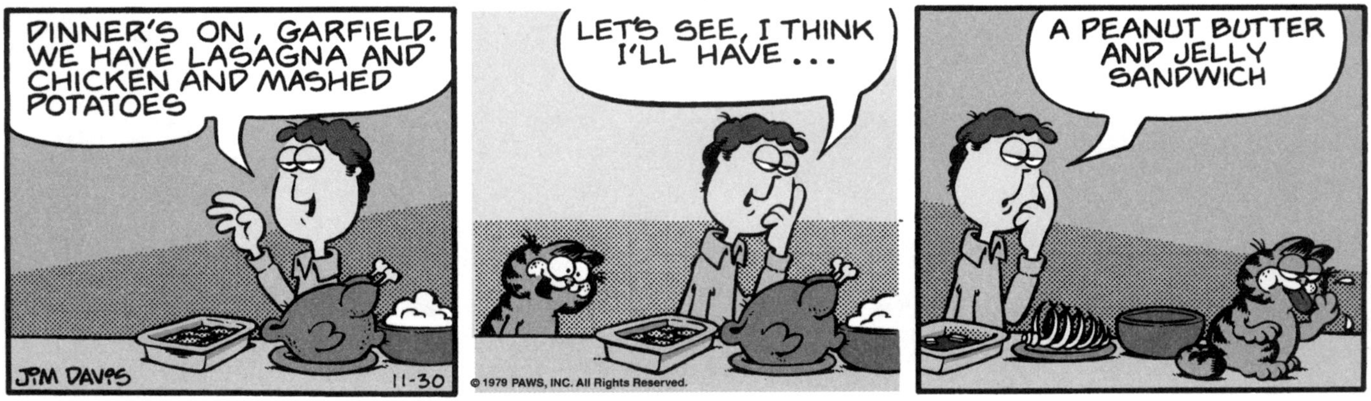
DINNER'S ON, GARFIELD. WE HAVE LASAGNA AND CHICKEN AND MASHED POTATOES
JIM DAVIS
11-30
LET'S SEE, I THINK I'LL HAVE . . .
© 1979 PAWS, INC. All Rights Reserved.
A PEANUT BUTTER AND JELLY SANDWICH

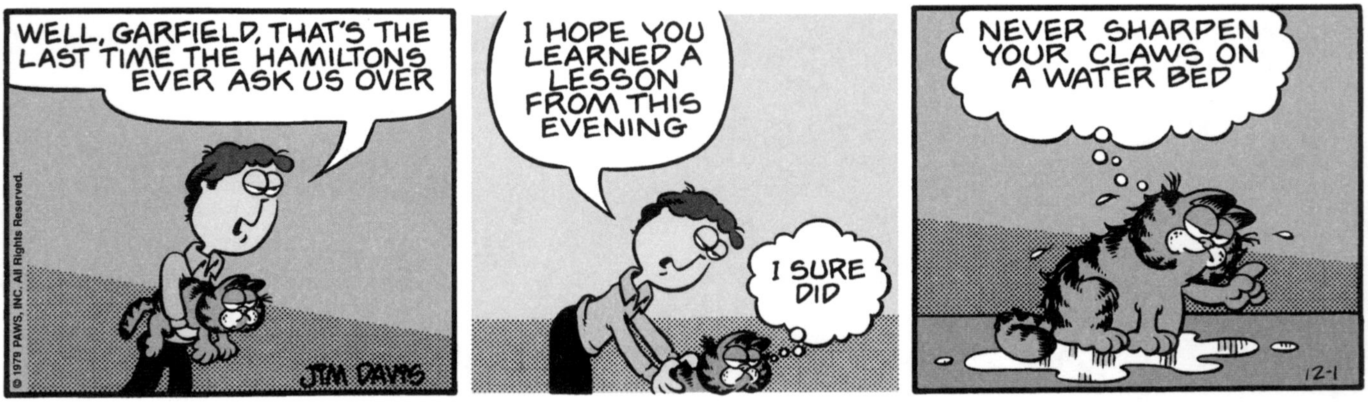
WELL, GARFIELD, THAT'S THE LAST TIME THE HAMILTONS EVER ASK US OVER
© 1979 PAWS, INC. All Rights Reserved.
JIM DAVIS
I HOPE YOU LEARNED A LESSON FROM THIS EVENING
I SURE DID
NEVER SHARPEN YOUR CLAWS ON A WATER BED
12-1

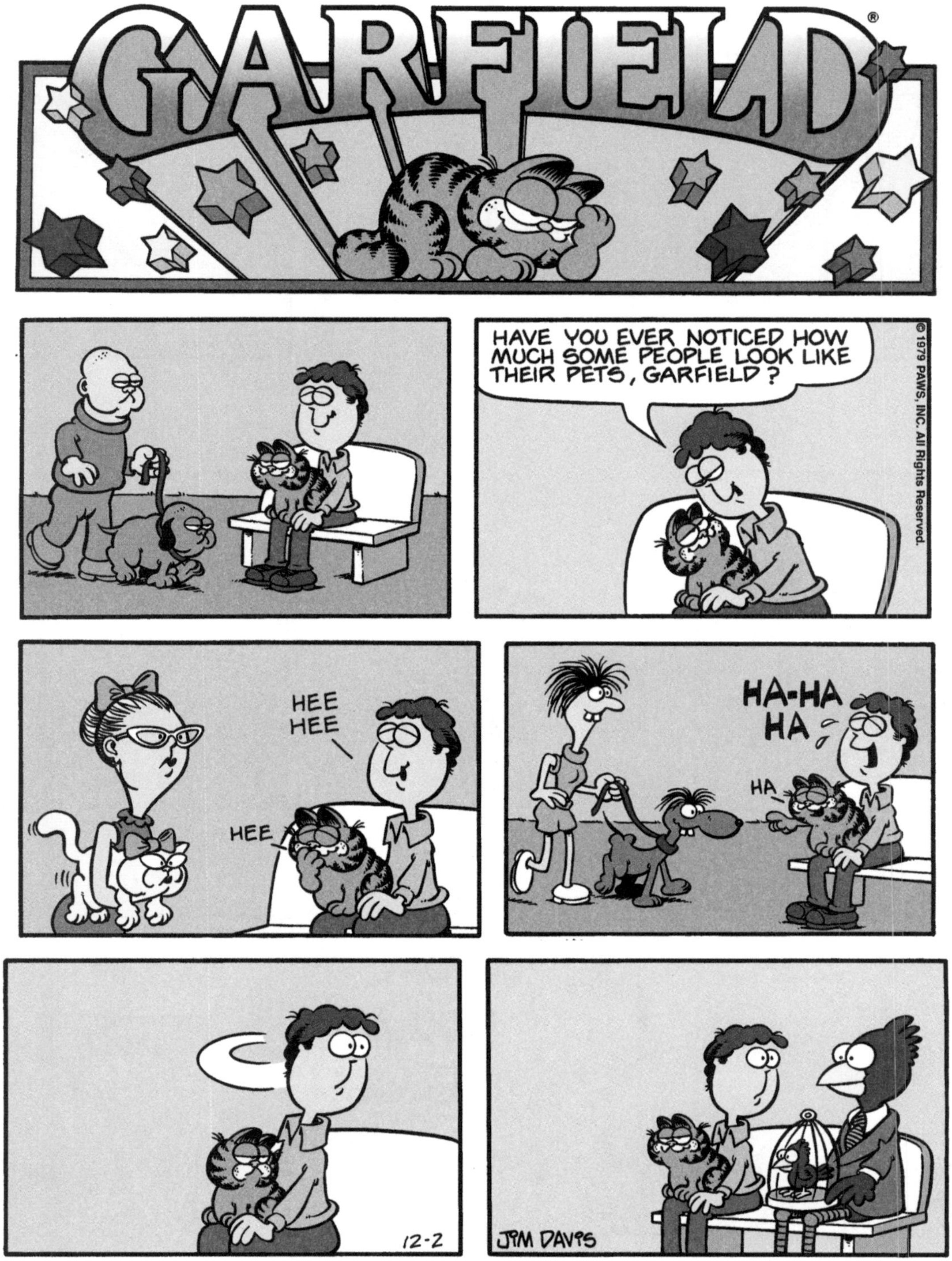
GARFIELD®
HAVE YOU EVER NOTICED HOW MUCH SOME PEOPLE LOOK LIKE THEIR PETS, GARFIELD?
© 1979 PAWS, INC. All Rights Reserved.
HEE HEE
HEE
HA-HA HA
HA
12-2
JIM DAVIS

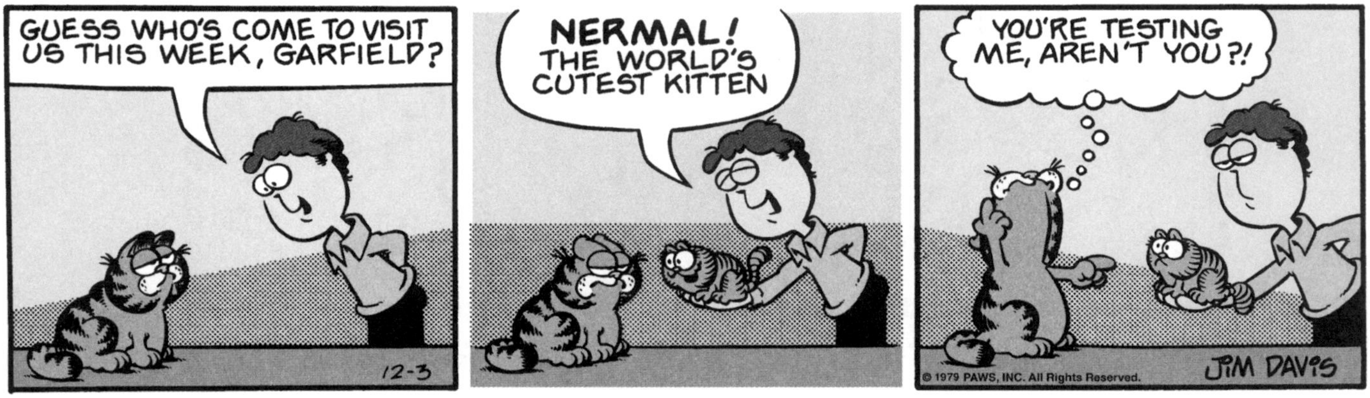
GUESS WHO'S COME TO VISIT US THIS WEEK, GARFIELD?
12-3
NERMAL! THE WORLD'S CUTEST KITTEN
YOU'RE TESTING ME, AREN'T YOU?!
© 1979 PAWS, INC. All Rights Reserved.
JIM DAVIS

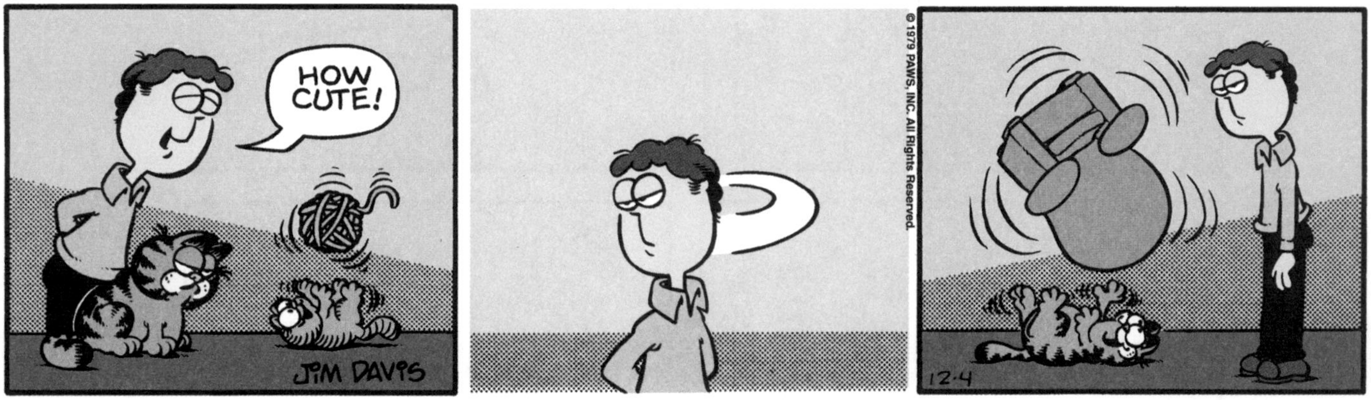
HOW CUTE!
JIM DAVIS
© 1979 PAWS, INC. All Rights Reserved.
12-4

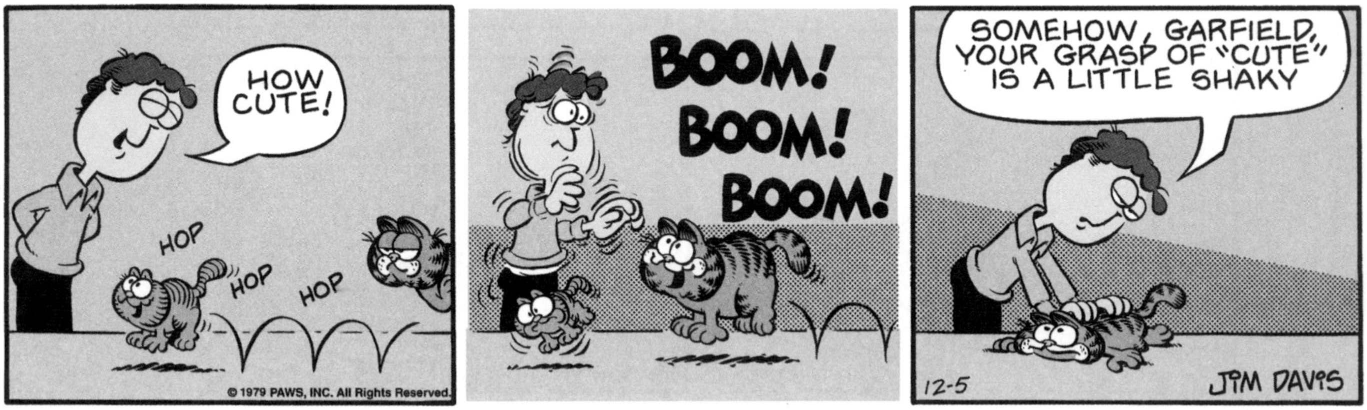
HOW CUTE!
HOP
HOP
HOP
© 1979 PAWS, INC. All Rights Reserved.
BOOM! BOOM! BOOM!
SOMEHOW, GARFIELD, YOUR GRASP OF "CUTE" IS A LITTLE SHAKY
12-5
JIM DAVIS

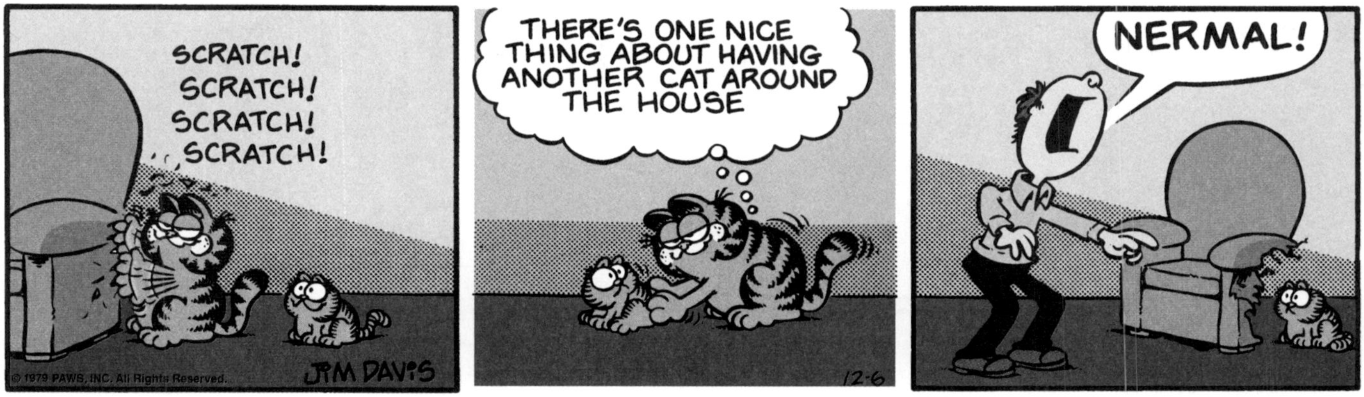
SCRATCH! SCRATCH! SCRATCH! SCRATCH!
© 1979 PAWS, INC. All Rights Reserved.
JIM DAVIS
THERE'S ONE NICE THING ABOUT HAVING ANOTHER CAT AROUND THE HOUSE
12-6
NERMAL!

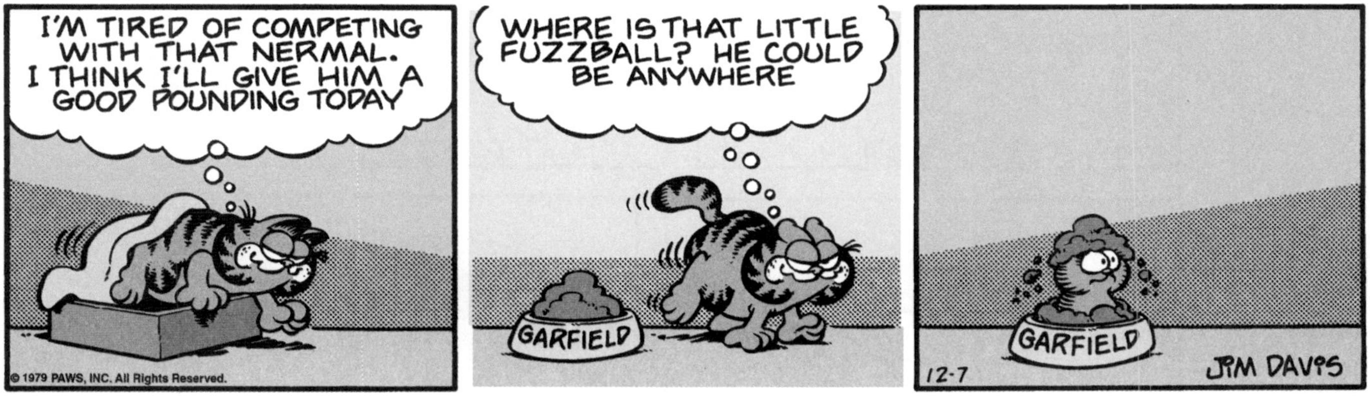
I'M TIRED OF COMPETING WITH THAT NERMAL. I THINK I'LL GIVE HIM A GOOD POUNDING TODAY
© 1979 PAWS, INC. All Rights Reserved.
WHERE IS THAT LITTLE FUZZBALL? HE COULD BE ANYWHERE
GARFIELD
GARFIELD
12-7
JIM DAVIS

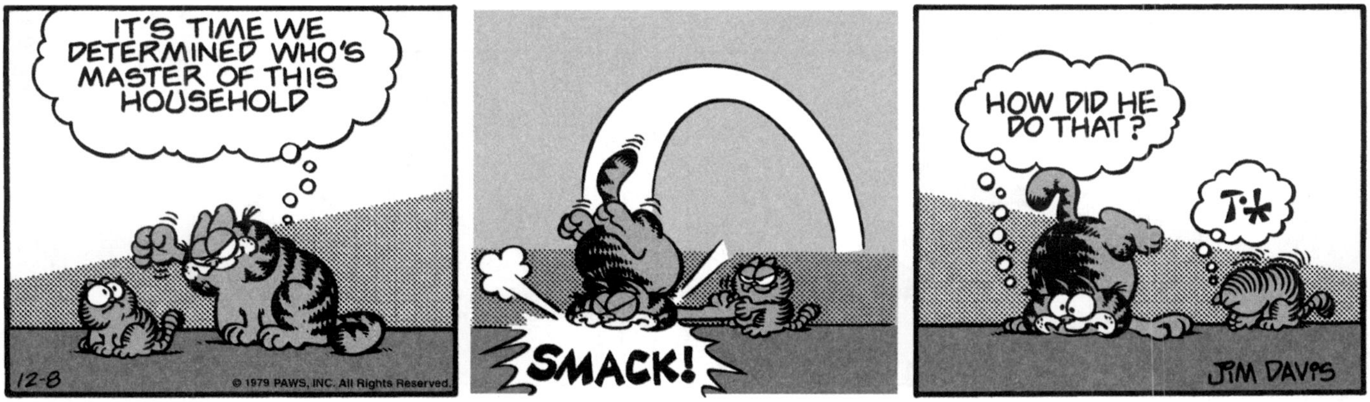
IT'S TIME WE DETERMINED WHO'S MASTER OF THIS HOUSEHOLD
12-8
© 1979 PAWS, INC. All Rights Reserved.
SMACK!
HOW DID HE DO THAT?
JIM DAVIS

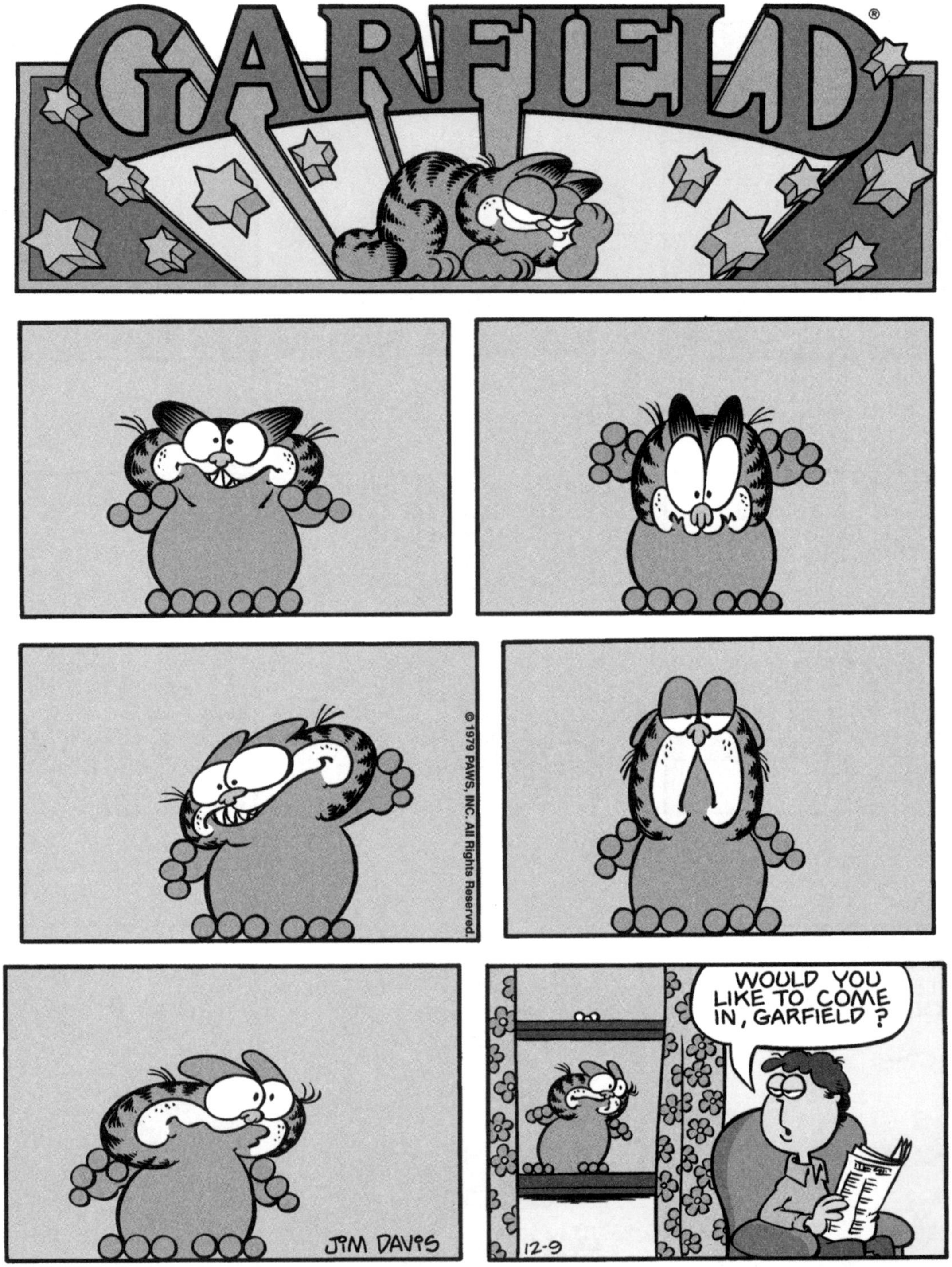
GARFIELD®
© 1979 PAWS, INC. All Rights Reserved.
JIM DAVIS
12-9
WOULD YOU LIKE TO COME IN, GARFIELD ?

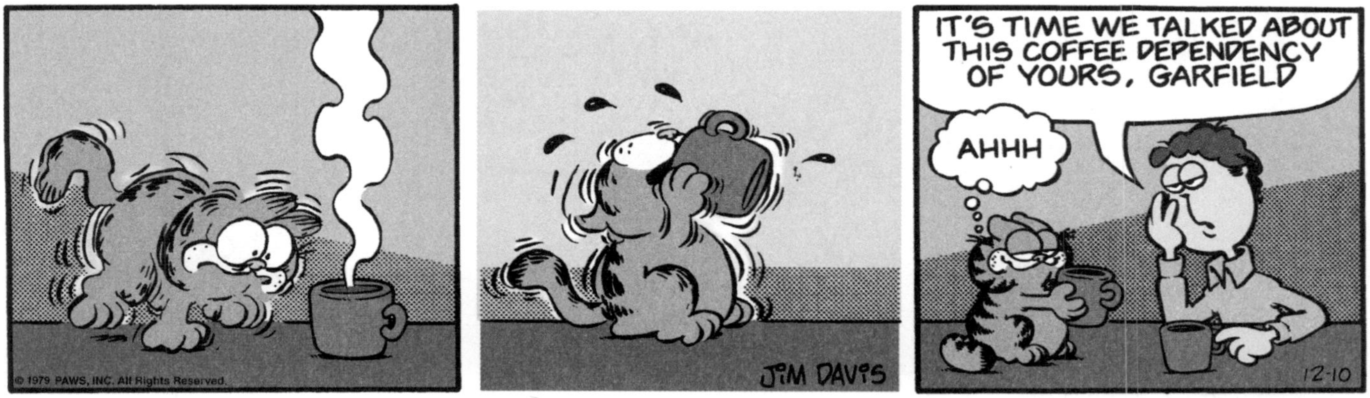
© 1979 PAWS, INC. All Rights Reserved.
JIM DAVIS
IT'S TIME WE TALKED ABOUT THIS COFFEE DEPENDENCY OF YOURS, GARFIELD
AHHH
12-10

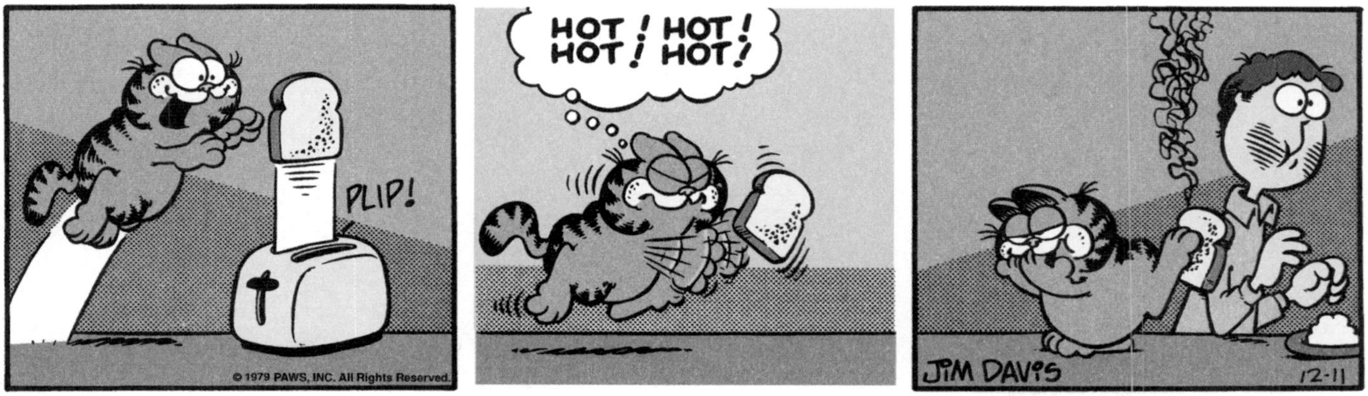
PLIP!
© 1979 PAWS, INC. All Rights Reserved.
HOT! HOT! HOT! HOT!
JIM DAVIS
12-11

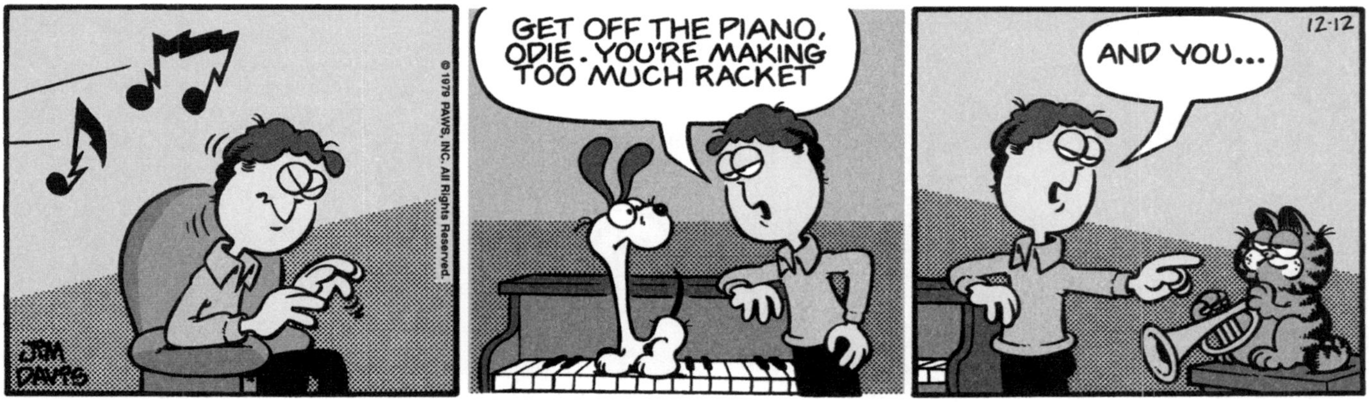
© 1979 PAWS, INC. All Rights Reserved.
JIM DAVIS
GET OFF THE PIANO, ODIE. YOU'RE MAKING TOO MUCH RACKET
12-12
AND YOU...

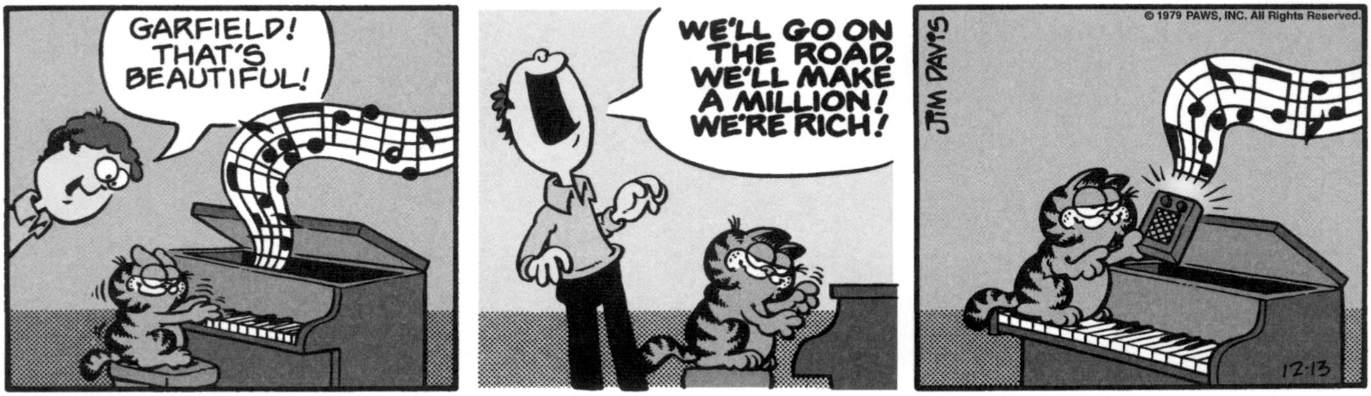
GARFIELD! THAT'S BEAUTIFUL!
WE'LL GO ON THE ROAD. WE'LL MAKE A MILLION! WE'RE RICH!
JIM DAVIS
© 1979 PAWS, INC. All Rights Reserved.
12-13

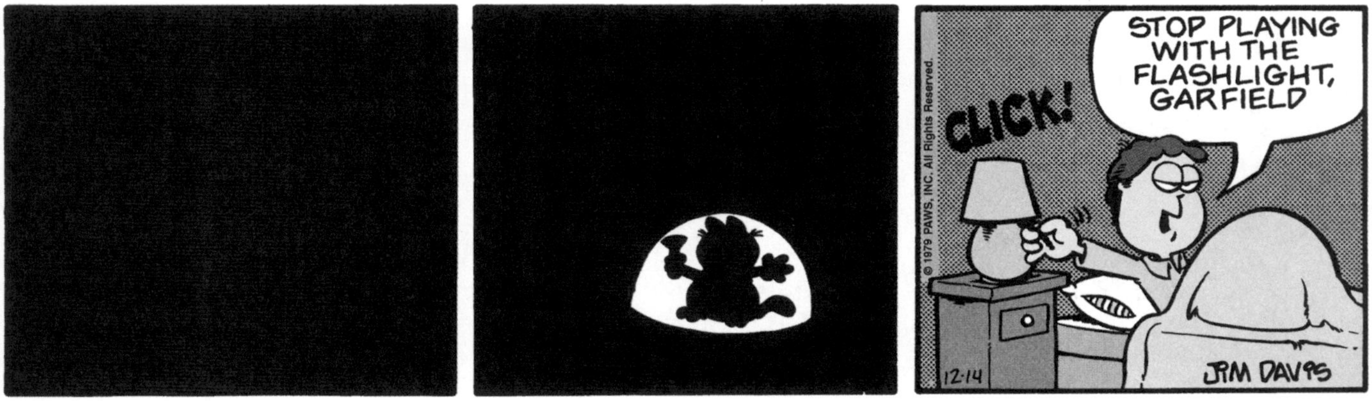
© 1979 PAWS, INC. All Rights Reserved.
CLICK!
STOP PLAYING WITH THE FLASHLIGHT, GARFIELD
12-14
JIM DAVIS

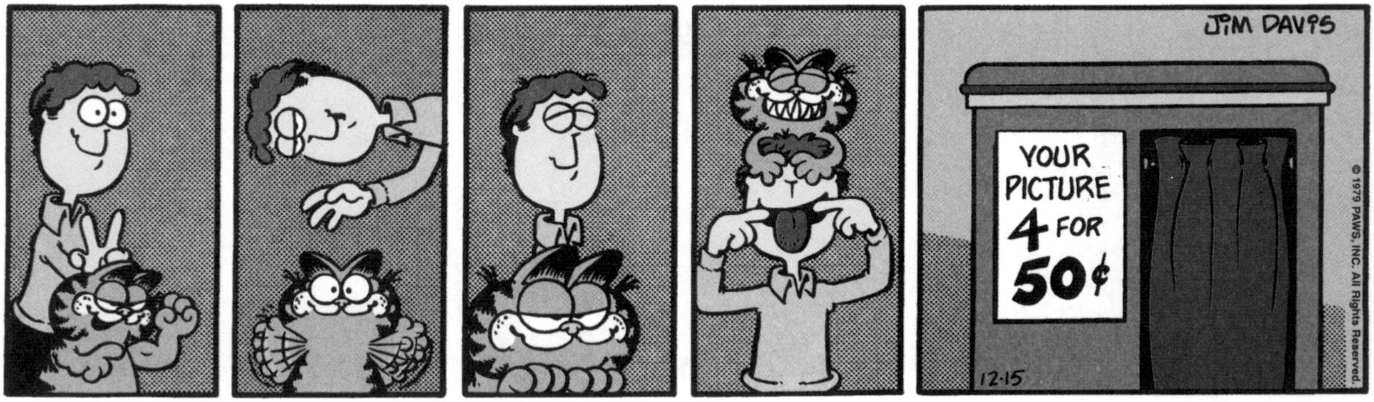
JIM DAVIS
YOUR PICTURE 4 FOR 50¢
© 1979 PAWS, INC. All Rights Reserved.
12-15

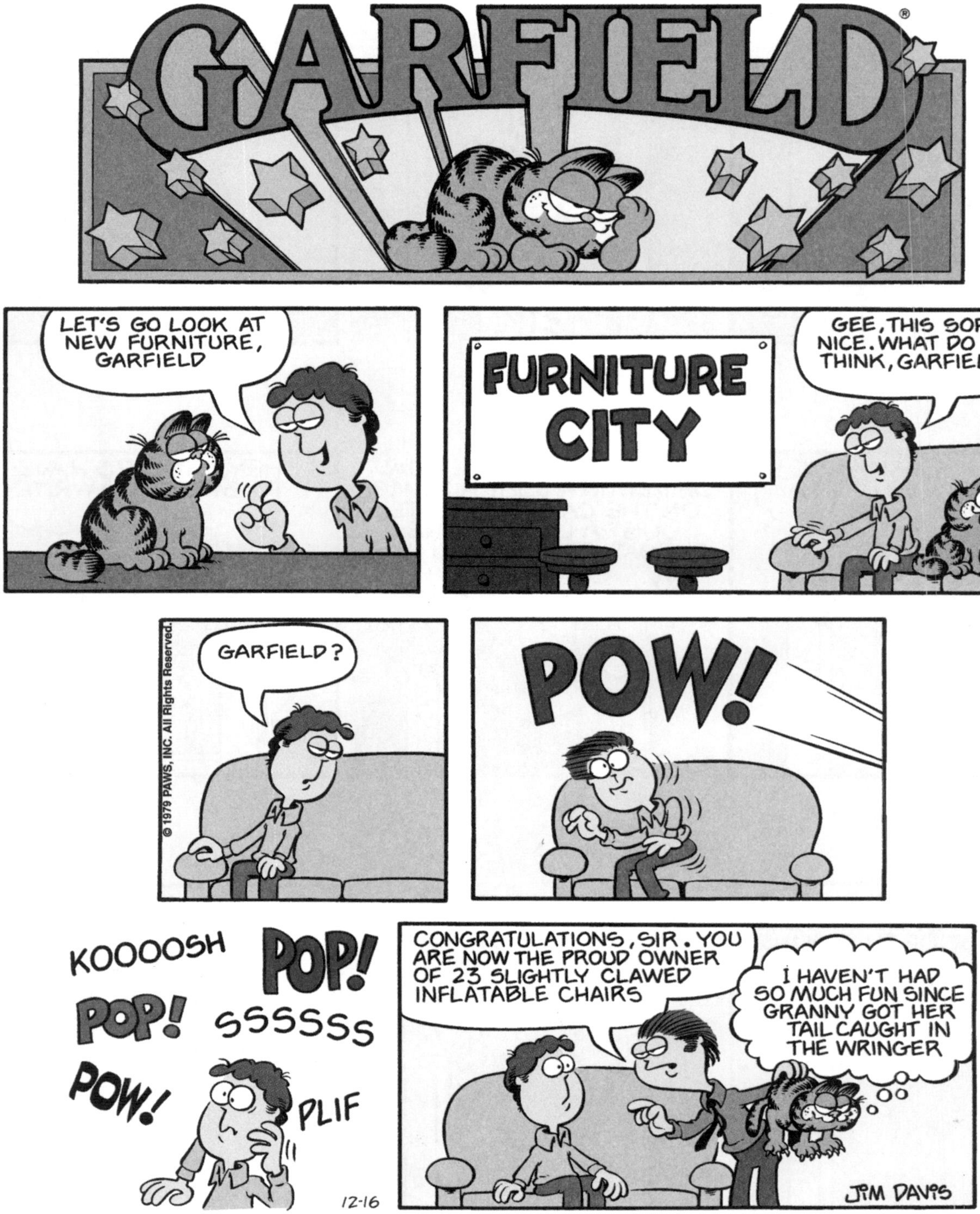
GARFIELD®
LET'S GO LOOK AT NEW FURNITURE, GARFIELD
FURNITURE CITY
GEE, THIS SOFA'S NICE. WHAT DO YOU THINK, GARFIELD?
GARFIELD?
POW!
KOOOOSH
POP!
POP!
SSSSSS
POW!
PLIF
CONGRATULATIONS, SIR. YOU ARE NOW THE PROUD OWNER OF 23 SLIGHTLY CLAWED INFLATABLE CHAIRS
I HAVEN'T HAD SO MUCH FUN SINCE GRANNY GOT HER TAIL CAUGHT IN THE WRINGER
JIM DAVIS
12-16

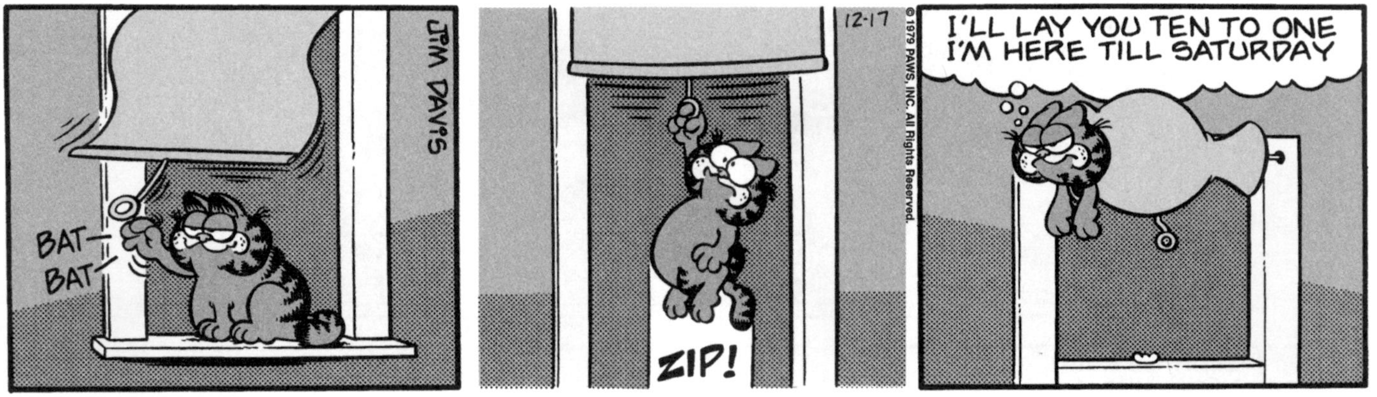
JIM DAVIS
BAT—
BAT—
12-17
© 1979 PAWS, INC. All Rights Reserved.
ZIP!
I'LL LAY YOU TEN TO ONE I'M HERE TILL SATURDAY

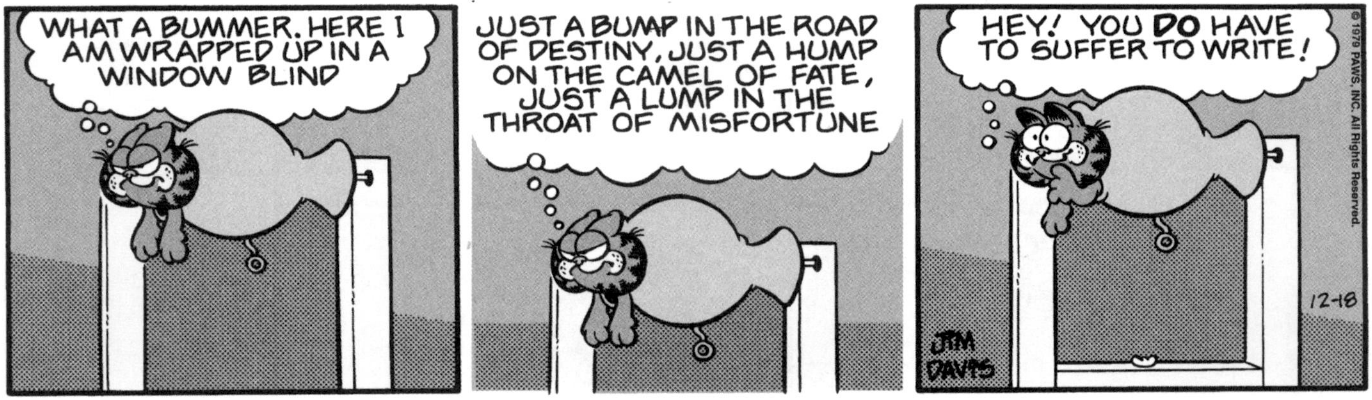
WHAT A BUMMER. HERE I AM WRAPPED UP IN A WINDOW BLIND
JUST A BUMP IN THE ROAD OF DESTINY, JUST A HUMP ON THE CAMEL OF FATE, JUST A LUMP IN THE THROAT OF MISFORTUNE
HEY! YOU **DO** HAVE TO SUFFER TO WRITE!
© 1979 PAWS, INC. All Rights Reserved.
12-18
JIM DAVIS

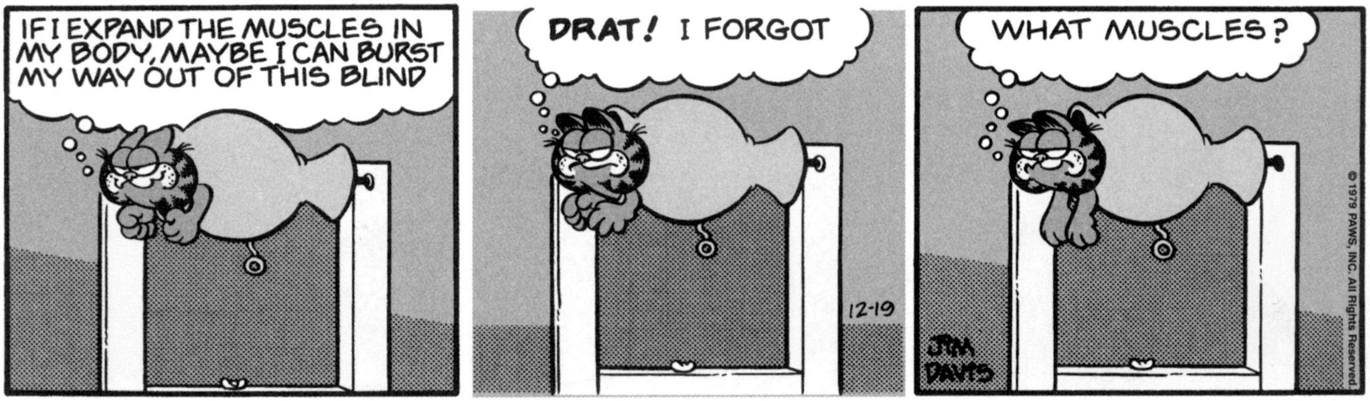
IF I EXPAND THE MUSCLES IN MY BODY, MAYBE I CAN BURST MY WAY OUT OF THIS BLIND
DRAT! I FORGOT
12-19
WHAT MUSCLES?
JIM DAVIS
© 1979 PAWS, INC. All Rights Reserved.

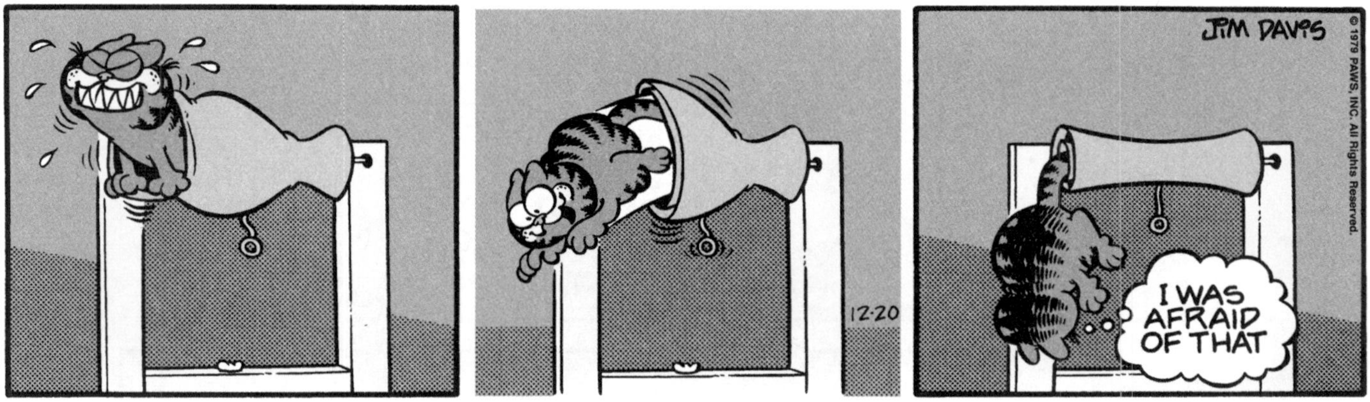
JIM DAVIS
12-20
I WAS AFRAID OF THAT
© 1979 PAWS, INC. All Rights Reserved.

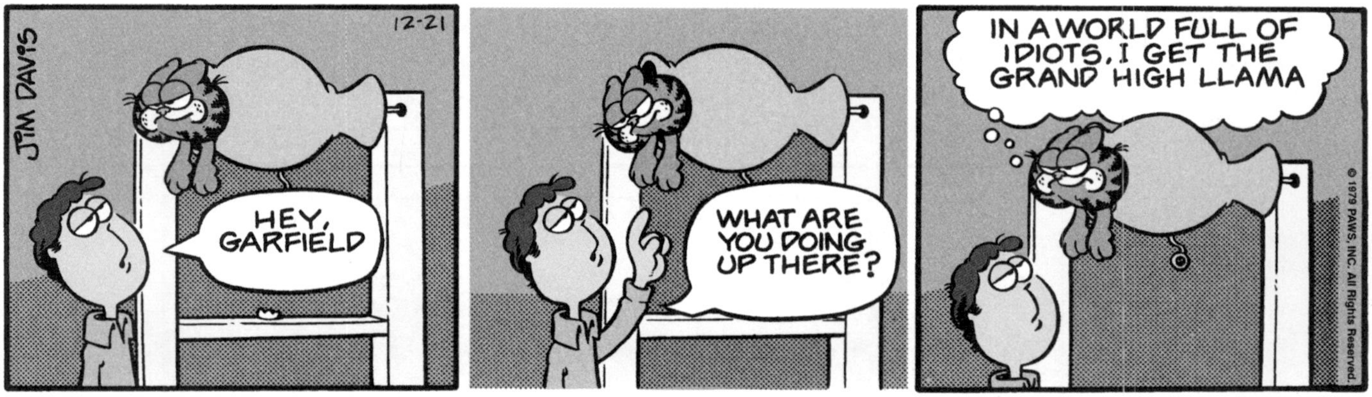
JIM DAVIS
12-21
HEY, GARFIELD
WHAT ARE YOU DOING UP THERE?
IN A WORLD FULL OF IDIOTS, I GET THE GRAND HIGH LLAMA
© 1979 PAWS, INC. All Rights Reserved.

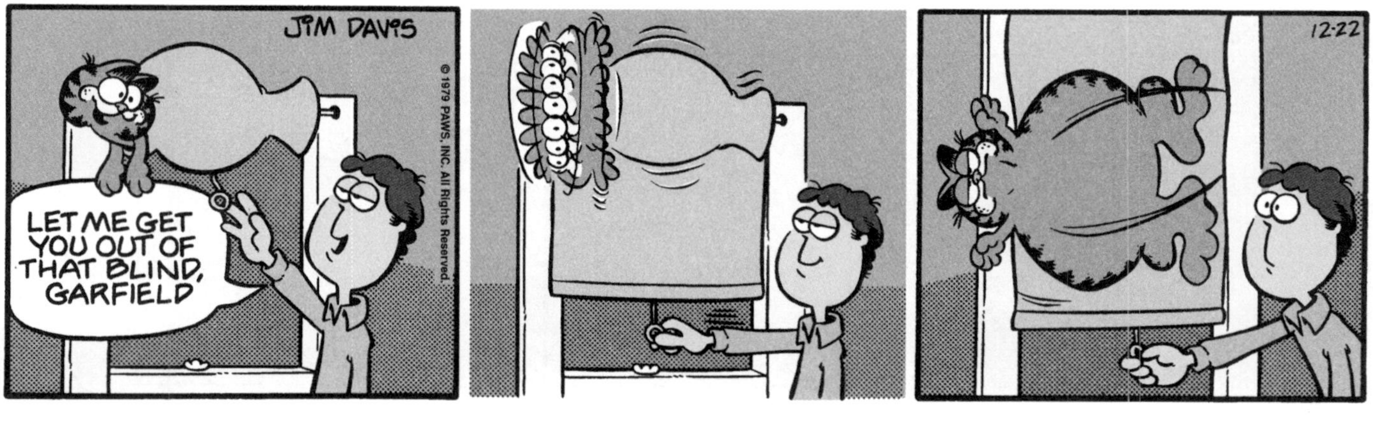
JIM DAVIS
© 1979 PAWS, INC. All Rights Reserved.
LET ME GET YOU OUT OF THAT BLIND, GARFIELD
12-22

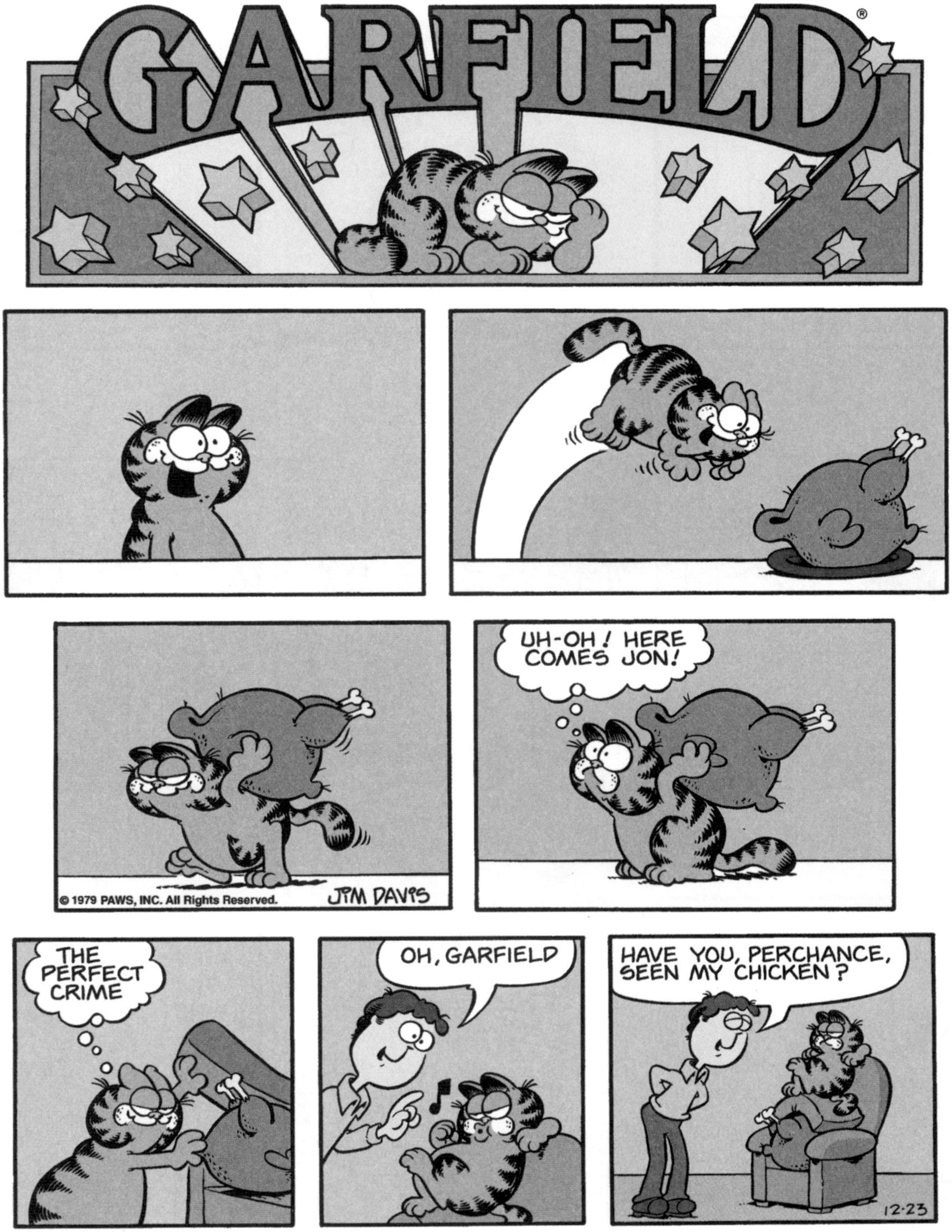
GARFIELD®
UH-OH! HERE COMES JON!
© 1979 PAWS, INC. All Rights Reserved.
JIM DAVIS
THE PERFECT CRIME
OH, GARFIELD
HAVE YOU, PERCHANCE, SEEN MY CHICKEN?
12·23

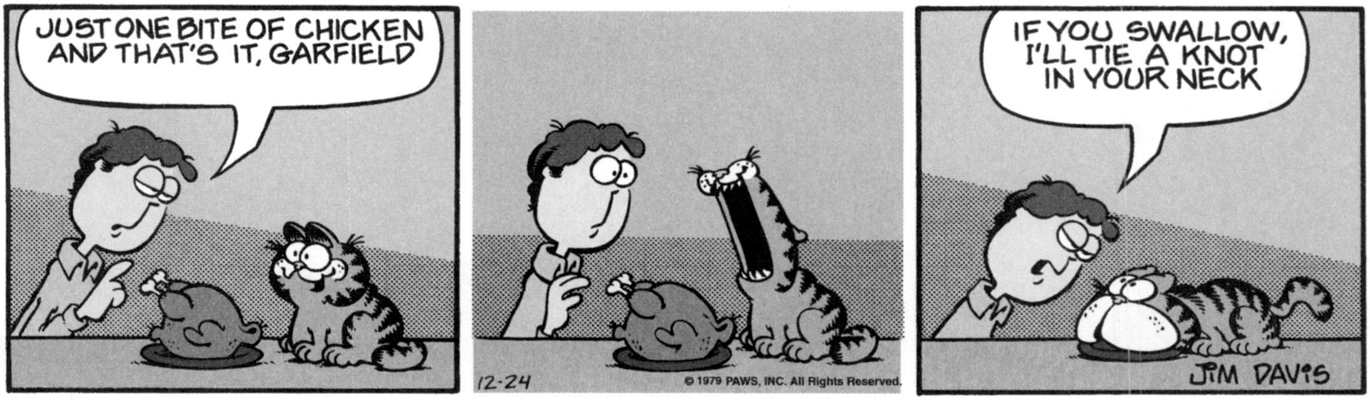
JUST ONE BITE OF CHICKEN AND THAT'S IT, GARFIELD
12-24
© 1979 PAWS, INC. All Rights Reserved.
IF YOU SWALLOW, I'LL TIE A KNOT IN YOUR NECK
JIM DAVIS

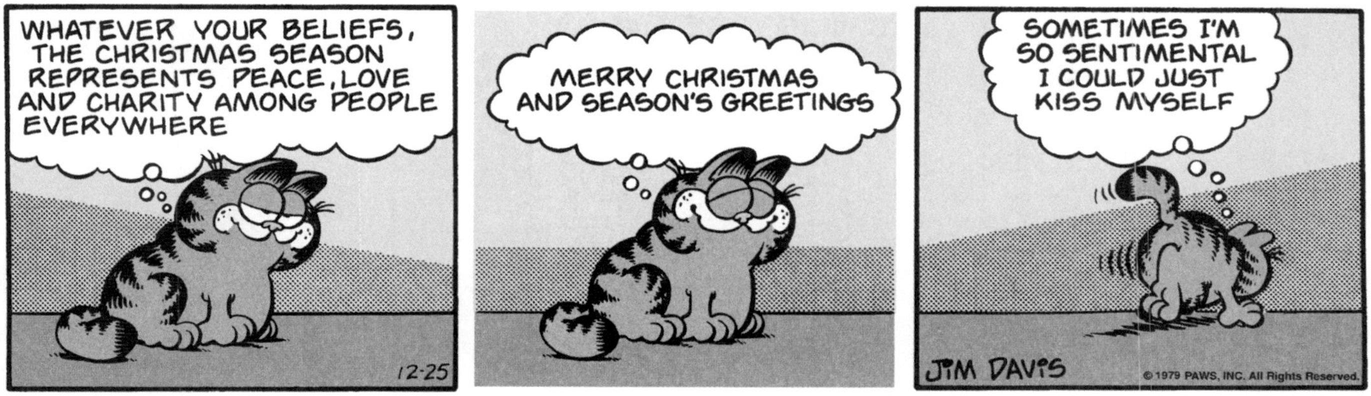
WHATEVER YOUR BELIEFS, THE CHRISTMAS SEASON REPRESENTS PEACE, LOVE AND CHARITY AMONG PEOPLE EVERYWHERE
12-25
MERRY CHRISTMAS AND SEASON'S GREETINGS
SOMETIMES I'M SO SENTIMENTAL I COULD JUST KISS MYSELF
JIM DAVIS
© 1979 PAWS, INC. All Rights Reserved.

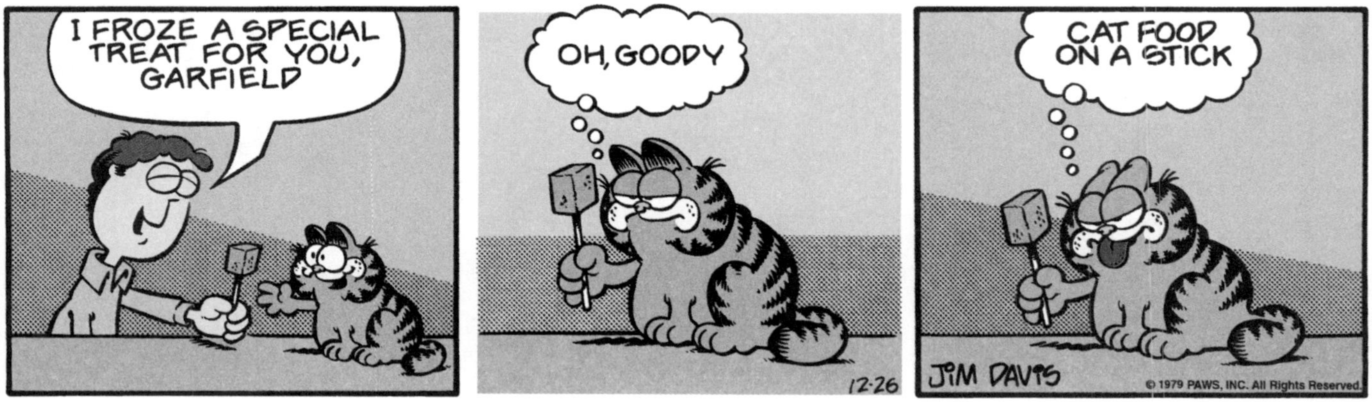
I FROZE A SPECIAL TREAT FOR YOU, GARFIELD
OH, GOODY
12-26
CAT FOOD ON A STICK
JIM DAVIS
© 1979 PAWS, INC. All Rights Reserved.

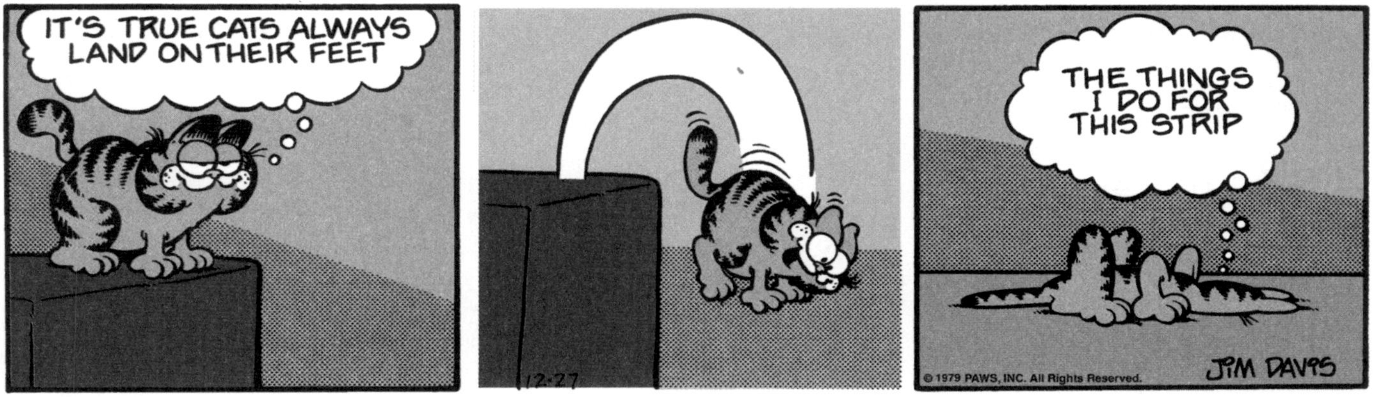
IT'S TRUE CATS ALWAYS LAND ON THEIR FEET
12-27
THE THINGS I DO FOR THIS STRIP
© 1979 PAWS, INC. All Rights Reserved.
JIM DAVIS

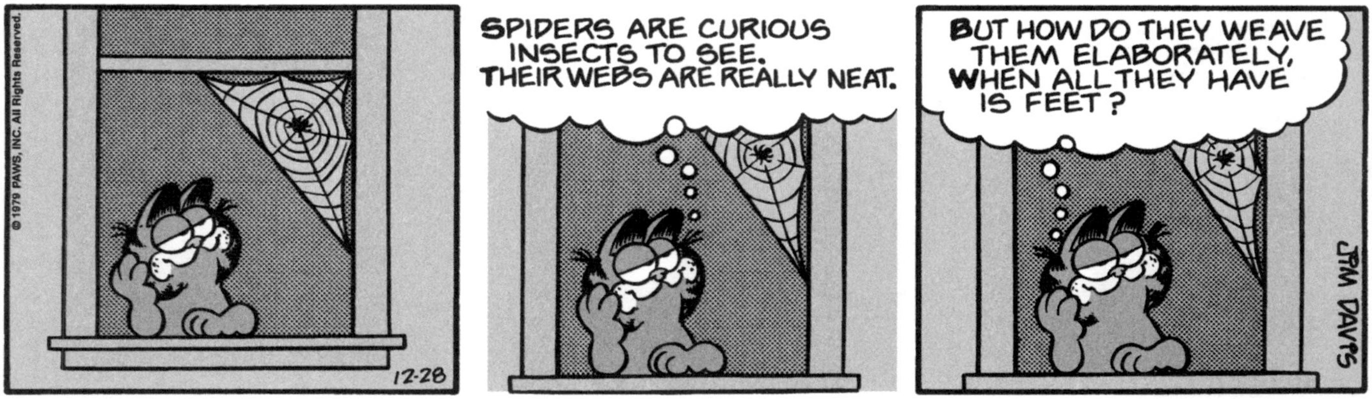
© 1979 PAWS, INC. All Rights Reserved.
12-28
SPIDERS ARE CURIOUS INSECTS TO SEE. THEIR WEBS ARE REALLY NEAT.
BUT HOW DO THEY WEAVE THEM ELABORATELY, WHEN ALL THEY HAVE IS FEET?
JIM DAVIS

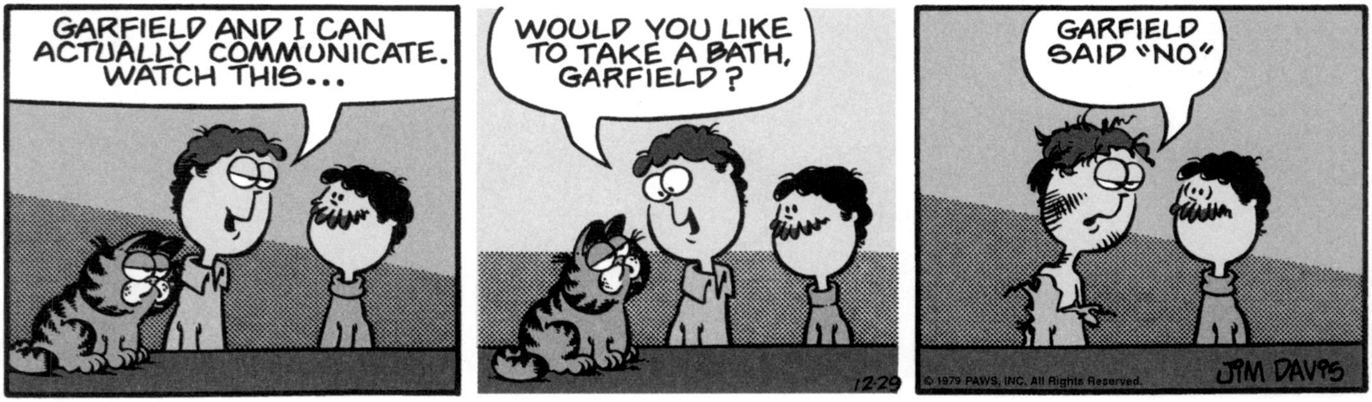
GARFIELD AND I CAN ACTUALLY COMMUNICATE. WATCH THIS...
WOULD YOU LIKE TO TAKE A BATH, GARFIELD?
12-29
GARFIELD SAID "NO"
© 1979 PAWS, INC. All Rights Reserved.
JIM DAVIS

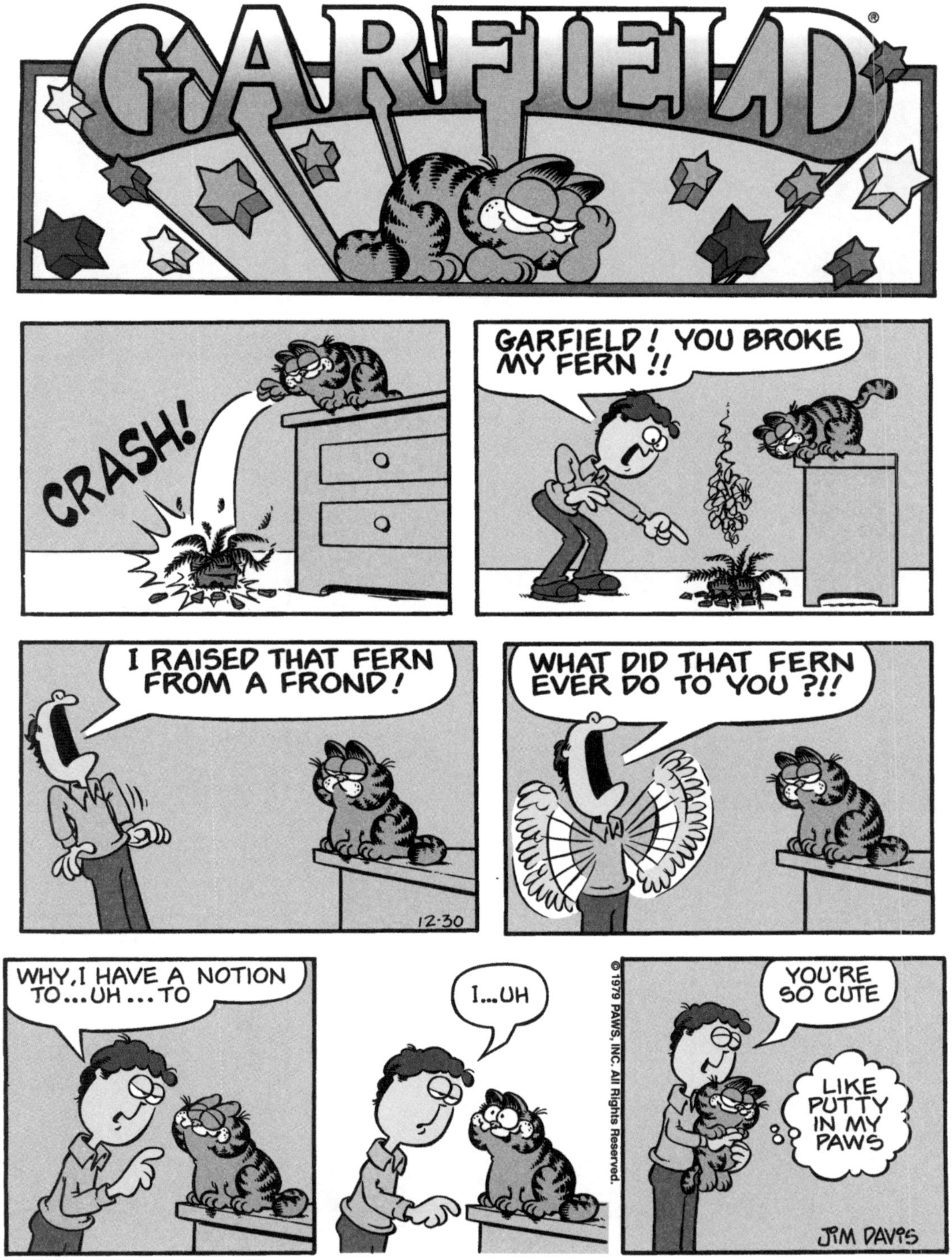
GARFIELD®
CRASH!
GARFIELD! YOU BROKE MY FERN!!
I RAISED THAT FERN FROM A FROND!
12-30
WHAT DID THAT FERN EVER DO TO YOU?!!
WHY, I HAVE A NOTION TO... UH... TO
I... UH
© 1979 PAWS, INC. All Rights Reserved.
YOU'RE SO CUTE
LIKE PUTTY IN MY PAWS
JIM DAVIS

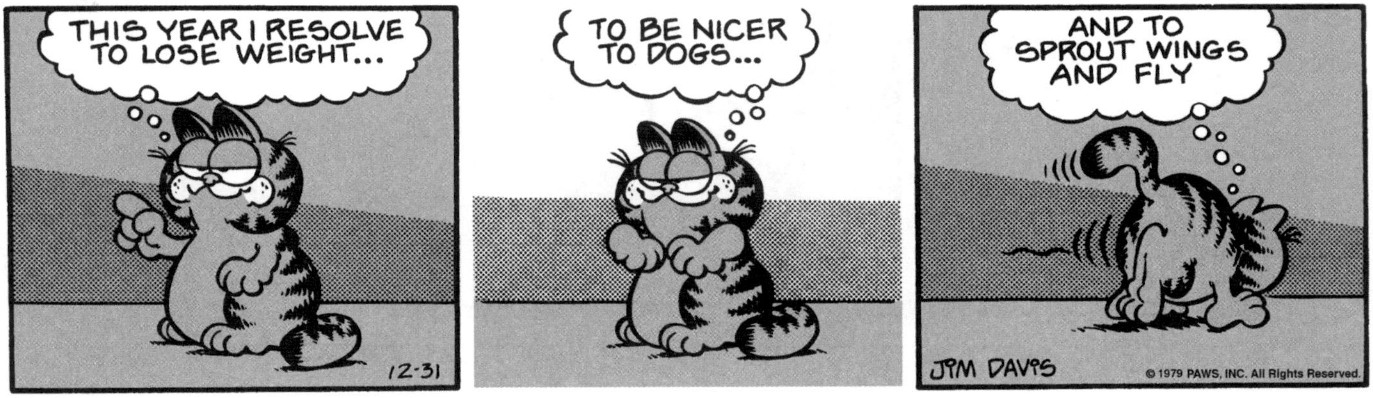
THIS YEAR I RESOLVE TO LOSE WEIGHT...
TO BE NICER TO DOGS...
AND TO SPROUT WINGS AND FLY
12-31
JIM DAVIS
© 1979 PAWS, INC. All Rights Reserved.

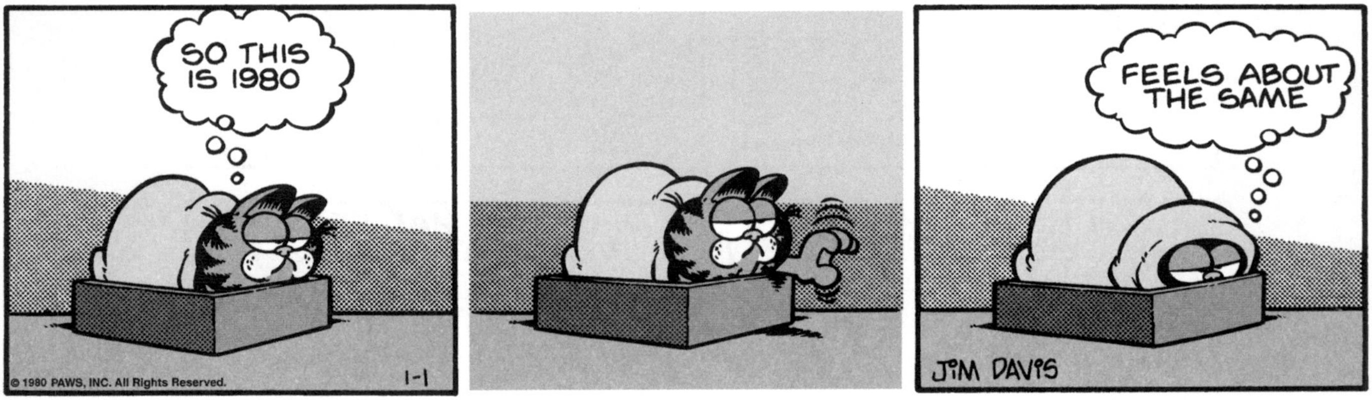
SO THIS IS 1980
© 1980 PAWS, INC. All Rights Reserved.
1-1
FEELS ABOUT THE SAME
JIM DAVIS

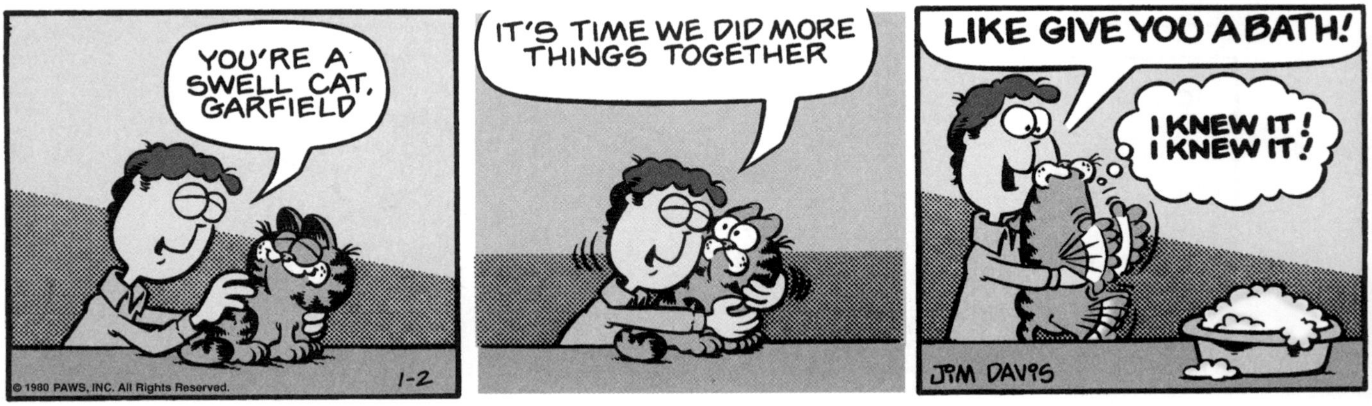
YOU'RE A SWELL CAT, GARFIELD
© 1980 PAWS, INC. All Rights Reserved.
1-2
IT'S TIME WE DID MORE THINGS TOGETHER
LIKE GIVE YOU A BATH!
I KNEW IT! I KNEW IT!
JIM DAVIS

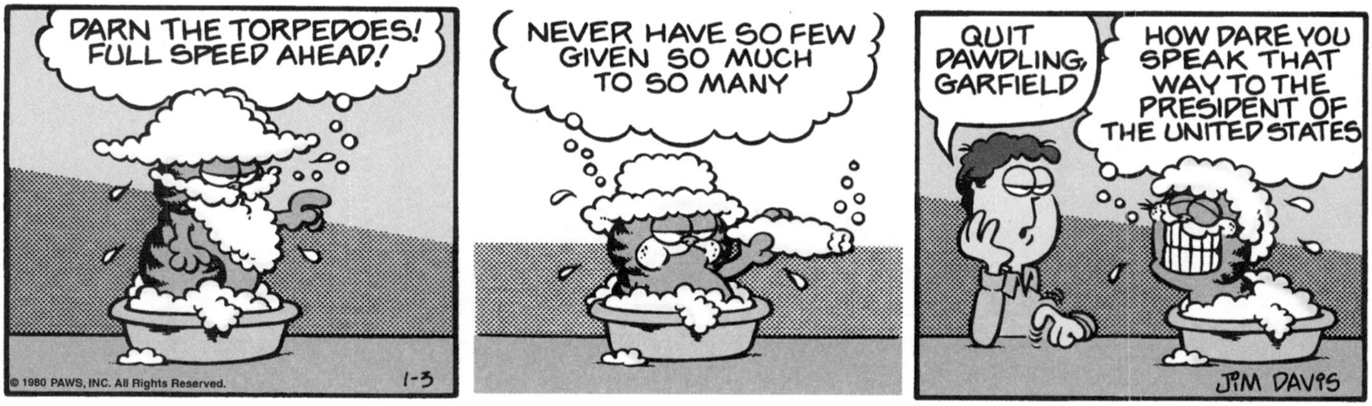
DARN THE TORPEDOES! FULL SPEED AHEAD!
© 1980 PAWS, INC. All Rights Reserved.
1-3
NEVER HAVE SO FEW GIVEN SO MUCH TO SO MANY
QUIT DAWDLING, GARFIELD
HOW DARE YOU SPEAK THAT WAY TO THE PRESIDENT OF THE UNITED STATES
JIM DAVIS

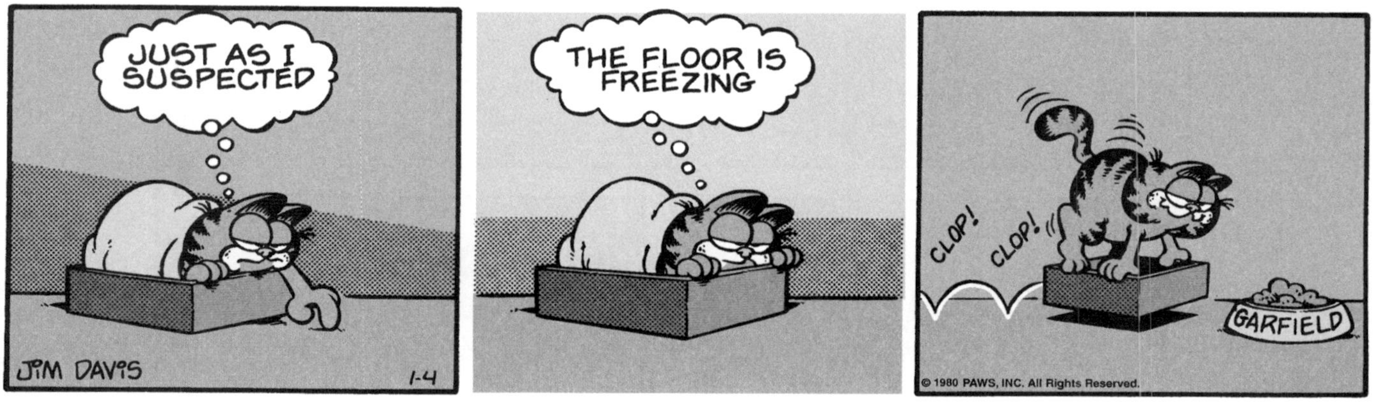
JUST AS I SUSPECTED
JIM DAVIS
1-4
THE FLOOR IS FREEZING
CLOP! CLOP!
GARFIELD
© 1980 PAWS, INC. All Rights Reserved.

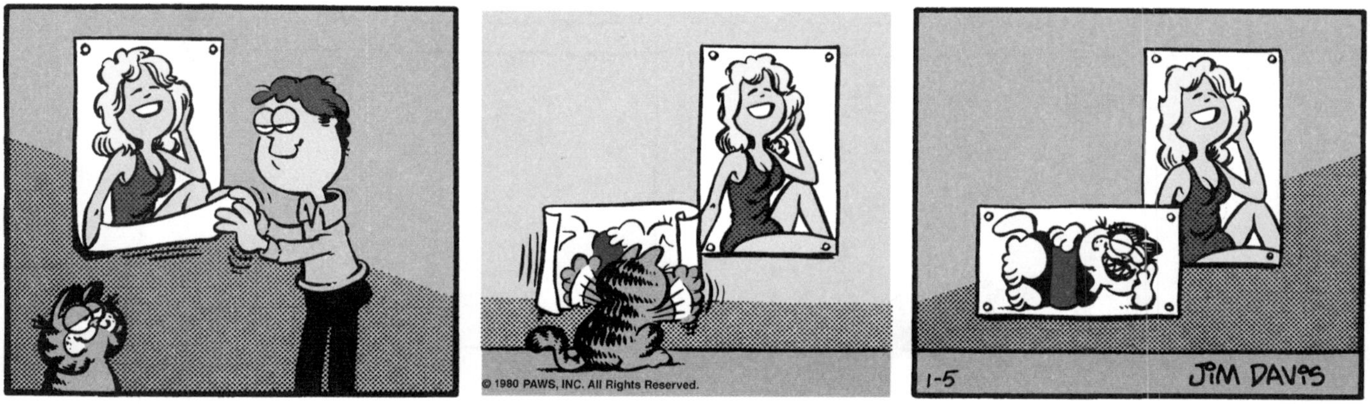
© 1980 PAWS, INC. All Rights Reserved.
1-5
JIM DAVIS

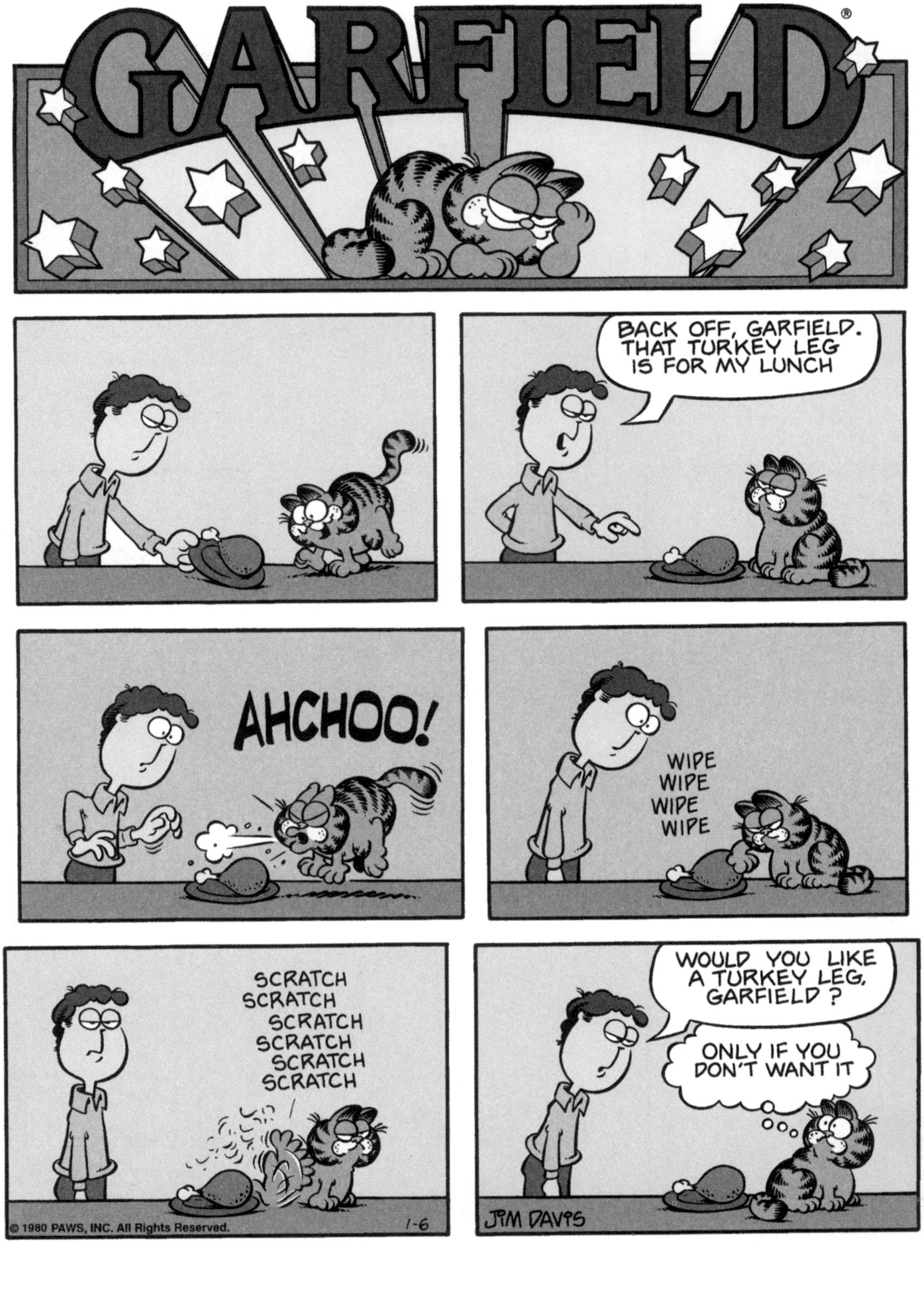
GARFIELD®
BACK OFF, GARFIELD. THAT TURKEY LEG IS FOR MY LUNCH
AHCHOO!
WIPE
WIPE
WIPE
WIPE
SCRATCH
SCRATCH
SCRATCH
SCRATCH
SCRATCH
SCRATCH
© 1980 PAWS, INC. All Rights Reserved.
1-6
JIM DAVIS
WOULD YOU LIKE A TURKEY LEG, GARFIELD?
ONLY IF YOU DON'T WANT IT

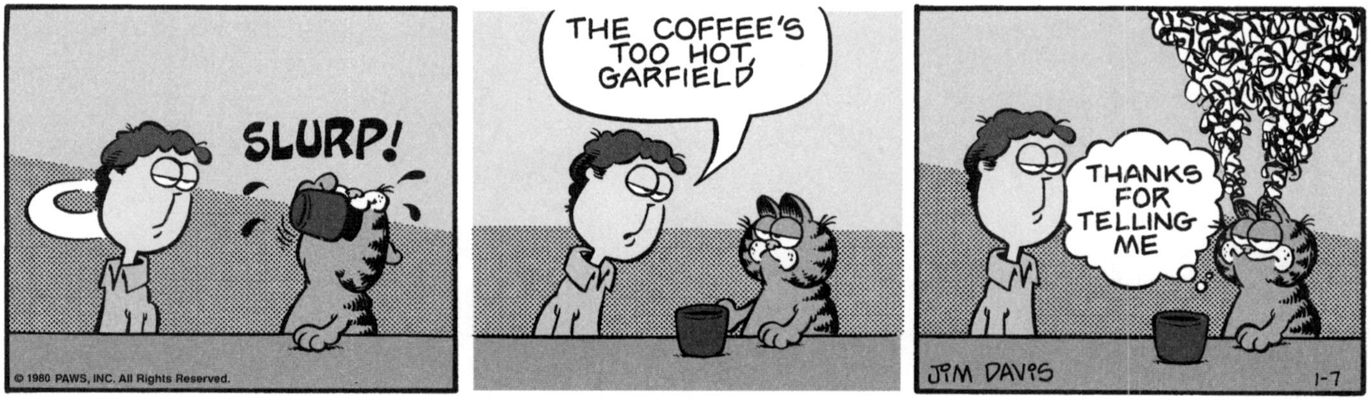
SLURP!
THE COFFEE'S TOO HOT, GARFIELD
THANKS FOR TELLING ME
© 1980 PAWS, INC. All Rights Reserved.
JIM DAVIS
1-7

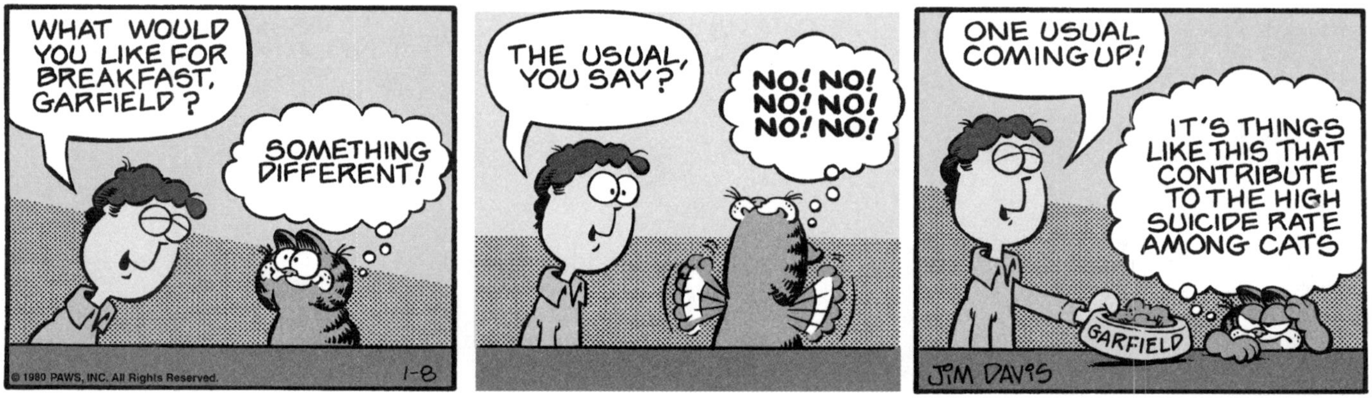
WHAT WOULD YOU LIKE FOR BREAKFAST, GARFIELD?
SOMETHING DIFFERENT!
THE USUAL, YOU SAY?
NO! NO! NO! NO! NO! NO!
ONE USUAL COMING UP!
IT'S THINGS LIKE THIS THAT CONTRIBUTE TO THE HIGH SUICIDE RATE AMONG CATS
GARFIELD
© 1980 PAWS, INC. All Rights Reserved.
1-8
JIM DAVIS

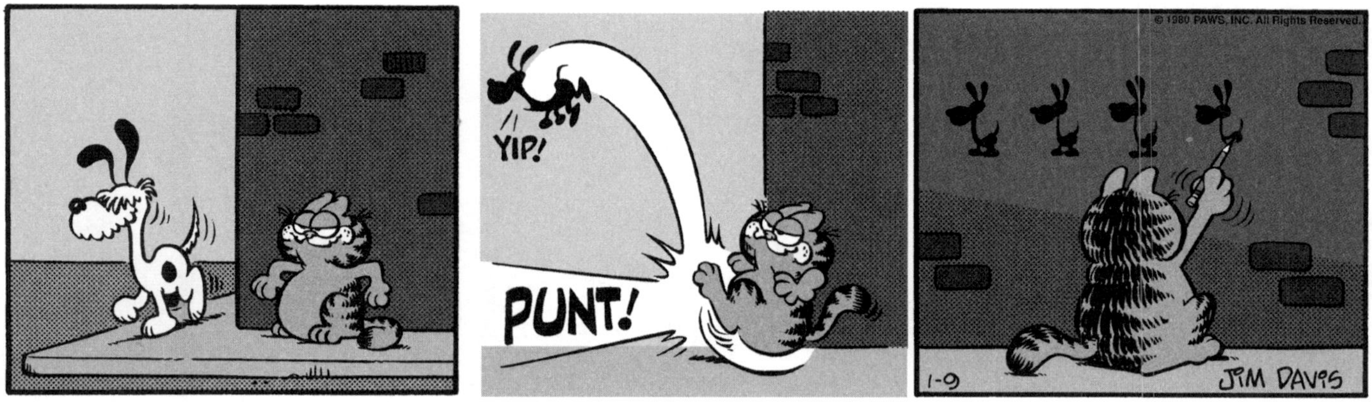
YIP!
PUNT!
© 1980 PAWS, INC. All Rights Reserved.
1-9
JIM DAVIS

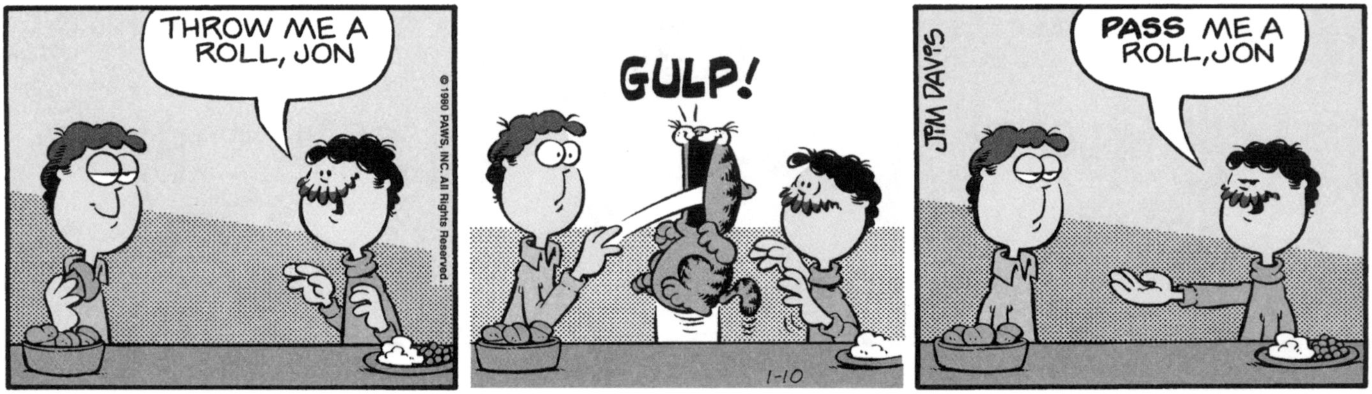
THROW ME A ROLL, JON
© 1980 PAWS, INC. All Rights Reserved.
GULP!
1-10
JIM DAVIS
PASS ME A ROLL, JON

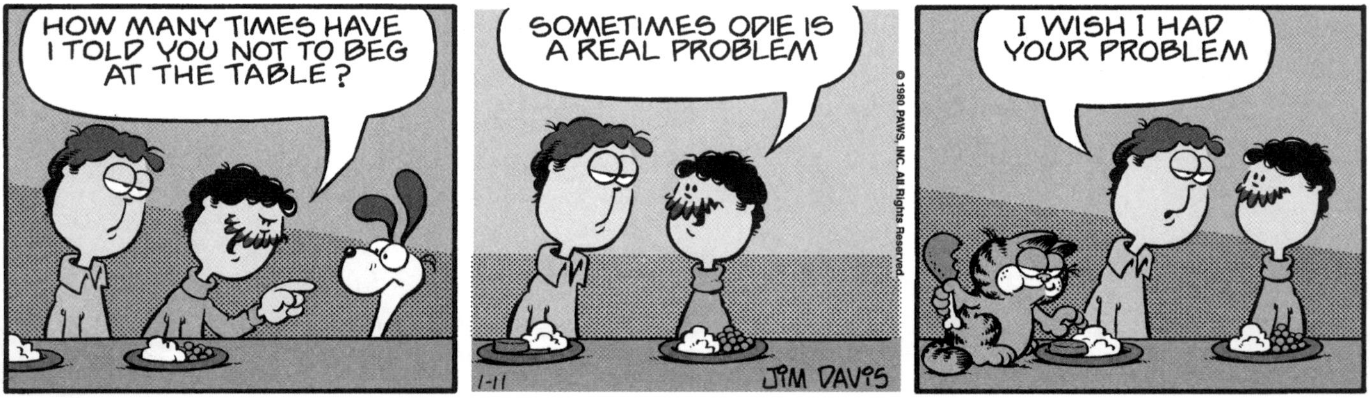
HOW MANY TIMES HAVE I TOLD YOU NOT TO BEG AT THE TABLE?
SOMETIMES ODIE IS A REAL PROBLEM
1-11
JIM DAVIS
© 1980 PAWS, INC. All Rights Reserved.
I WISH I HAD YOUR PROBLEM

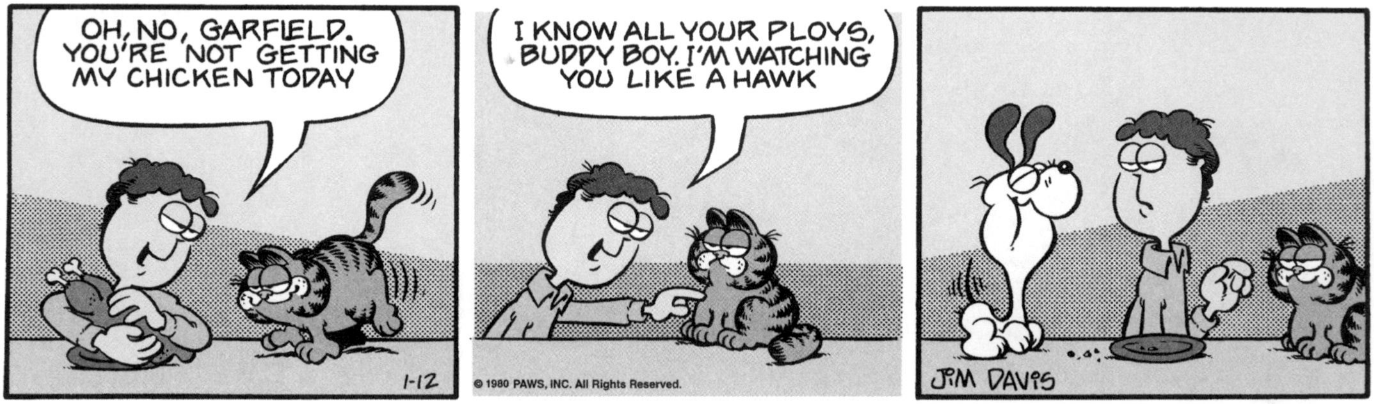
OH, NO, GARFIELD. YOU'RE NOT GETTING MY CHICKEN TODAY
1-12
I KNOW ALL YOUR PLOYS, BUDDY BOY. I'M WATCHING YOU LIKE A HAWK
© 1980 PAWS, INC. All Rights Reserved.
JIM DAVIS

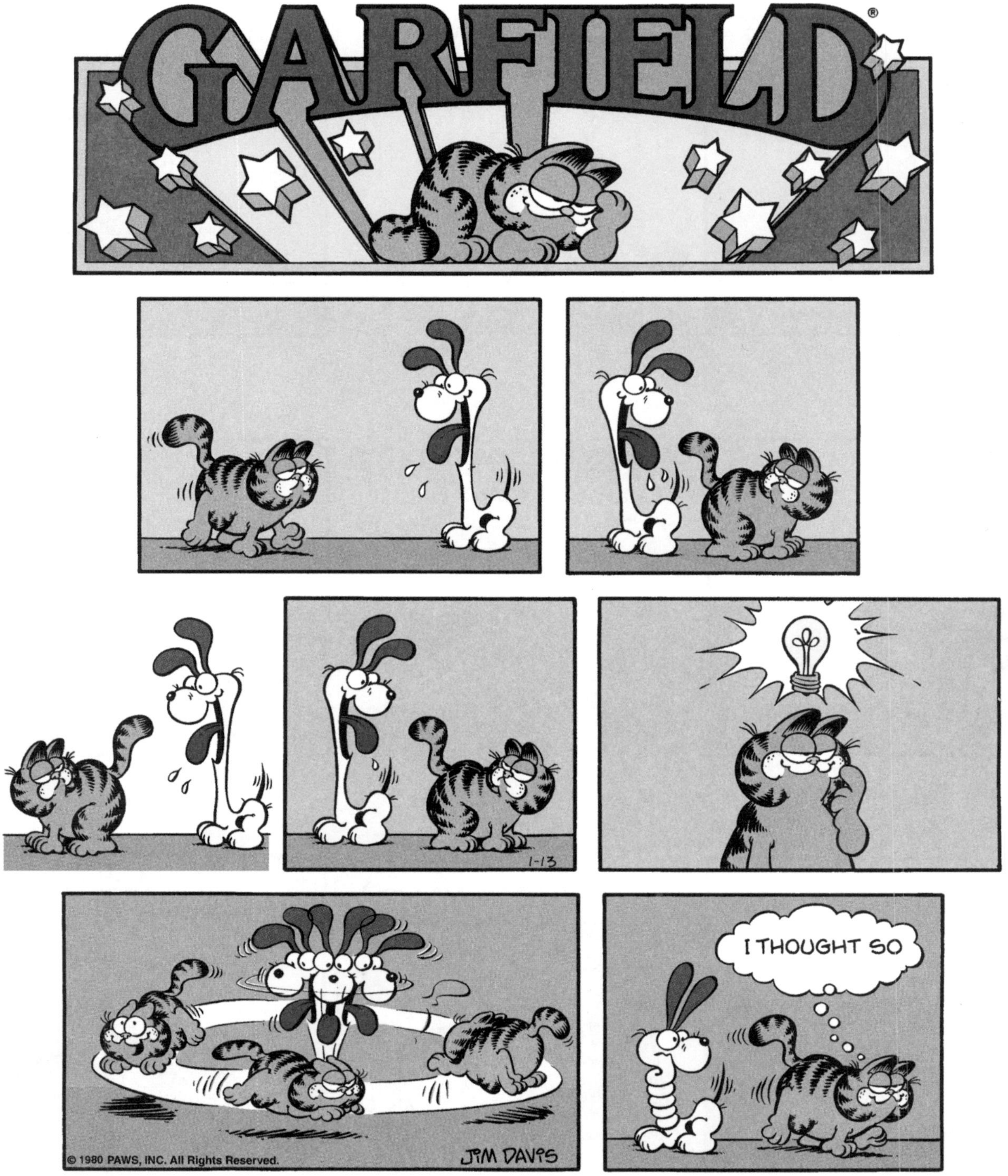
GARFIELD®
1-13
I THOUGHT SO
JIM DAVIS

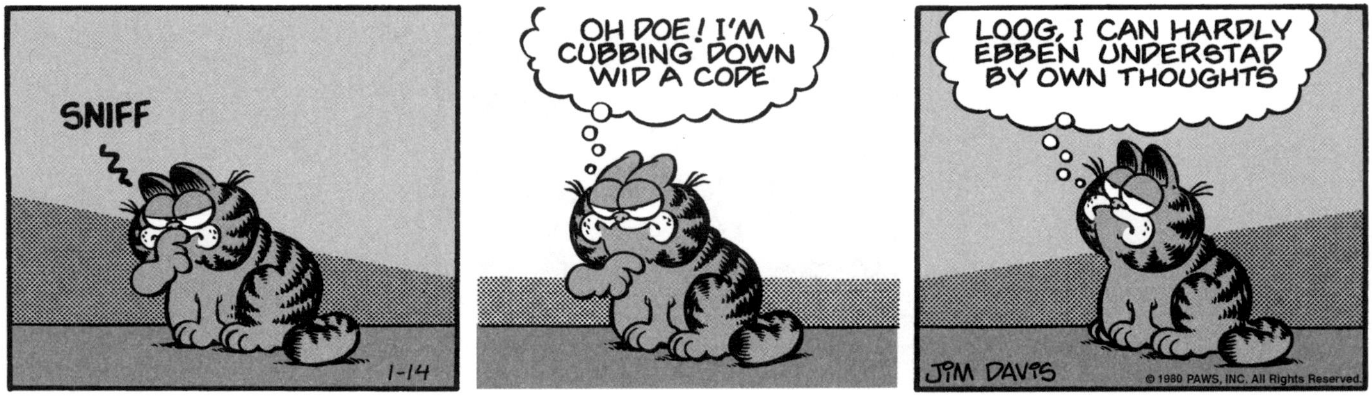
SNIFF
1-14
OH DOE! I'M CUBBING DOWN WID A CODE
LOOG, I CAN HARDLY EBBEN UNDERSTAD BY OWN THOUGHTS
JIM DAVIS
© 1980 PAWS, INC. All Rights Reserved.

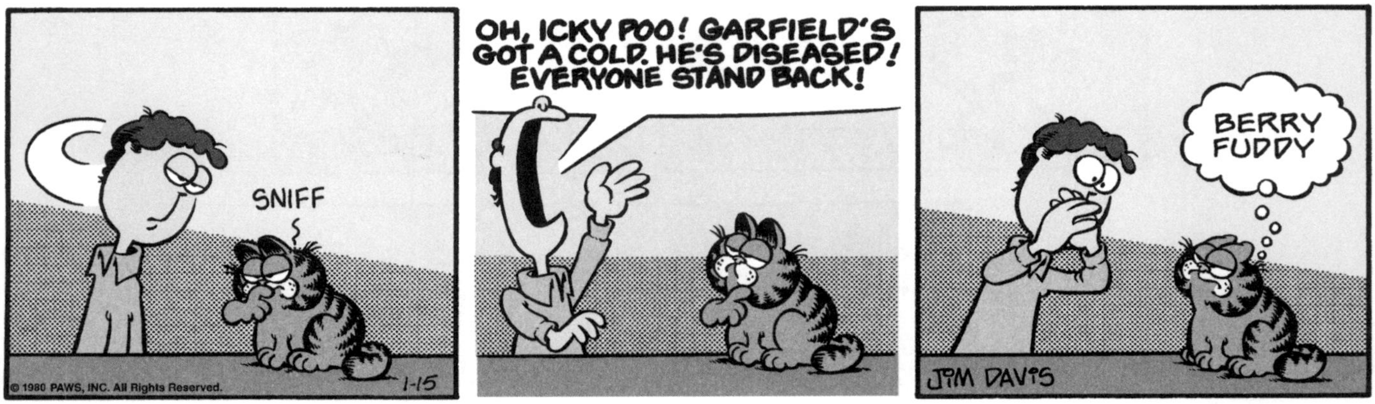
SNIFF
© 1980 PAWS, INC. All Rights Reserved.
1-15
OH, ICKY POO! GARFIELD'S GOT A COLD. HE'S DISEASED! EVERYONE STAND BACK!
BERRY FUDDY
JIM DAVIS

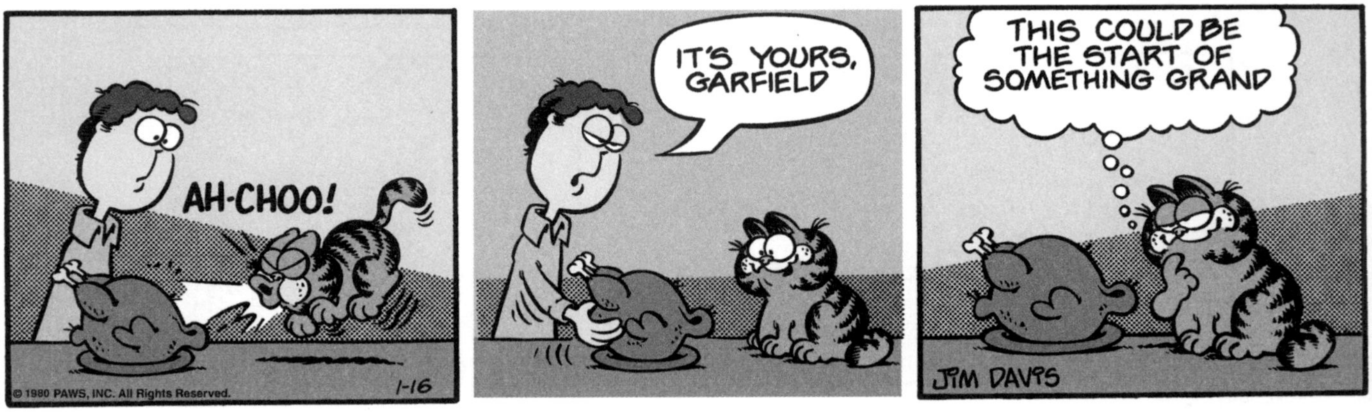
AH-CHOO!
© 1980 PAWS, INC. All Rights Reserved.
1-16
IT'S YOURS, GARFIELD
THIS COULD BE THE START OF SOMETHING GRAND
JIM DAVIS

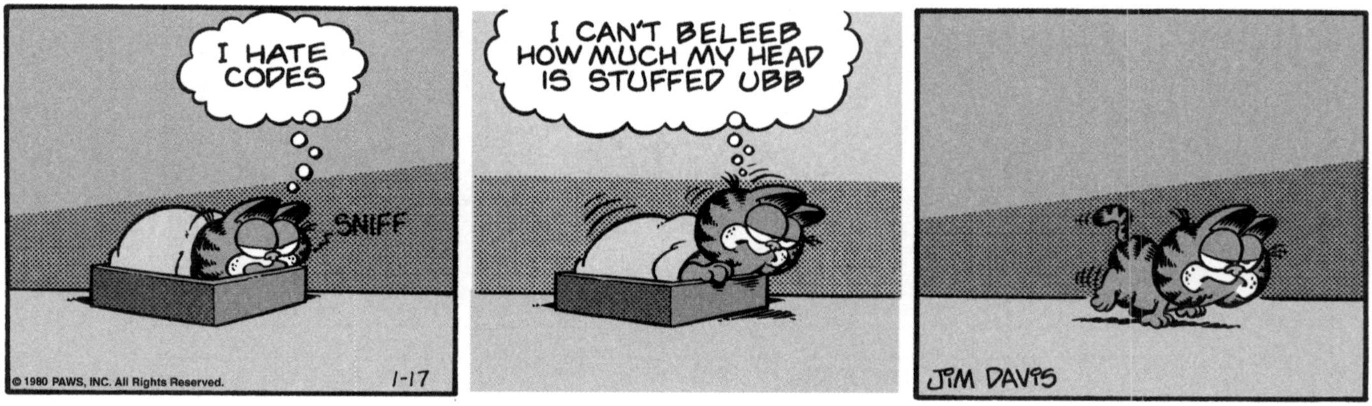
I HATE CODES
SNIFF
© 1980 PAWS, INC. All Rights Reserved.
1-17
I CAN'T BELEEB HOW MUCH MY HEAD IS STUFFED UBB
JIM DAVIS

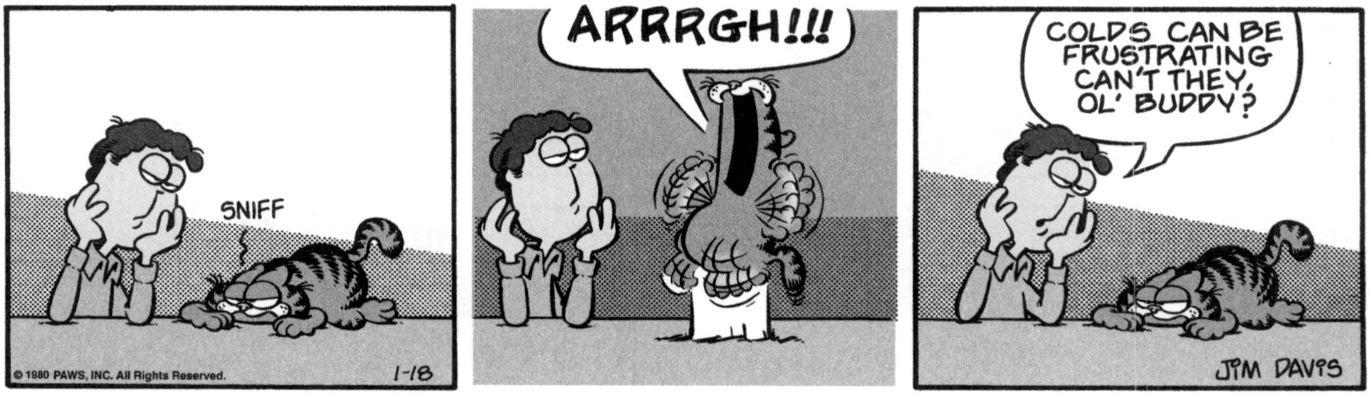
SNIFF
© 1980 PAWS, INC. All Rights Reserved.
1-18
ARRRGH!!!
COLDS CAN BE FRUSTRATING CAN'T THEY, OL' BUDDY?
JIM DAVIS

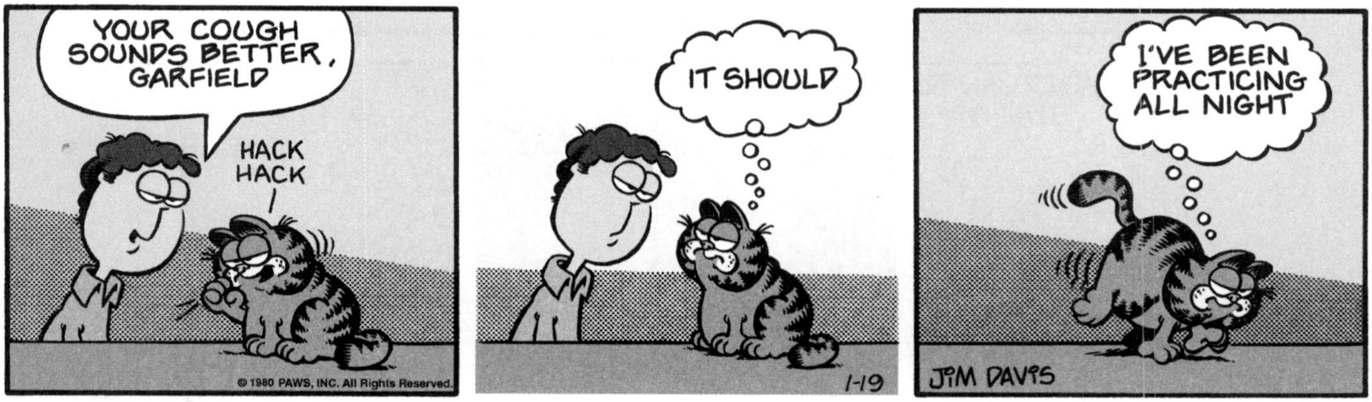
YOUR COUGH SOUNDS BETTER, GARFIELD
HACK HACK
© 1980 PAWS, INC. All Rights Reserved.
IT SHOULD
1-19
I'VE BEEN PRACTICING ALL NIGHT
JIM DAVIS

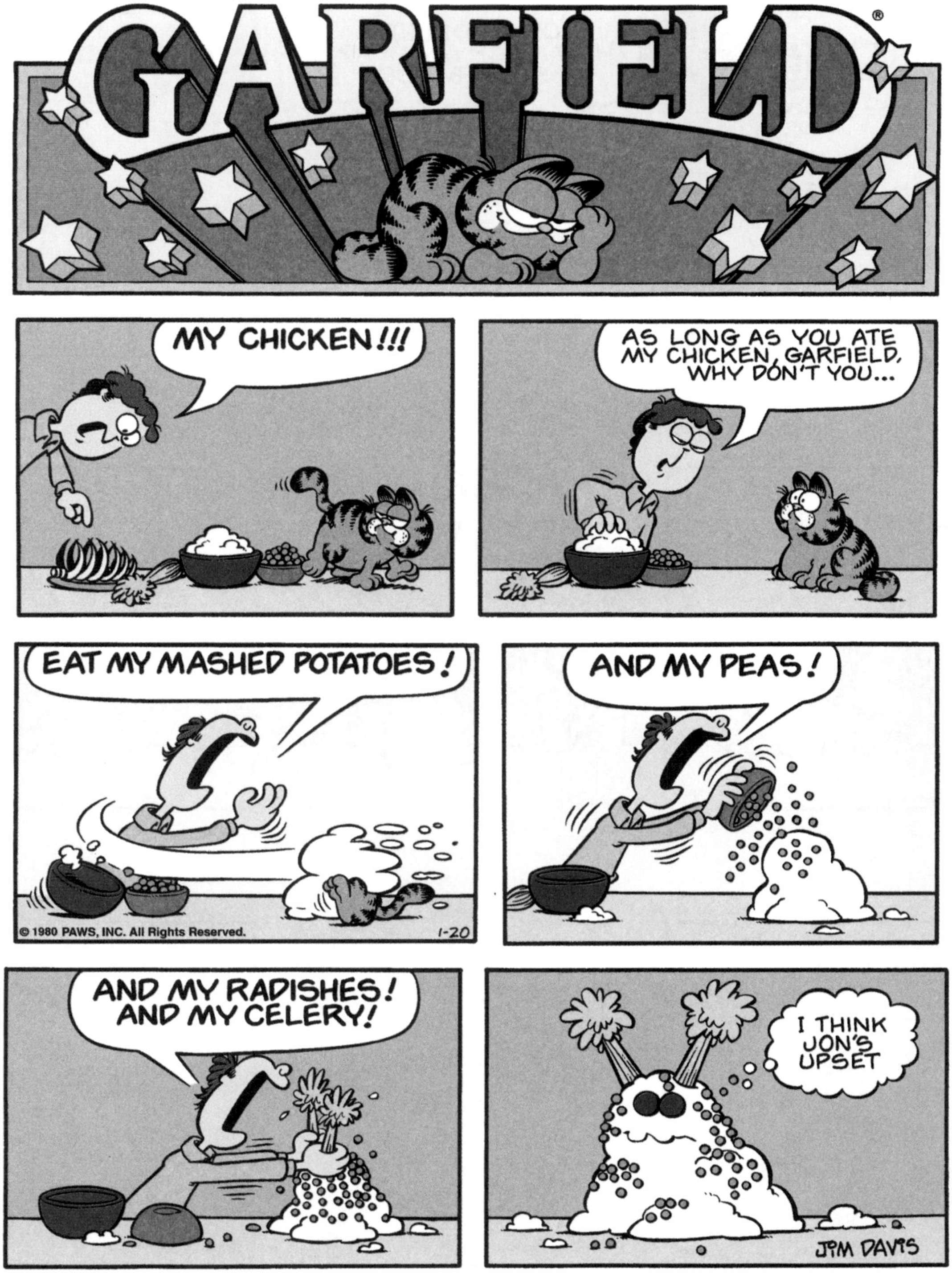
GARFIELD®
MY CHICKEN!!!
AS LONG AS YOU ATE MY CHICKEN, GARFIELD, WHY DON'T YOU...
EAT MY MASHED POTATOES!
© 1980 PAWS, INC. All Rights Reserved.
1-20
AND MY PEAS!
AND MY RADISHES! AND MY CELERY!
I THINK JON'S UPSET
JIM DAVIS

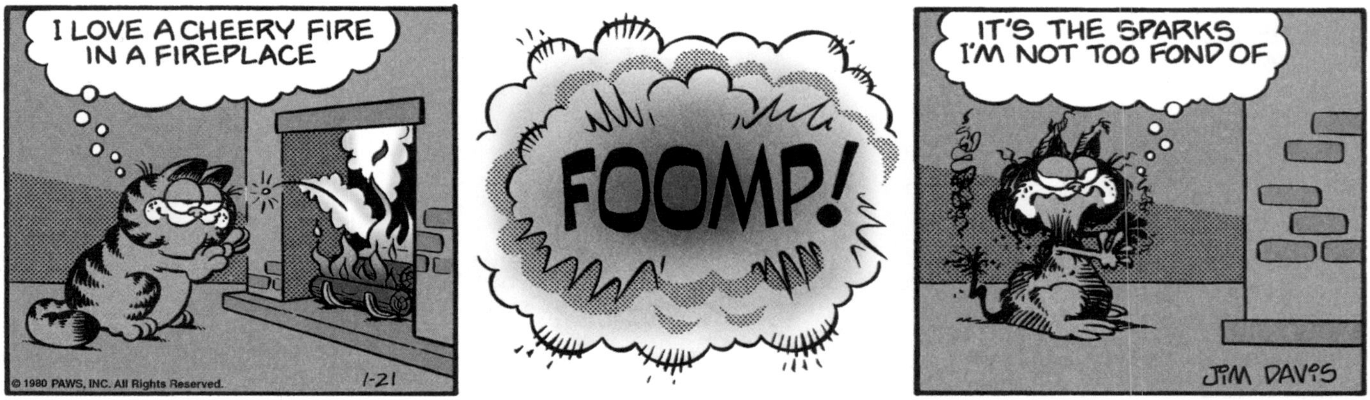
I LOVE A CHEERY FIRE IN A FIREPLACE
© 1980 PAWS, INC. All Rights Reserved.
1-21
FOOMP!
IT'S THE SPARKS I'M NOT TOO FOND OF
JIM DAVIS

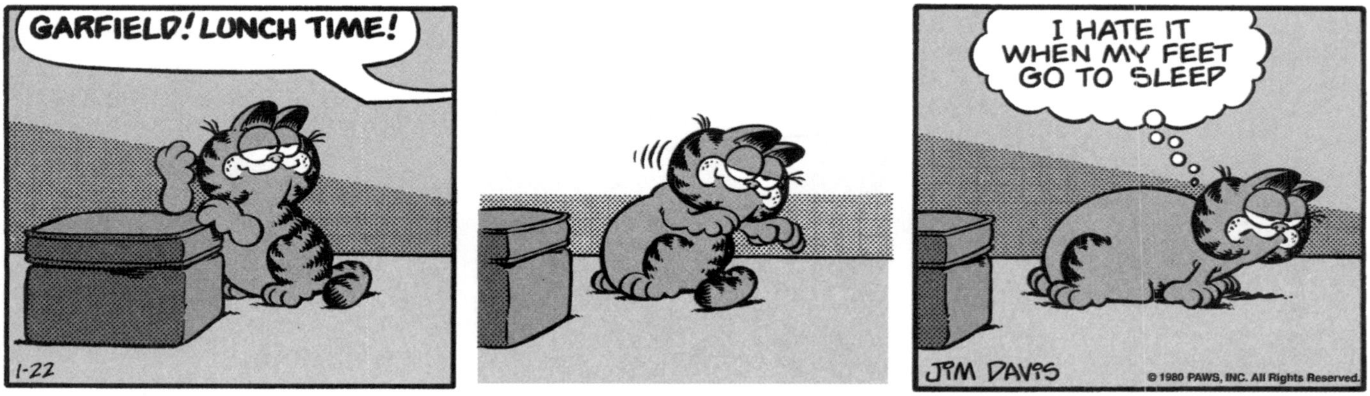
GARFIELD! LUNCH TIME!
1-22
I HATE IT WHEN MY FEET GO TO SLEEP
JIM DAVIS
© 1980 PAWS, INC. All Rights Reserved.

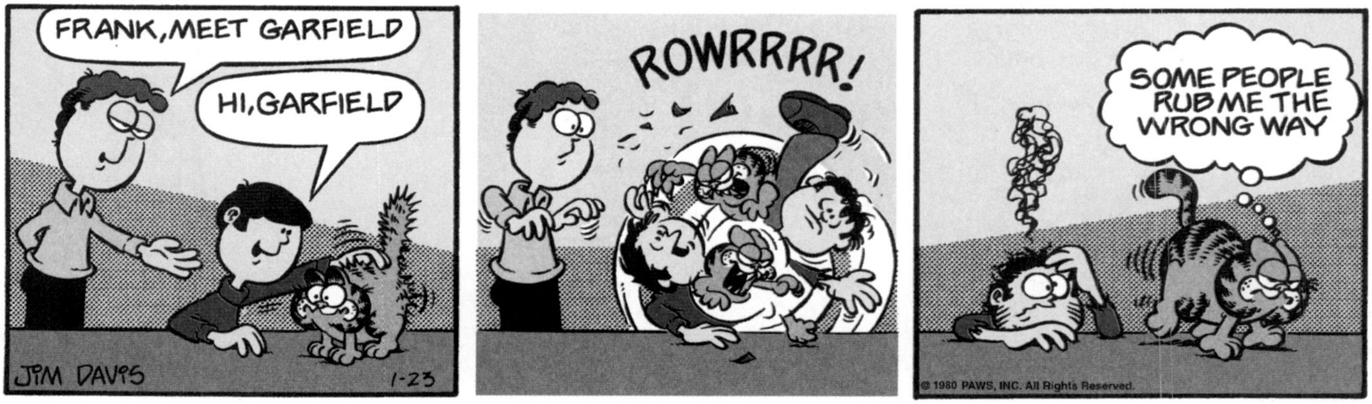
FRANK, MEET GARFIELD
HI, GARFIELD
JIM DAVIS
1-23
ROWRRRR!
SOME PEOPLE RUB ME THE WRONG WAY
© 1980 PAWS, INC. All Rights Reserved.

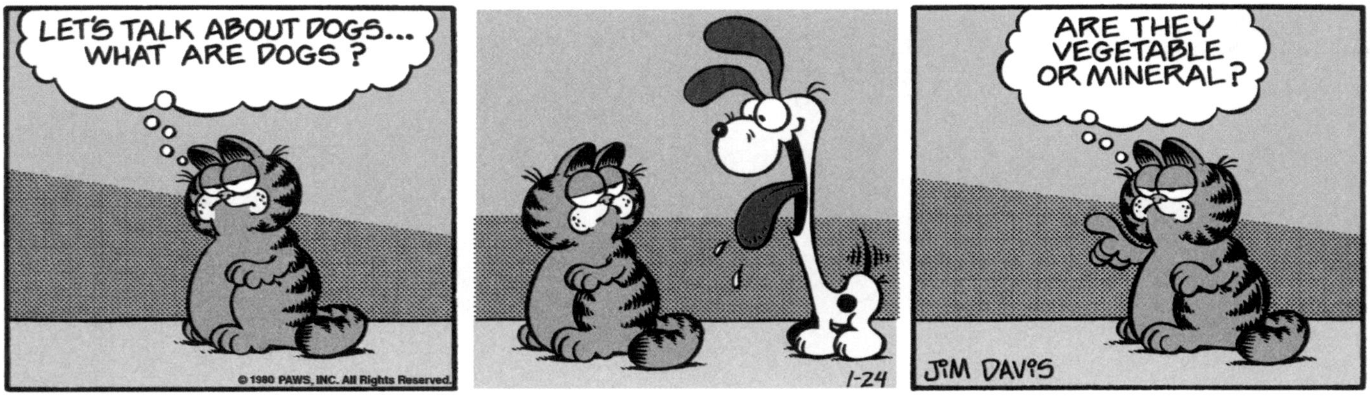
LET'S TALK ABOUT DOGS... WHAT ARE DOGS?
ARE THEY VEGETABLE OR MINERAL?
© 1980 PAWS, INC. All Rights Reserved.
1-24
JIM DAVIS

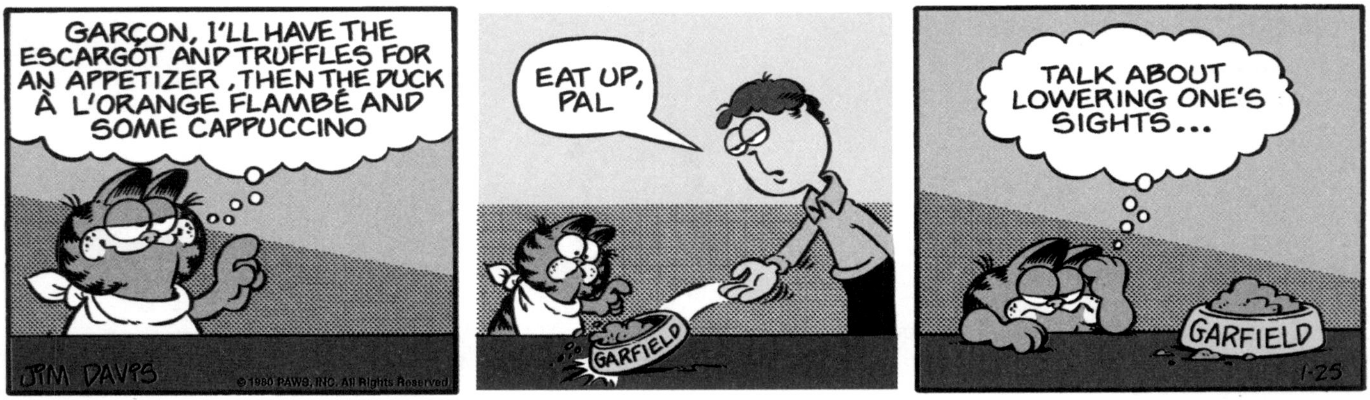
GARÇON, I'LL HAVE THE ESCARGÔT AND TRUFFLES FOR AN APPETIZER, THEN THE DUCK À L'ORANGE FLAMBÉ AND SOME CAPPUCCINO
JIM DAVIS
© 1980 PAWS, INC. All Rights Reserved.
EAT UP, PAL
GARFIELD
TALK ABOUT LOWERING ONE'S SIGHTS...
GARFIELD
1-25

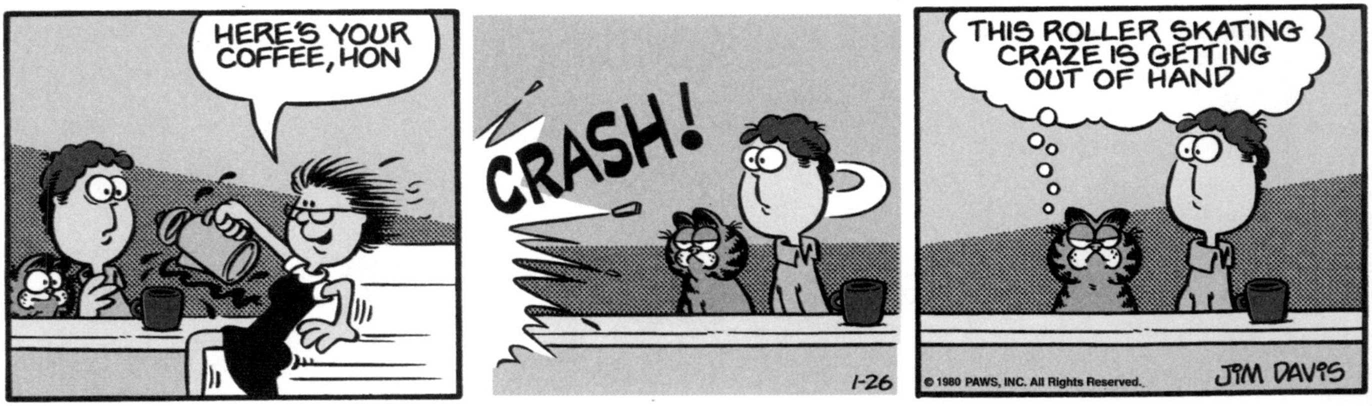
HERE'S YOUR COFFEE, HON
CRASH!
1-26
THIS ROLLER SKATING CRAZE IS GETTING OUT OF HAND
© 1980 PAWS, INC. All Rights Reserved.
JIM DAVIS

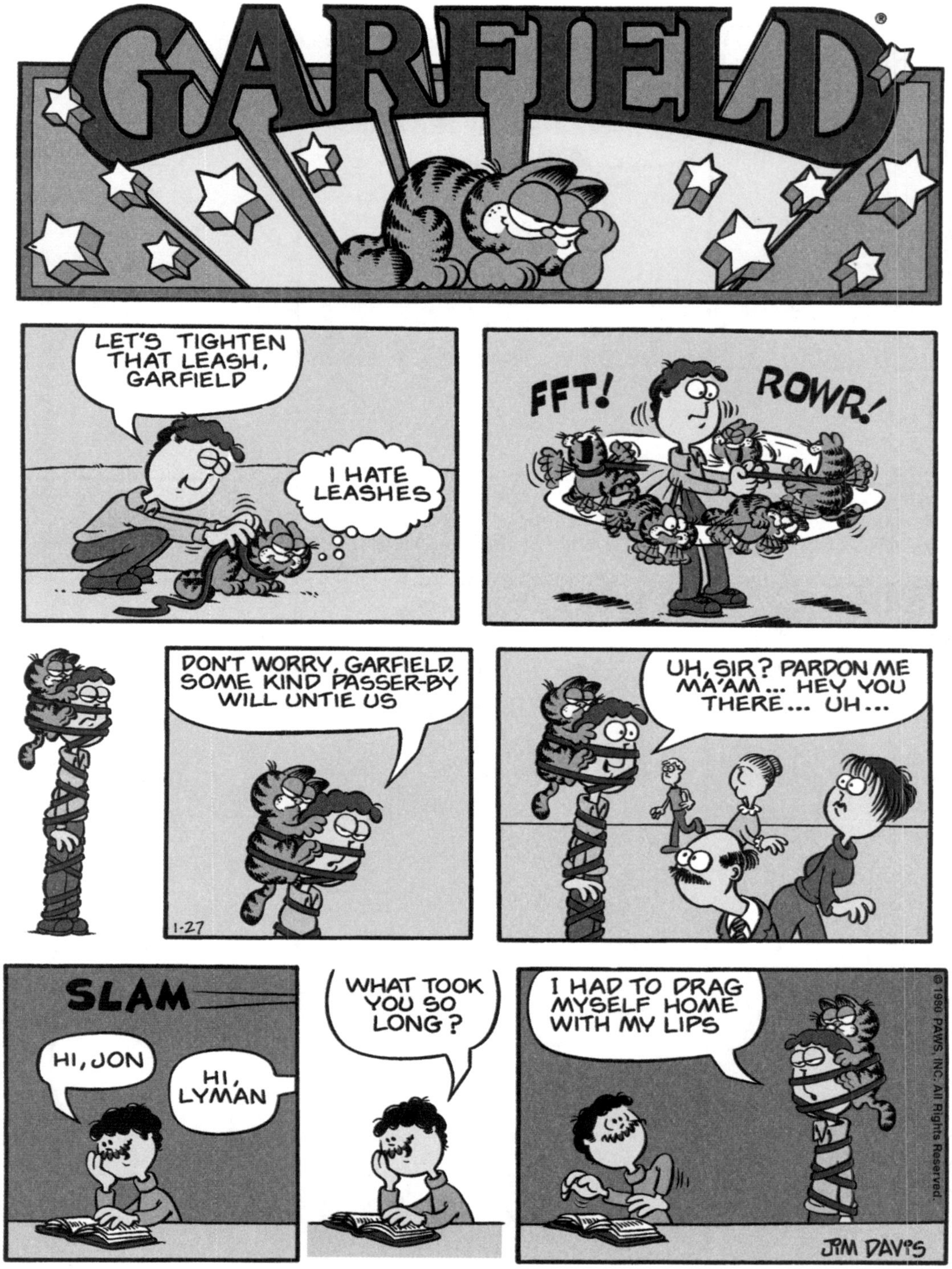
GARFIELD
LET'S TIGHTEN THAT LEASH, GARFIELD
I HATE LEASHES
FFT!
ROWR!
DON'T WORRY, GARFIELD. SOME KIND PASSER-BY WILL UNTIE US
1-27
UH, SIR? PARDON ME MA'AM... HEY YOU THERE... UH...
SLAM
HI, JON
HI, LYMAN
WHAT TOOK YOU SO LONG?
I HAD TO DRAG MYSELF HOME WITH MY LIPS
© 1980 PAWS, INC. All Rights Reserved.
JIM DAVIS

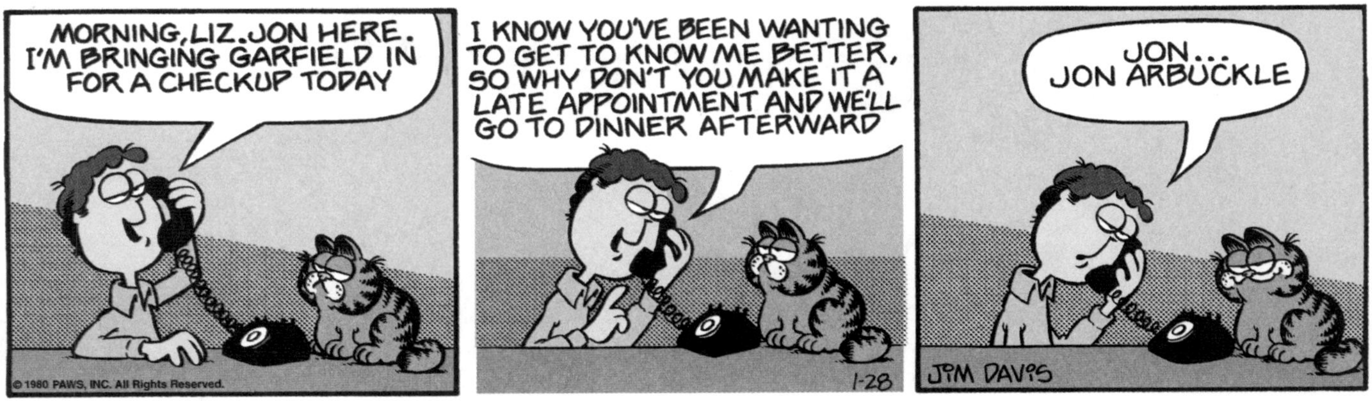
MORNING, LIZ. JON HERE. I'M BRINGING GARFIELD IN FOR A CHECKUP TODAY
I KNOW YOU'VE BEEN WANTING TO GET TO KNOW ME BETTER, SO WHY DON'T YOU MAKE IT A LATE APPOINTMENT AND WE'LL GO TO DINNER AFTERWARD
JON... JON ARBUCKLE
© 1980 PAWS, INC. All Rights Reserved.
1-28
JIM DAVIS

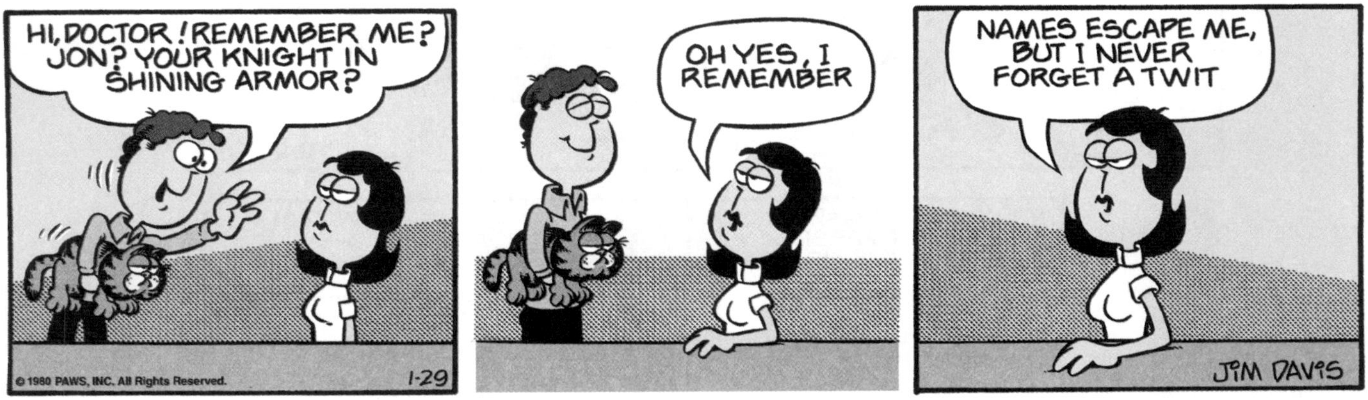
HI, DOCTOR! REMEMBER ME? JON? YOUR KNIGHT IN SHINING ARMOR?
OH YES, I REMEMBER
NAMES ESCAPE ME, BUT I NEVER FORGET A TWIT
© 1980 PAWS, INC. All Rights Reserved.
1-29
JIM DAVIS

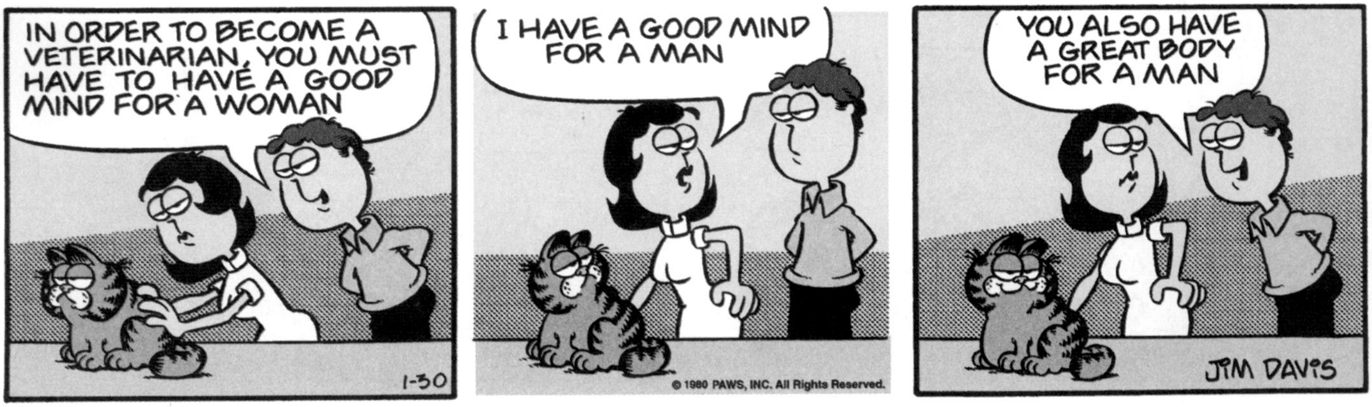
IN ORDER TO BECOME A VETERINARIAN, YOU MUST HAVE TO HAVE A GOOD MIND FOR A WOMAN
I HAVE A GOOD MIND FOR A MAN
YOU ALSO HAVE A GREAT BODY FOR A MAN
1-30
© 1980 PAWS, INC. All Rights Reserved.
JIM DAVIS

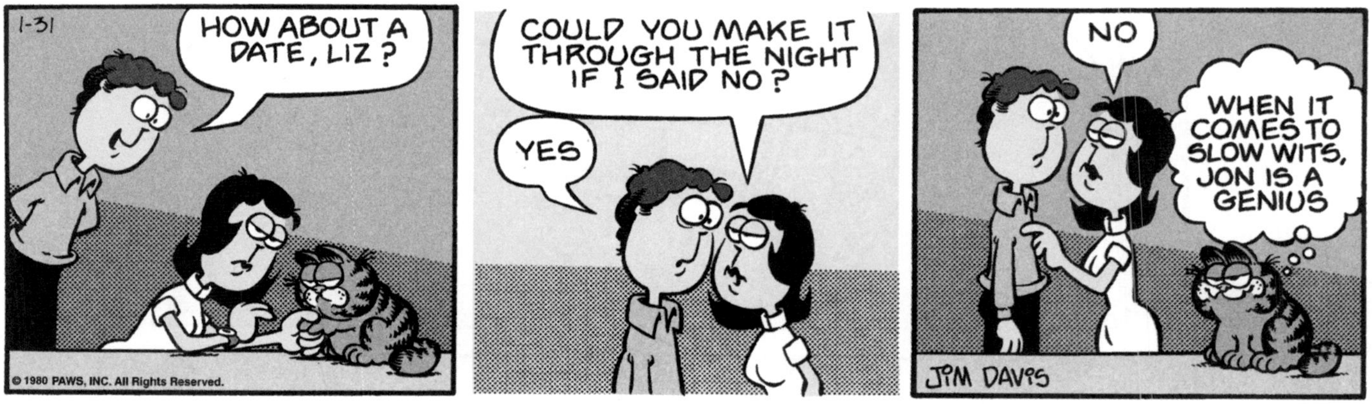
1-31
HOW ABOUT A DATE, LIZ?
© 1980 PAWS, INC. All Rights Reserved.
COULD YOU MAKE IT THROUGH THE NIGHT IF I SAID NO?
YES
NO
WHEN IT COMES TO SLOW WITS, JON IS A GENIUS
JIM DAVIS

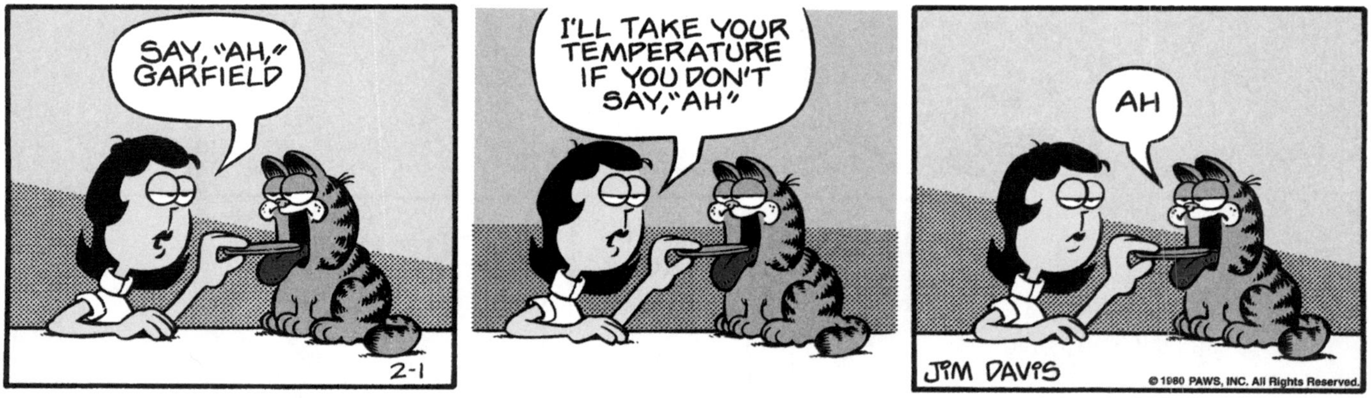
SAY, "AH," GARFIELD
2-1
I'LL TAKE YOUR TEMPERATURE IF YOU DON'T SAY, "AH"
AH
JIM DAVIS
© 1980 PAWS, INC. All Rights Reserved.

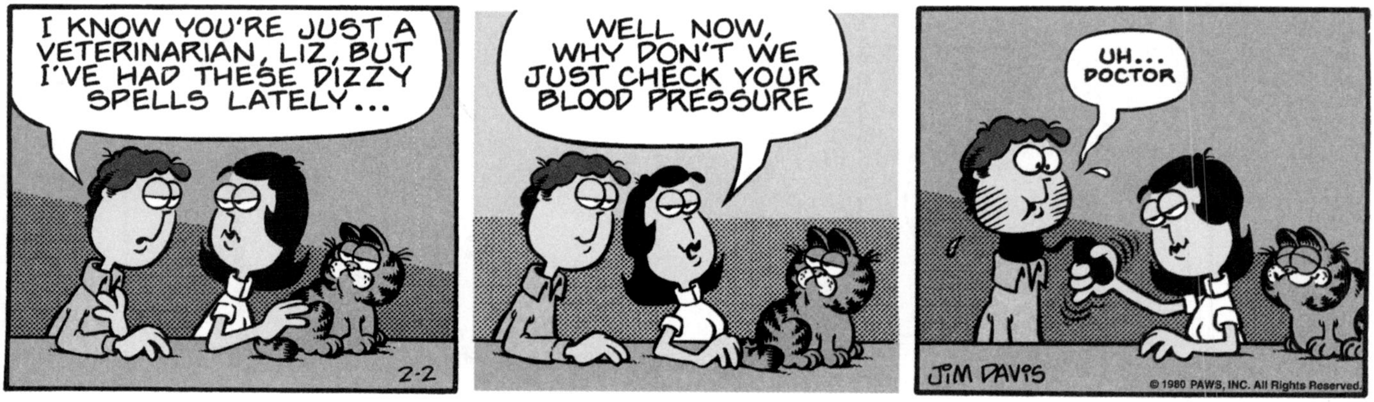
I KNOW YOU'RE JUST A VETERINARIAN, LIZ, BUT I'VE HAD THESE DIZZY SPELLS LATELY...
2-2
WELL NOW, WHY DON'T WE JUST CHECK YOUR BLOOD PRESSURE
UH... DOCTOR
JIM DAVIS
© 1980 PAWS, INC. All Rights Reserved.

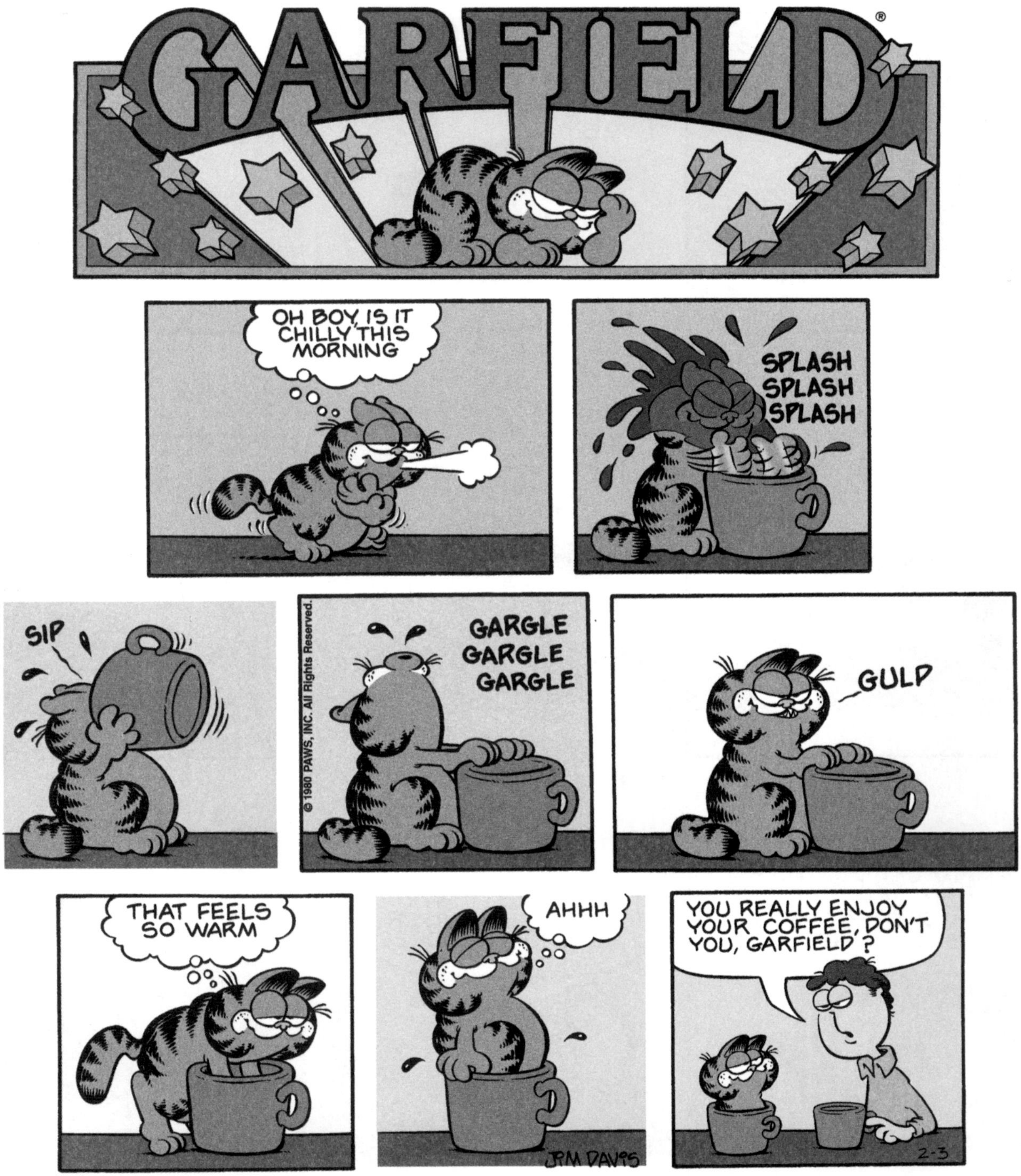
GARFIELD®
OH BOY, IS IT CHILLY THIS MORNING
SPLASH SPLASH SPLASH
SIP
GARGLE GARGLE GARGLE
© 1980 PAWS, INC. All Rights Reserved.
GULP
THAT FEELS SO WARM
AHHH
JPM DAVIS
YOU REALLY ENJOY YOUR COFFEE, DON'T YOU, GARFIELD?
2-3

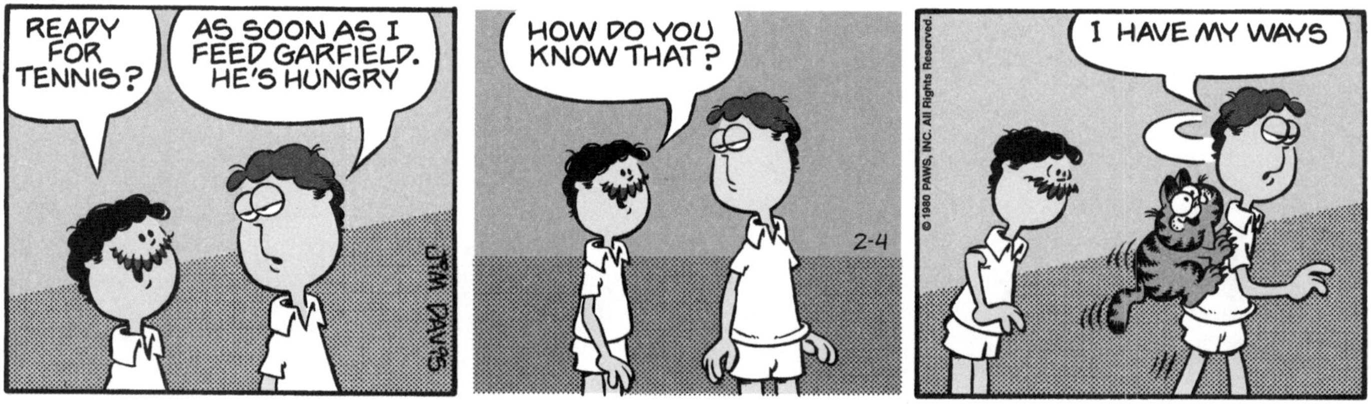
READY FOR TENNIS?
AS SOON AS I FEED GARFIELD. HE'S HUNGRY
JIM DAVIS
HOW DO YOU KNOW THAT?
2-4
I HAVE MY WAYS
© 1980 PAWS, INC. All Rights Reserved.

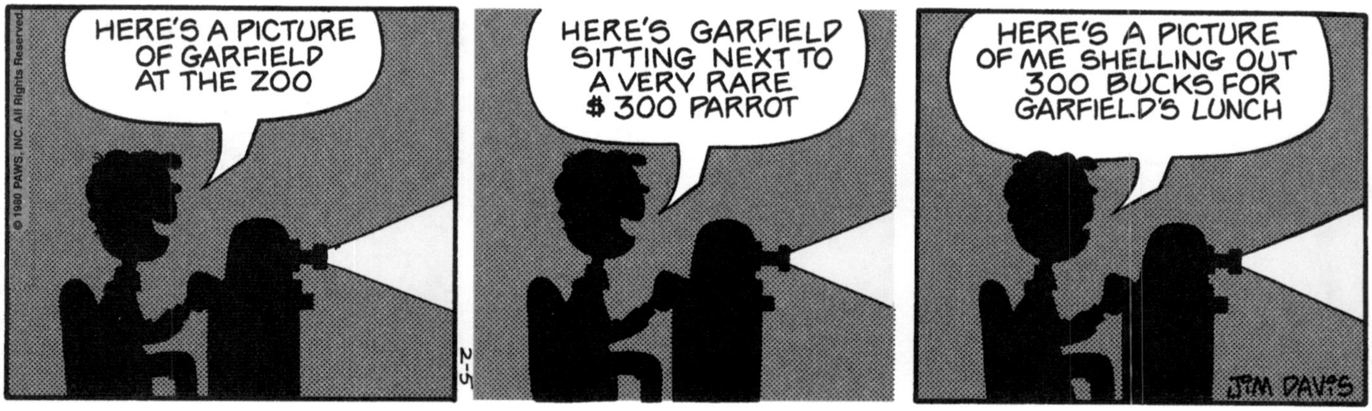
© 1980 PAWS, INC. All Rights Reserved.
HERE'S A PICTURE OF GARFIELD AT THE ZOO
2-5
HERE'S GARFIELD SITTING NEXT TO A VERY RARE $ 300 PARROT
HERE'S A PICTURE OF ME SHELLING OUT 300 BUCKS FOR GARFIELD'S LUNCH
JIM DAVIS

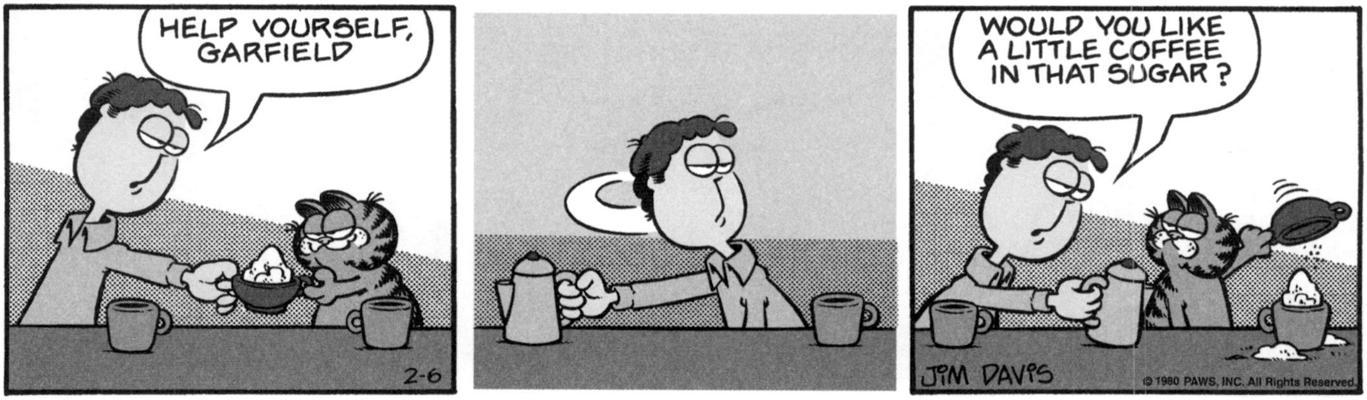
HELP YOURSELF, GARFIELD
2-6
WOULD YOU LIKE A LITTLE COFFEE IN THAT SUGAR?
JIM DAVIS
© 1980 PAWS, INC. All Rights Reserved.

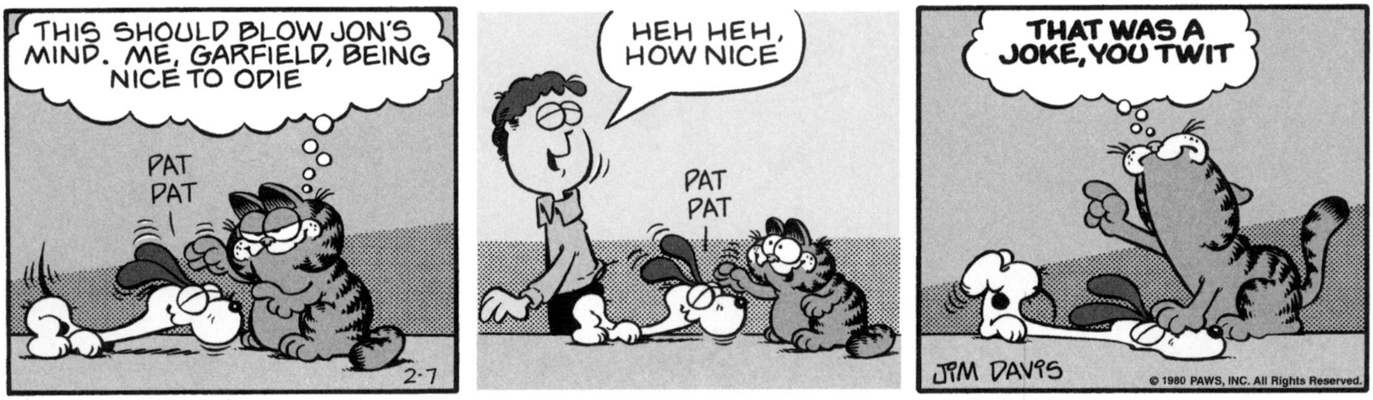
THIS SHOULD BLOW JON'S MIND. ME, GARFIELD, BEING NICE TO ODIE
PAT PAT
2-7
HEH HEH, HOW NICE
PAT PAT
THAT WAS A JOKE, YOU TWIT
JIM DAVIS
© 1980 PAWS, INC. All Rights Reserved.

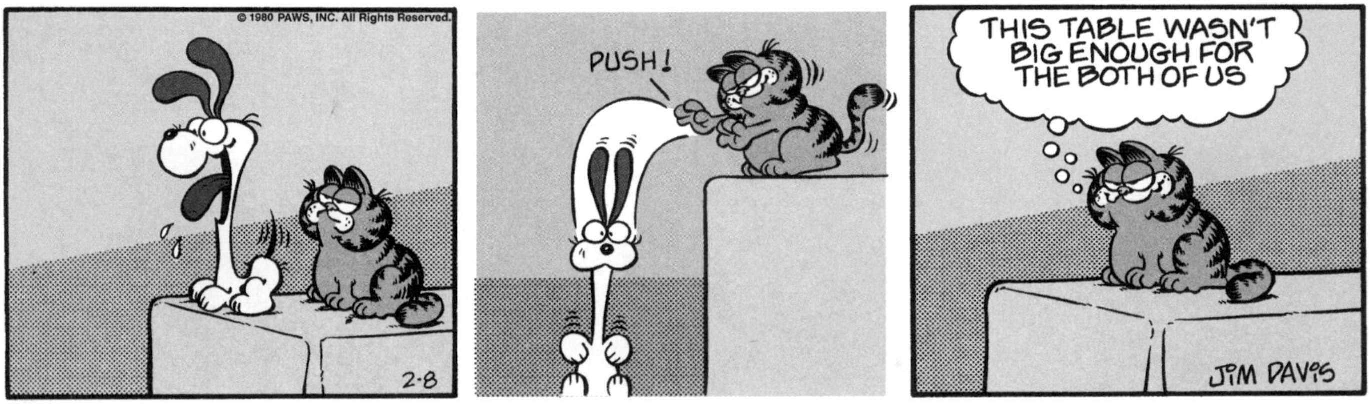
© 1980 PAWS, INC. All Rights Reserved.
2-8
PUSH!
THIS TABLE WASN'T BIG ENOUGH FOR THE BOTH OF US
JIM DAVIS

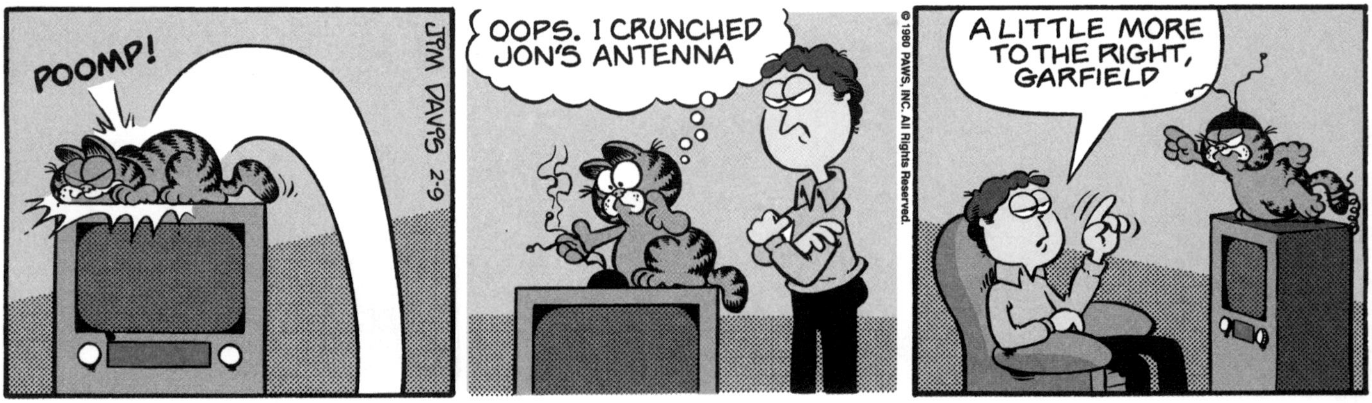
POOMP!
JIM DAVIS 2-9
OOPS. I CRUNCHED JON'S ANTENNA
© 1980 PAWS, INC. All Rights Reserved.
A LITTLE MORE TO THE RIGHT, GARFIELD

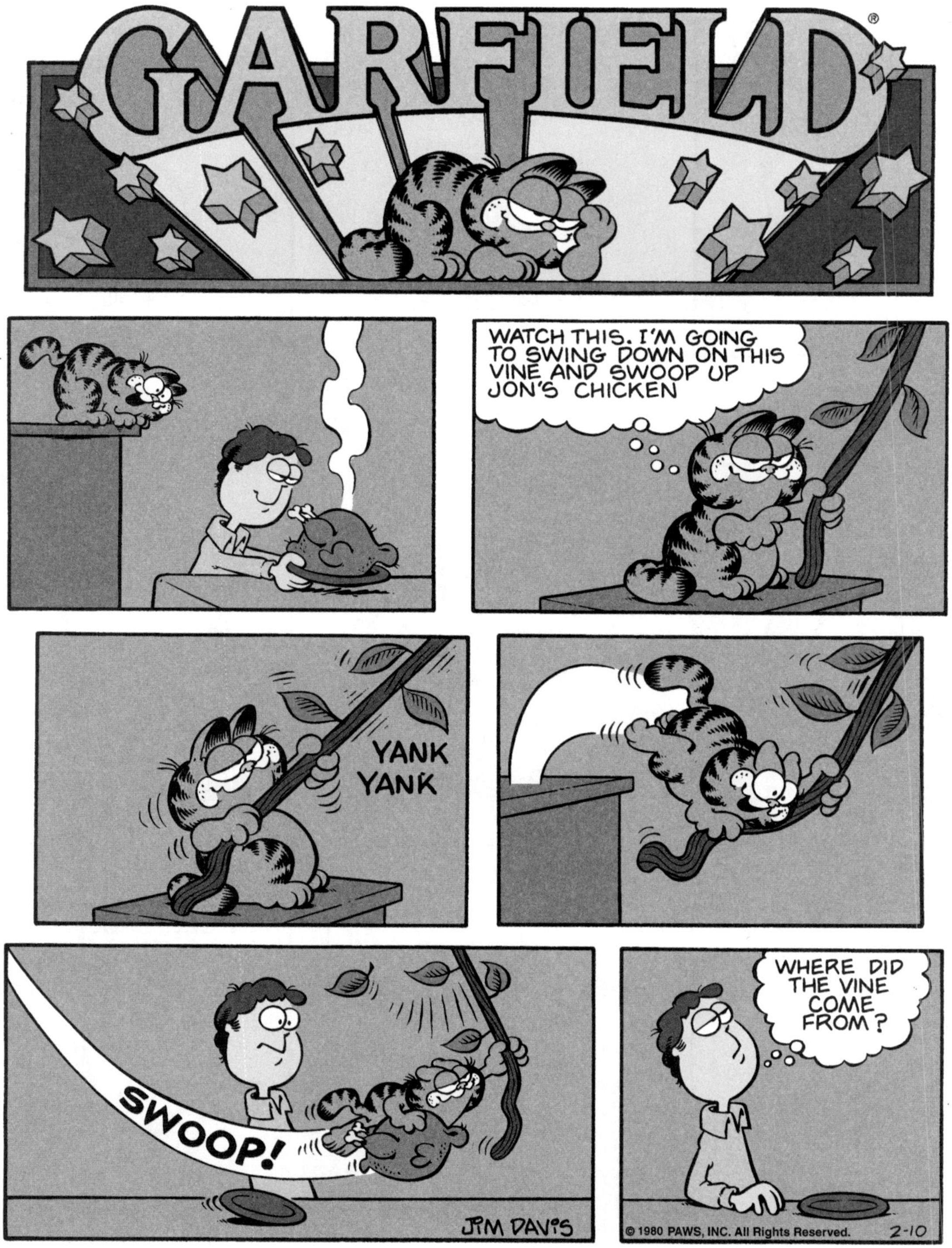
GARFIELD®
WATCH THIS. I'M GOING TO SWING DOWN ON THIS VINE AND SWOOP UP JON'S CHICKEN
YANK YANK
SWOOP!
WHERE DID THE VINE COME FROM?
JIM DAVIS
© 1980 PAWS, INC. All Rights Reserved.
2-10

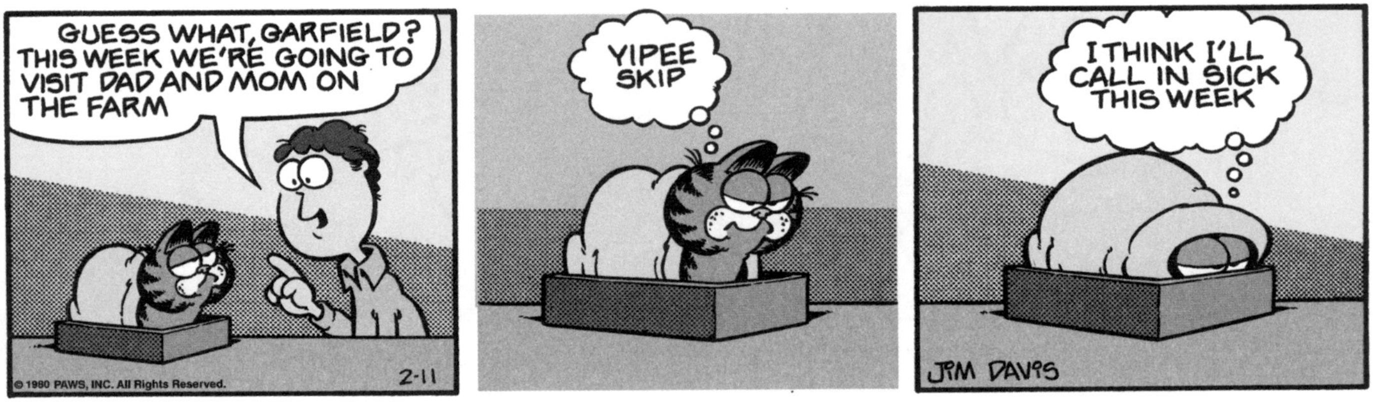
GUESS WHAT, GARFIELD? THIS WEEK WE'RE GOING TO VISIT DAD AND MOM ON THE FARM
© 1980 PAWS, INC. All Rights Reserved.
2-11
YIPEE SKIP
I THINK I'LL CALL IN SICK THIS WEEK
JIM DAVIS

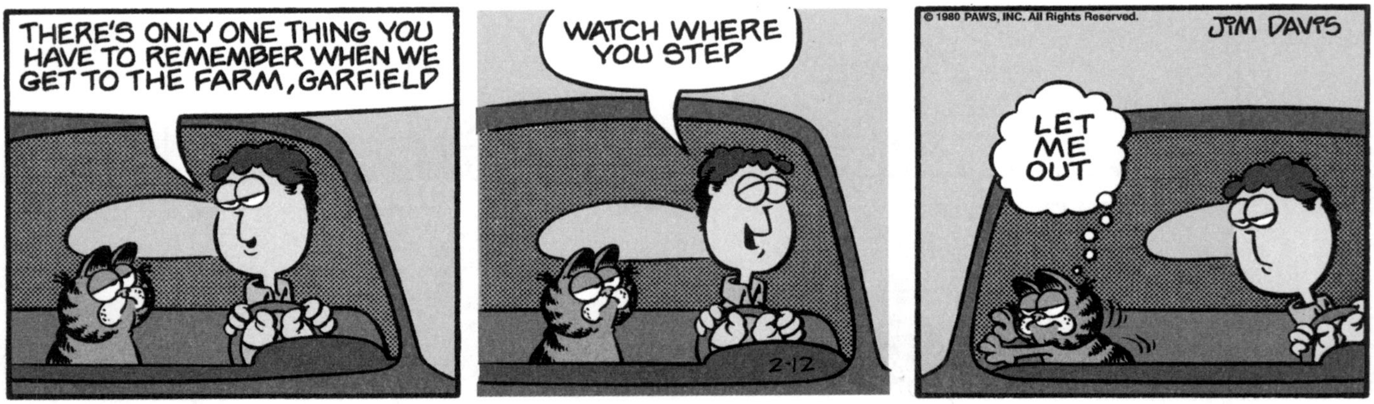
THERE'S ONLY ONE THING YOU HAVE TO REMEMBER WHEN WE GET TO THE FARM, GARFIELD
WATCH WHERE YOU STEP
2-12
© 1980 PAWS, INC. All Rights Reserved.
JIM DAVIS
LET ME OUT

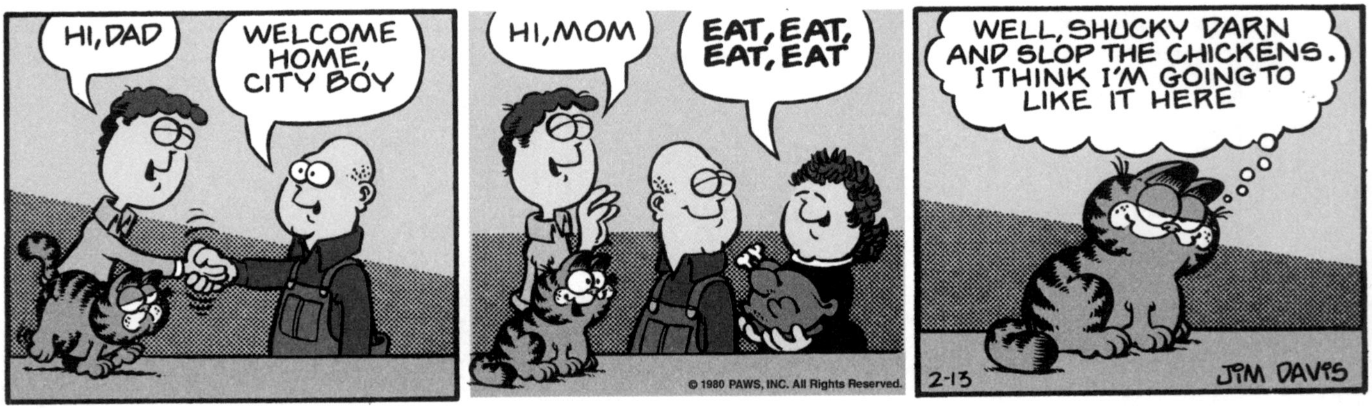
HI, DAD
WELCOME HOME, CITY BOY
HI, MOM
EAT, EAT, EAT, EAT
© 1980 PAWS, INC. All Rights Reserved.
WELL, SHUCKY DARN AND SLOP THE CHICKENS. I THINK I'M GOING TO LIKE IT HERE
2-13
JIM DAVIS

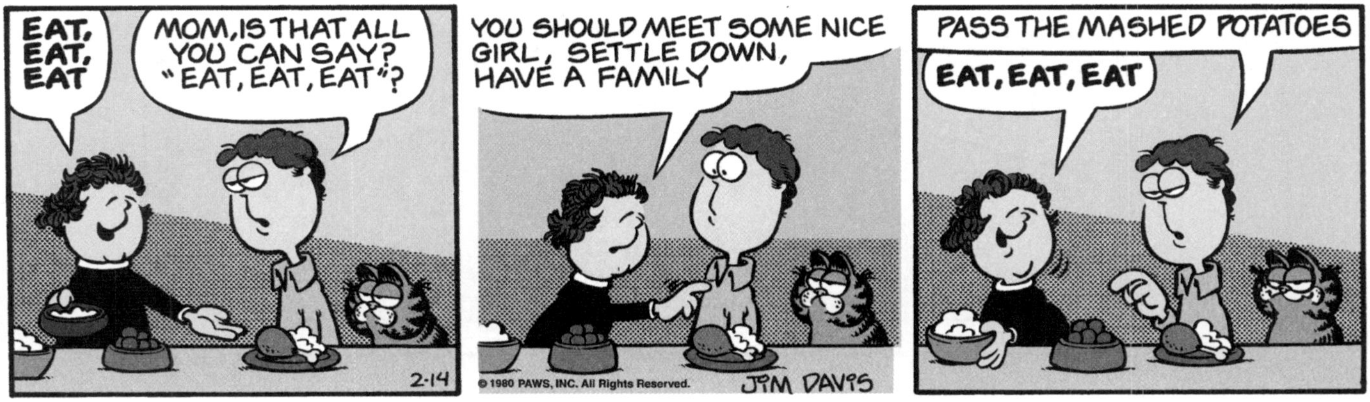
EAT, EAT, EAT
MOM, IS THAT ALL YOU CAN SAY? "EAT, EAT, EAT"?
2-14
YOU SHOULD MEET SOME NICE GIRL, SETTLE DOWN, HAVE A FAMILY
© 1980 PAWS, INC. All Rights Reserved.
JIM DAVIS
PASS THE MASHED POTATOES
EAT, EAT, EAT

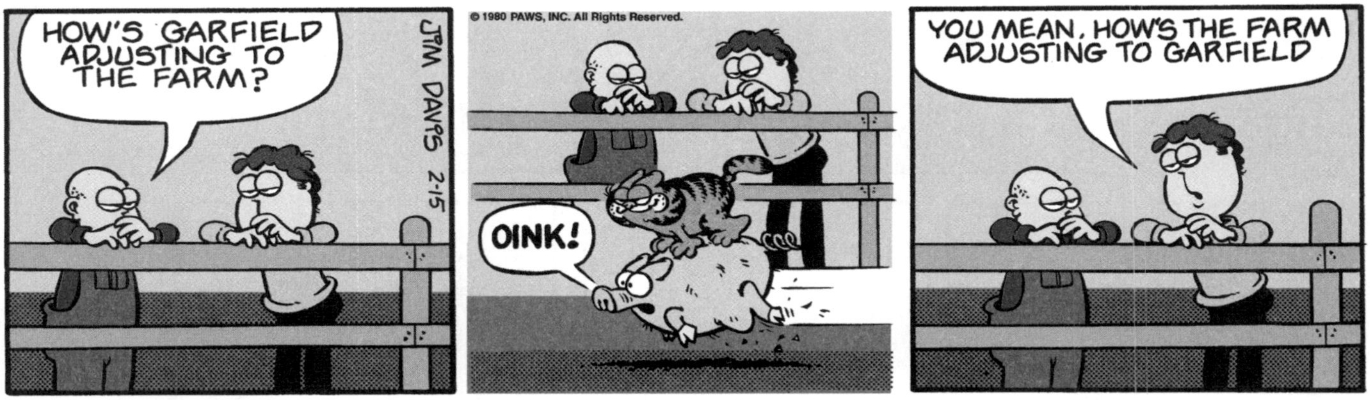
HOW'S GARFIELD ADJUSTING TO THE FARM?
JIM DAVIS 2-15
© 1980 PAWS, INC. All Rights Reserved.
OINK!
YOU MEAN, HOW'S THE FARM ADJUSTING TO GARFIELD

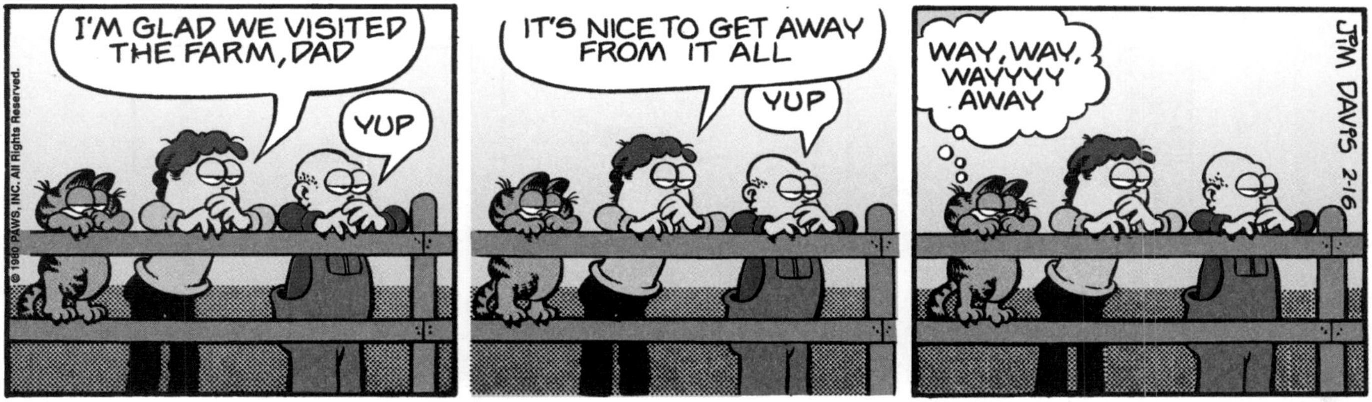
I'M GLAD WE VISITED THE FARM, DAD
YUP
© 1980 PAWS, INC. All Rights Reserved.
IT'S NICE TO GET AWAY FROM IT ALL
YUP
WAY, WAY, WAYYYY AWAY
JIM DAVIS 2-16

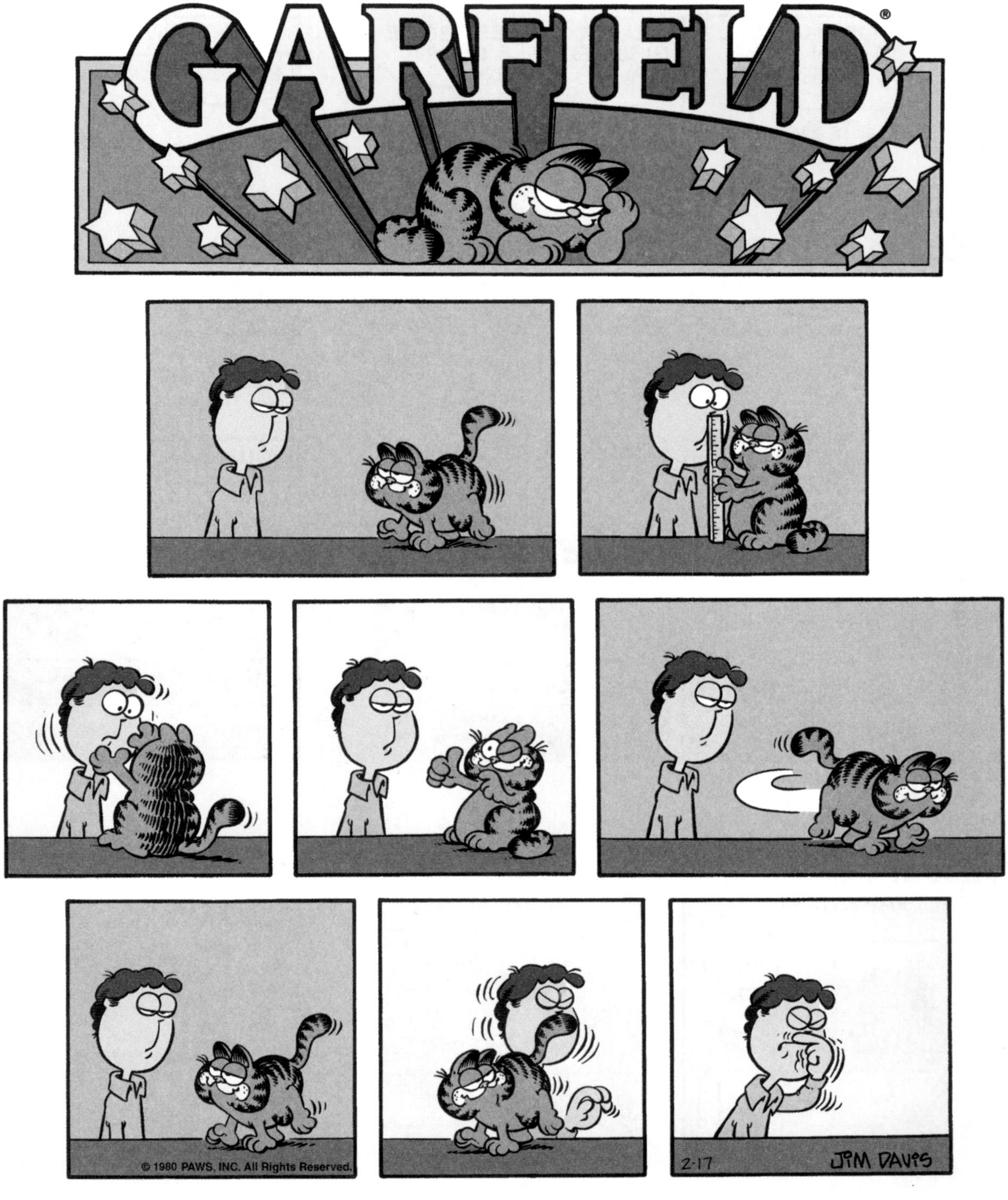
GARFIELD®
© 1980 PAWS, INC. All Rights Reserved.
2-17
JIM DAVIS

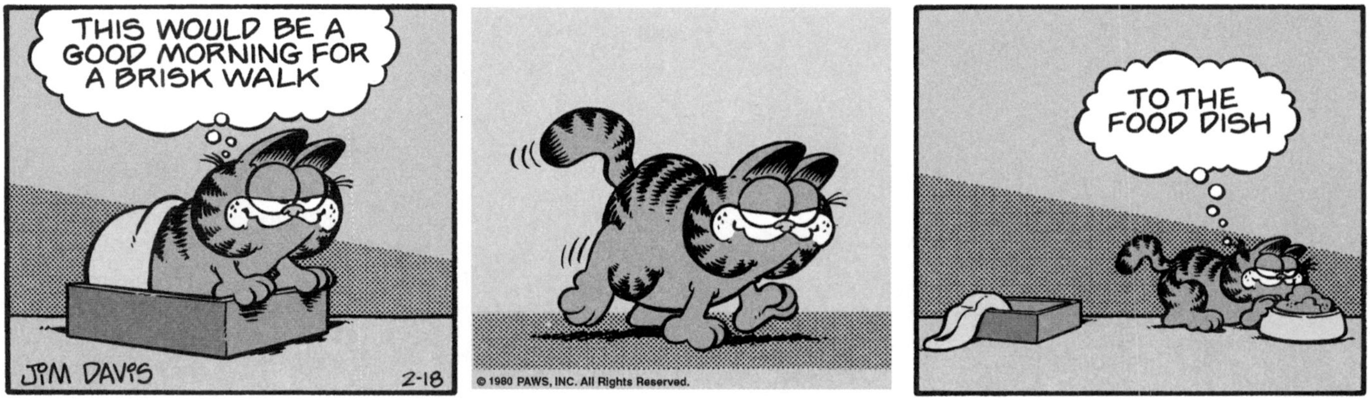
THIS WOULD BE A GOOD MORNING FOR A BRISK WALK
JIM DAVIS
2-18
© 1980 PAWS, INC. All Rights Reserved.
TO THE FOOD DISH

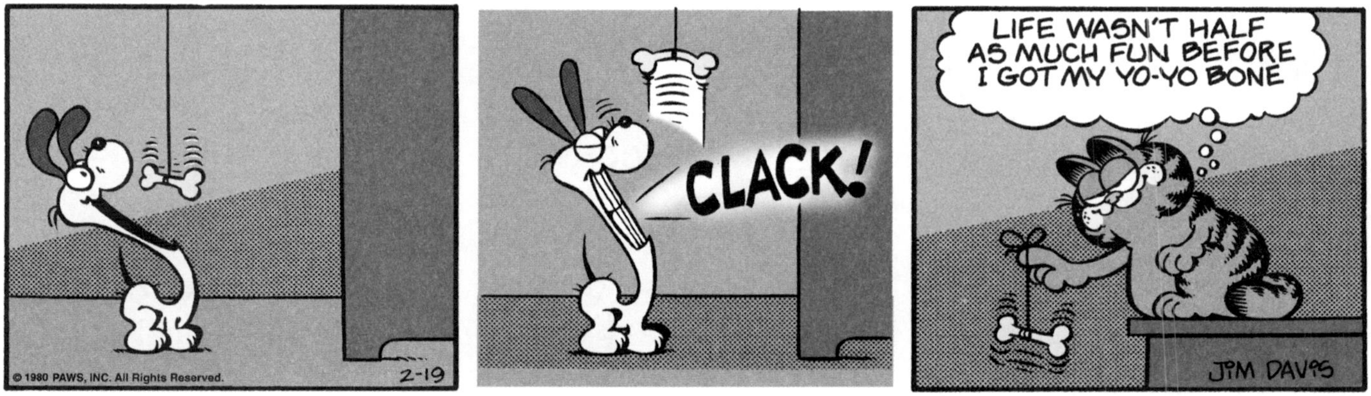
© 1980 PAWS, INC. All Rights Reserved.
2-19
CLACK!
LIFE WASN'T HALF AS MUCH FUN BEFORE I GOT MY YO-YO BONE
JIM DAVIS

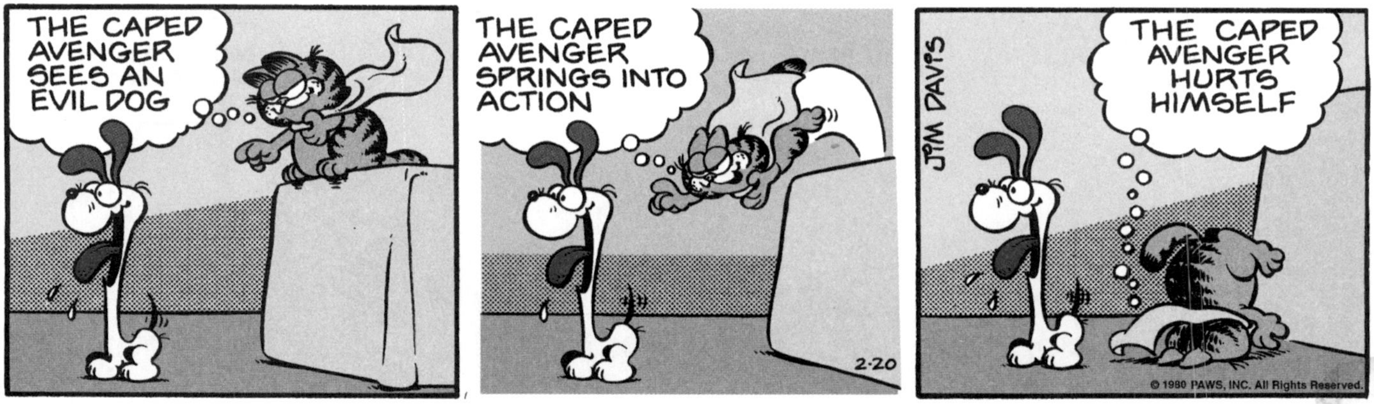
THE CAPED AVENGER SEES AN EVIL DOG
THE CAPED AVENGER SPRINGS INTO ACTION
2-20
JIM DAVIS
THE CAPED AVENGER HURTS HIMSELF
© 1980 PAWS, INC. All Rights Reserved.

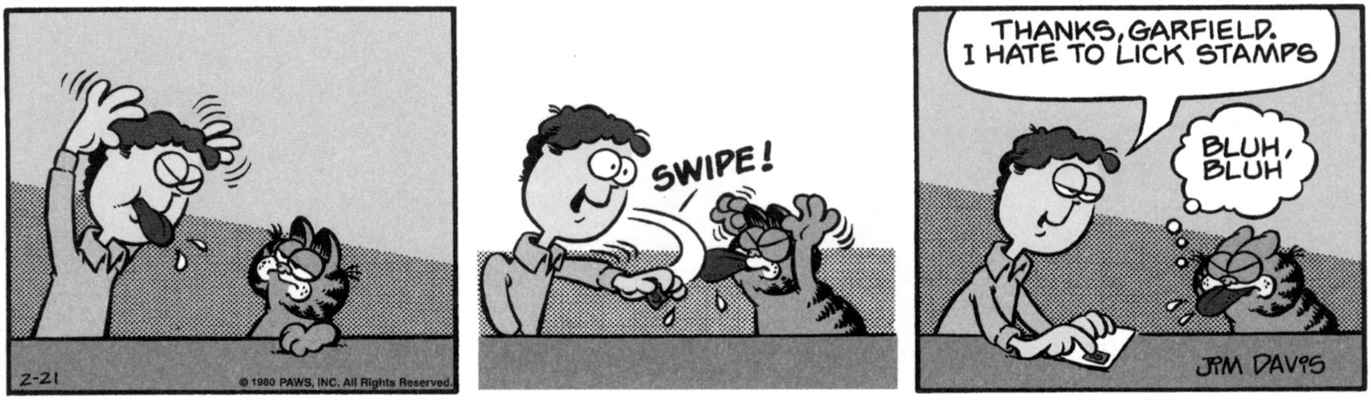
2-21
© 1980 PAWS, INC. All Rights Reserved.
SWIPE!
THANKS, GARFIELD. I HATE TO LICK STAMPS
BLUH, BLUH
JIM DAVIS

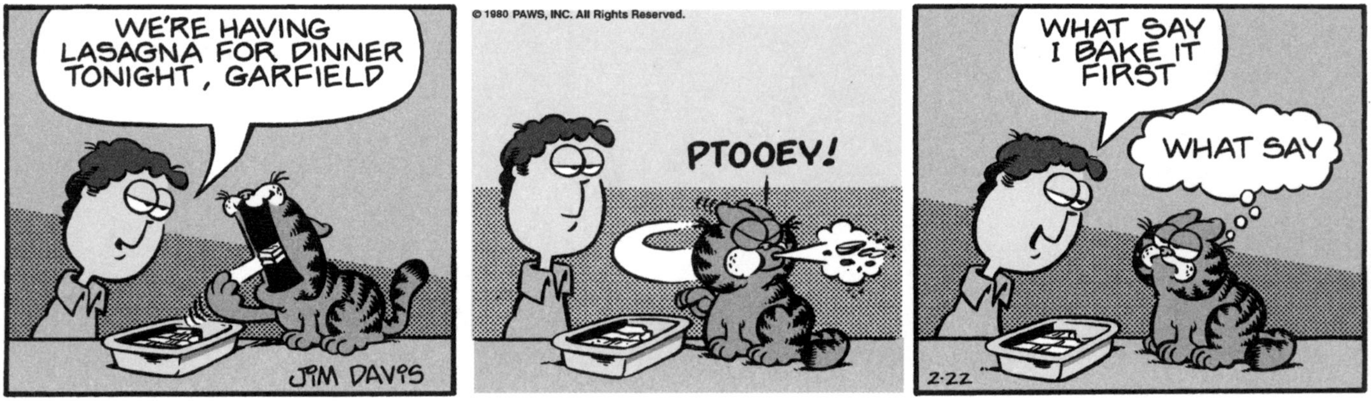
WE'RE HAVING LASAGNA FOR DINNER TONIGHT, GARFIELD
JIM DAVIS
© 1980 PAWS, INC. All Rights Reserved.
PTOOEY!
WHAT SAY I BAKE IT FIRST
WHAT SAY
2-22

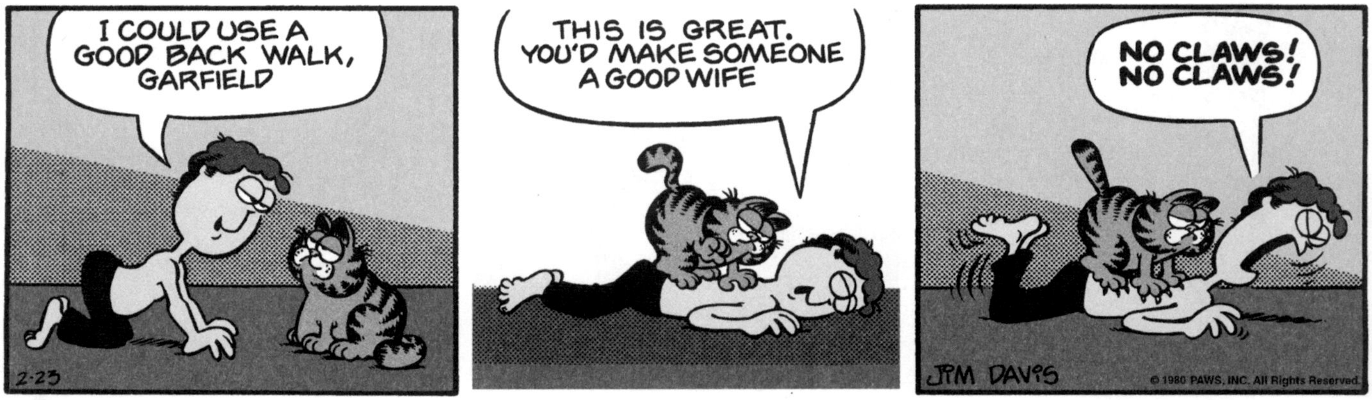
I COULD USE A GOOD BACK WALK, GARFIELD
2-23
THIS IS GREAT. YOU'D MAKE SOMEONE A GOOD WIFE
NO CLAWS! NO CLAWS!
JIM DAVIS
© 1980 PAWS, INC. All Rights Reserved.

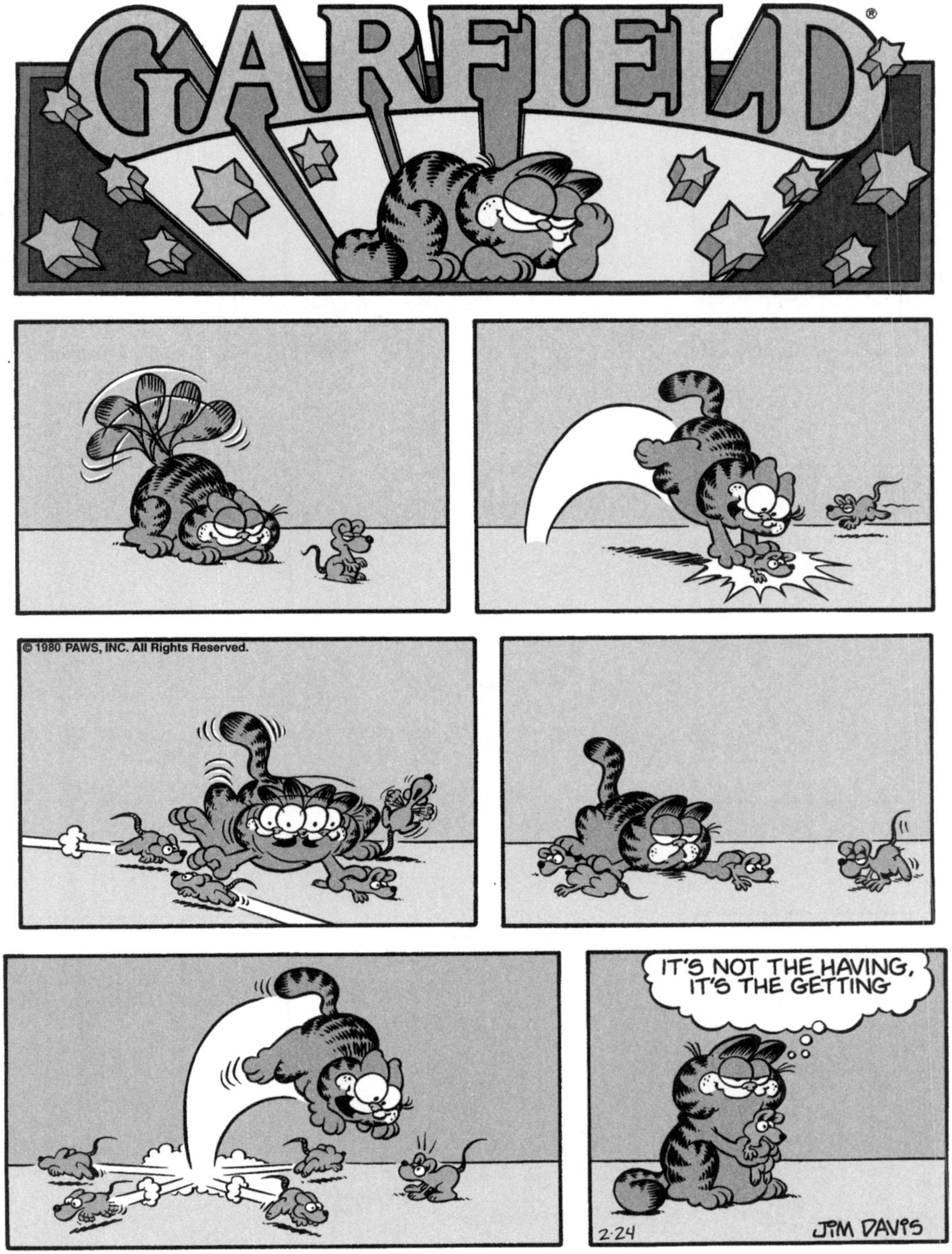
GARFIELD®
© 1980 PAWS, INC. All Rights Reserved.
IT'S NOT THE HAVING, IT'S THE GETTING
2·24
JIM DAVIS

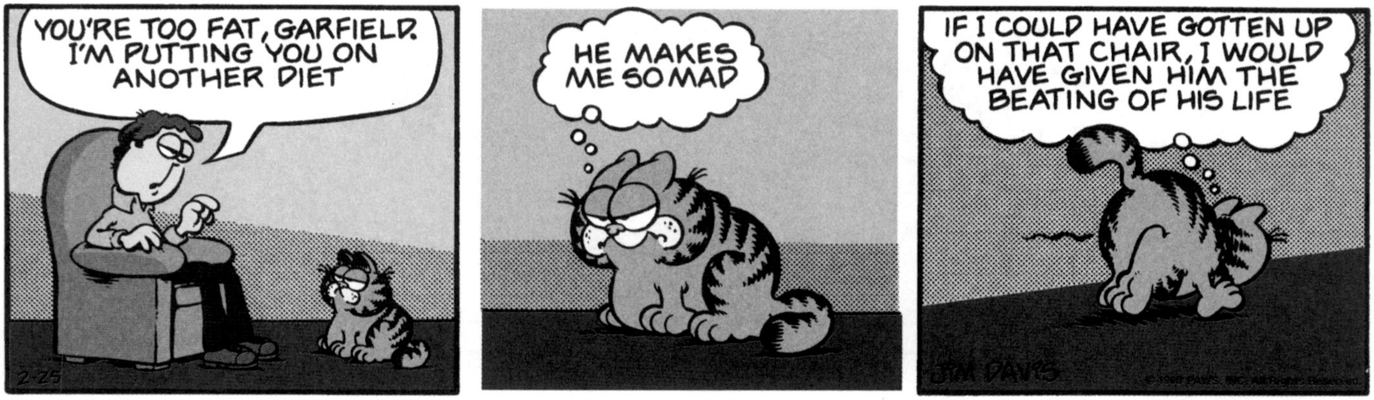
YOU'RE TOO FAT, GARFIELD. I'M PUTTING YOU ON ANOTHER DIET
2-25
HE MAKES ME SO MAD
IF I COULD HAVE GOTTEN UP ON THAT CHAIR, I WOULD HAVE GIVEN HIM THE BEATING OF HIS LIFE
JIM DAVIS

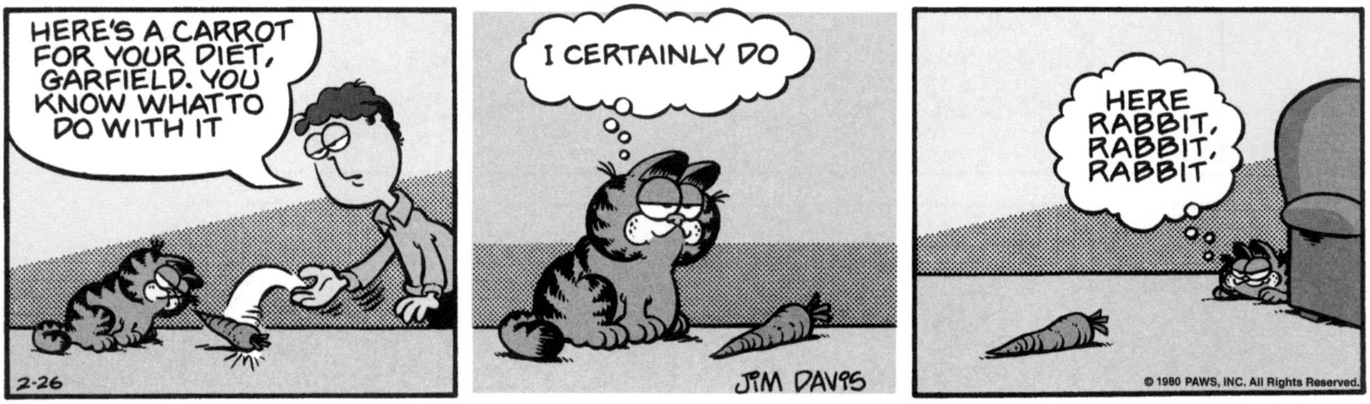
HERE'S A CARROT FOR YOUR DIET, GARFIELD. YOU KNOW WHAT TO DO WITH IT
2-26
I CERTAINLY DO
JIM DAVIS
HERE RABBIT, RABBIT, RABBIT
© 1980 PAWS, INC. All Rights Reserved.

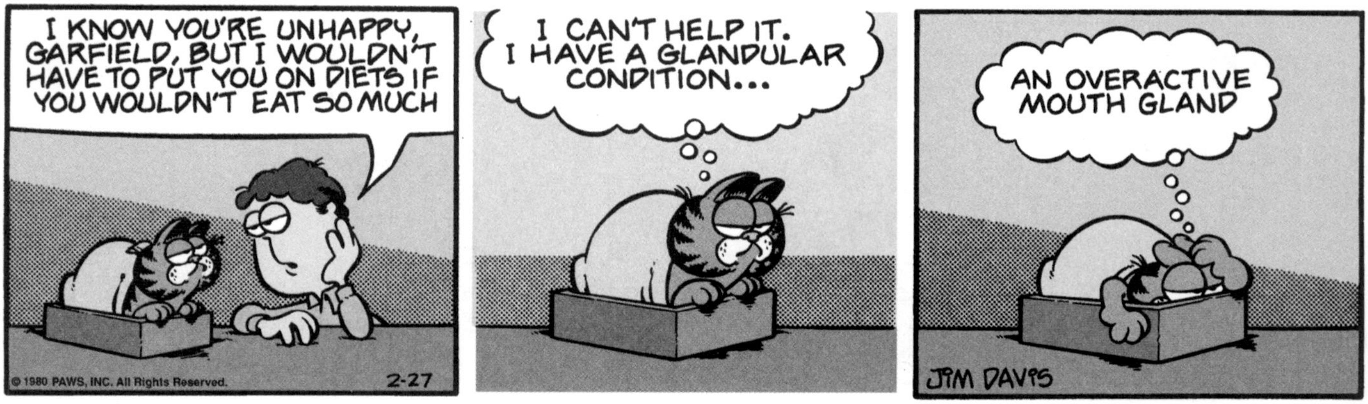
I KNOW YOU'RE UNHAPPY, GARFIELD, BUT I WOULDN'T HAVE TO PUT YOU ON DIETS IF YOU WOULDN'T EAT SO MUCH
© 1980 PAWS, INC. All Rights Reserved.
2-27
I CAN'T HELP IT. I HAVE A GLANDULAR CONDITION...
AN OVERACTIVE MOUTH GLAND
JIM DAVIS

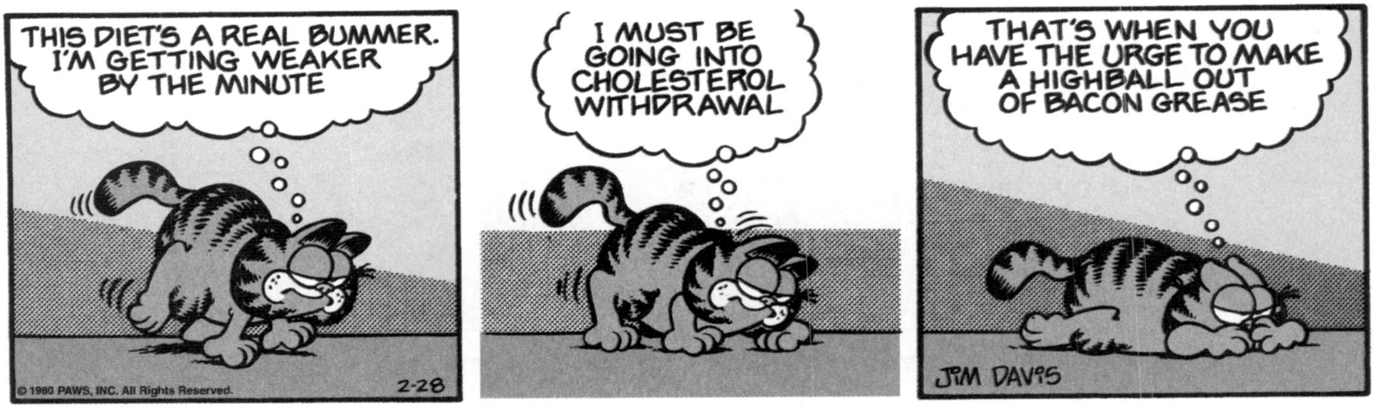
THIS DIET'S A REAL BUMMER. I'M GETTING WEAKER BY THE MINUTE
© 1980 PAWS, INC. All Rights Reserved.
2-28
I MUST BE GOING INTO CHOLESTEROL WITHDRAWAL
THAT'S WHEN YOU HAVE THE URGE TO MAKE A HIGHBALL OUT OF BACON GREASE
JIM DAVIS

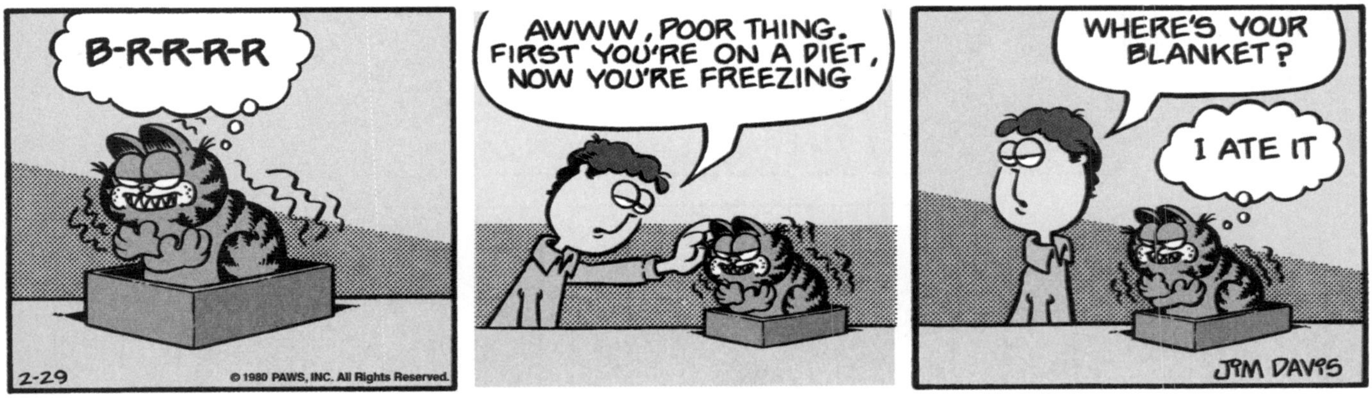
B-R-R-R-R
2-29
© 1980 PAWS, INC. All Rights Reserved.
AWWW, POOR THING. FIRST YOU'RE ON A DIET, NOW YOU'RE FREEZING
WHERE'S YOUR BLANKET?
I ATE IT
JIM DAVIS

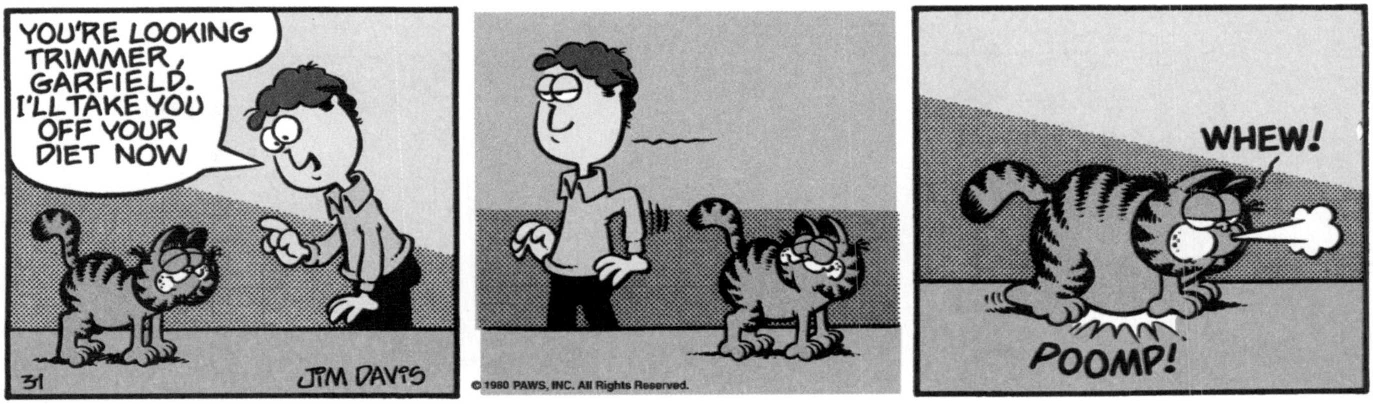
YOU'RE LOOKING TRIMMER, GARFIELD. I'LL TAKE YOU OFF YOUR DIET NOW
31
JIM DAVIS
© 1980 PAWS, INC. All Rights Reserved.
WHEW!
POOMP!

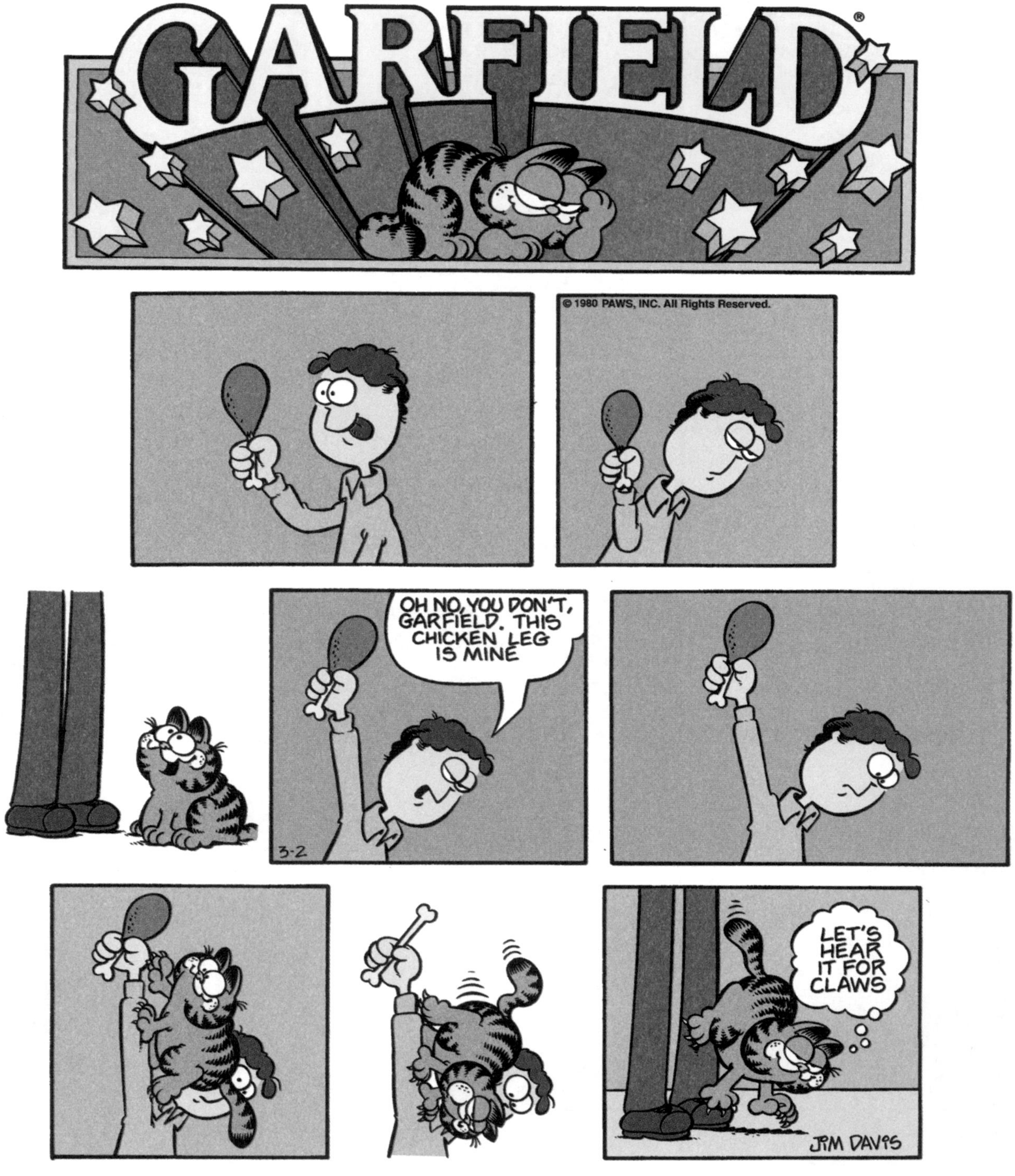
GARFIELD®
© 1980 PAWS, INC. All Rights Reserved.
OH NO, YOU DON'T, GARFIELD. THIS CHICKEN LEG IS MINE
3-2
LET'S HEAR IT FOR CLAWS
JIM DAVIS

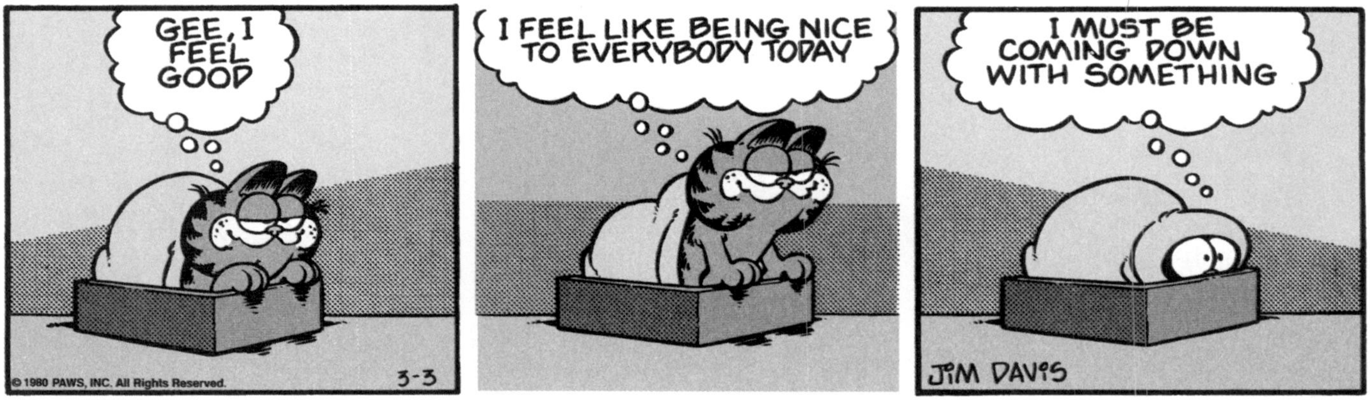
GEE, I FEEL GOOD
© 1980 PAWS, INC. All Rights Reserved.
3-3
I FEEL LIKE BEING NICE TO EVERYBODY TODAY
I MUST BE COMING DOWN WITH SOMETHING
JIM DAVIS

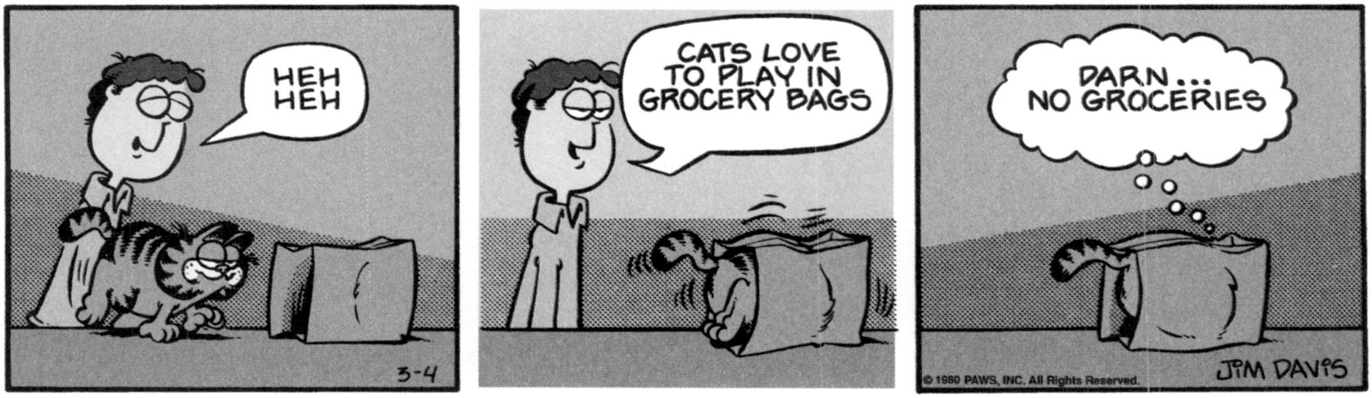
HEH HEH
3-4
CATS LOVE TO PLAY IN GROCERY BAGS
DARN... NO GROCERIES
© 1980 PAWS, INC. All Rights Reserved.
JIM DAVIS

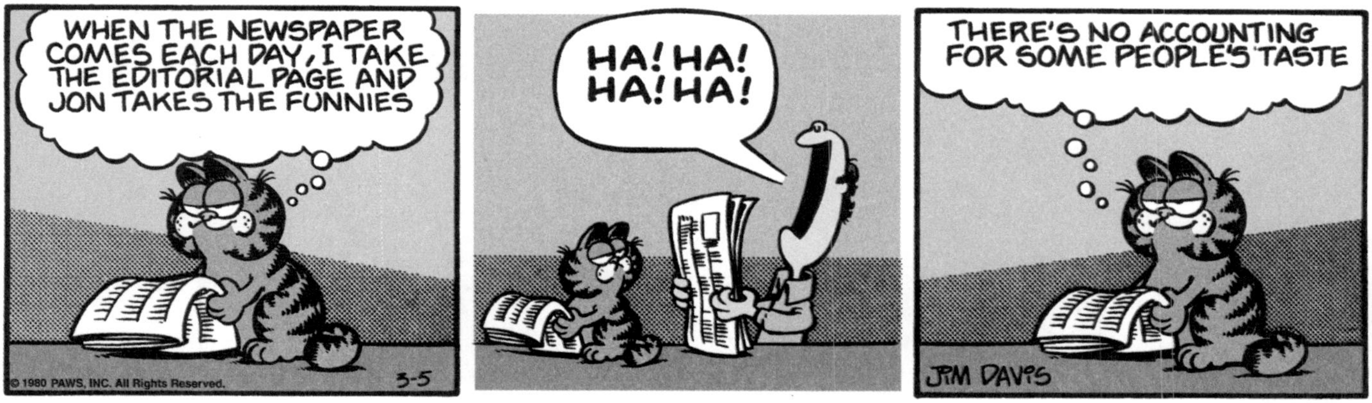
WHEN THE NEWSPAPER COMES EACH DAY, I TAKE THE EDITORIAL PAGE AND JON TAKES THE FUNNIES
© 1980 PAWS, INC. All Rights Reserved.
3-5
HA! HA! HA! HA!
THERE'S NO ACCOUNTING FOR SOME PEOPLE'S TASTE
JIM DAVIS

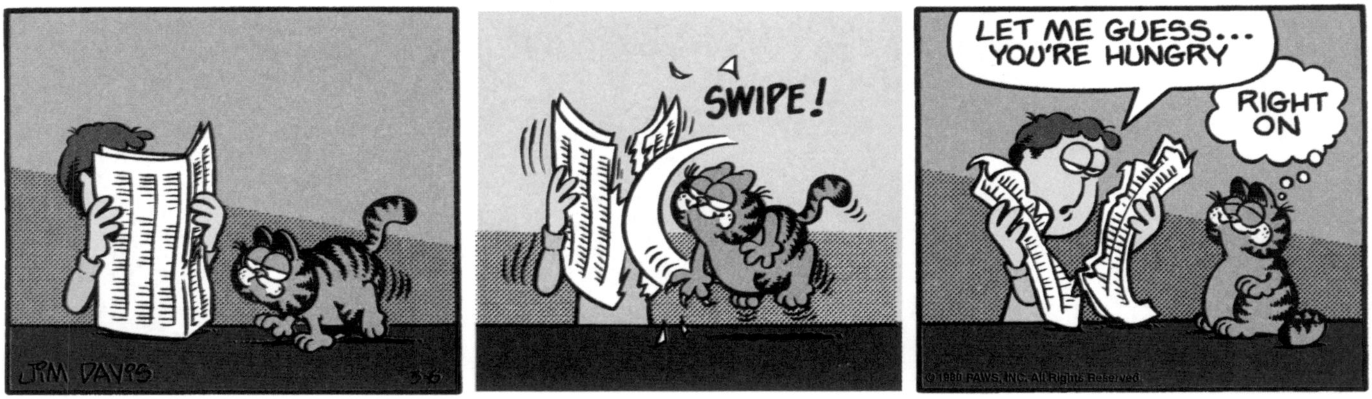
JIM DAVIS
3-6
SWIPE!
LET ME GUESS... YOU'RE HUNGRY
RIGHT ON
© 1980 PAWS, INC. All Rights Reserved.

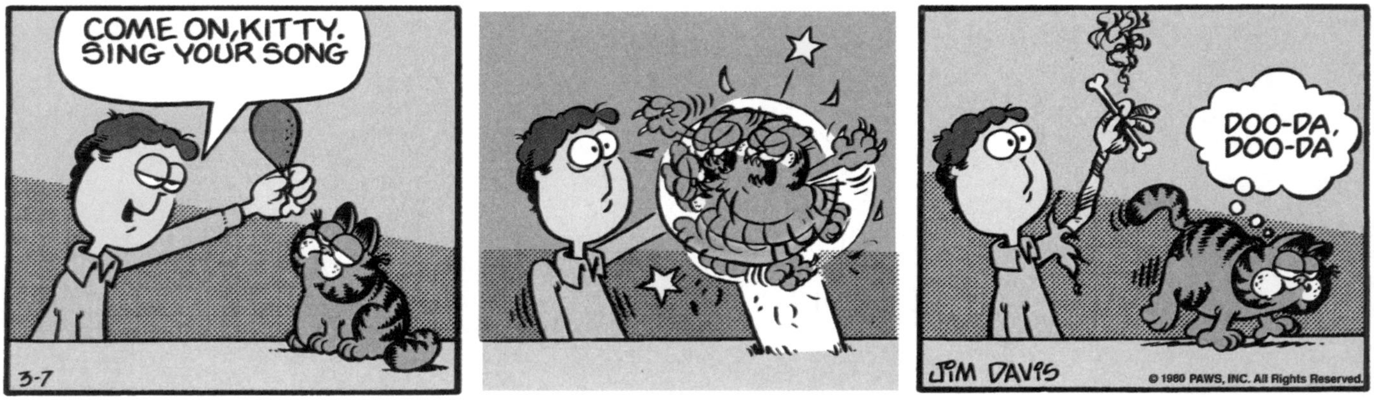
COME ON, KITTY. SING YOUR SONG
3-7
DOO-DA, DOO-DA
JIM DAVIS
© 1980 PAWS, INC. All Rights Reserved.

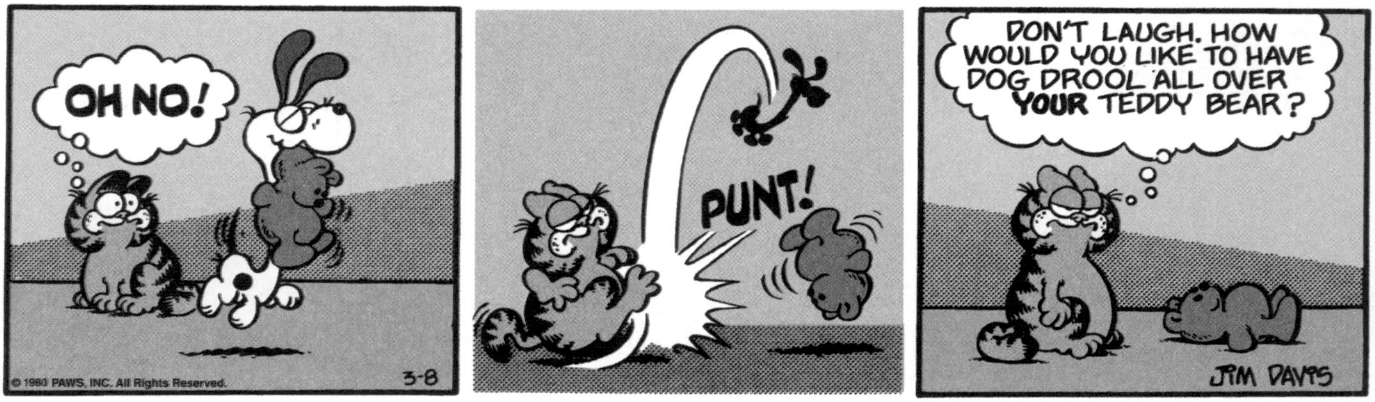
OH NO!
© 1980 PAWS, INC. All Rights Reserved.
3-8
PUNT!
DON'T LAUGH. HOW WOULD YOU LIKE TO HAVE DOG DROOL ALL OVER **YOUR** TEDDY BEAR?
JIM DAVIS

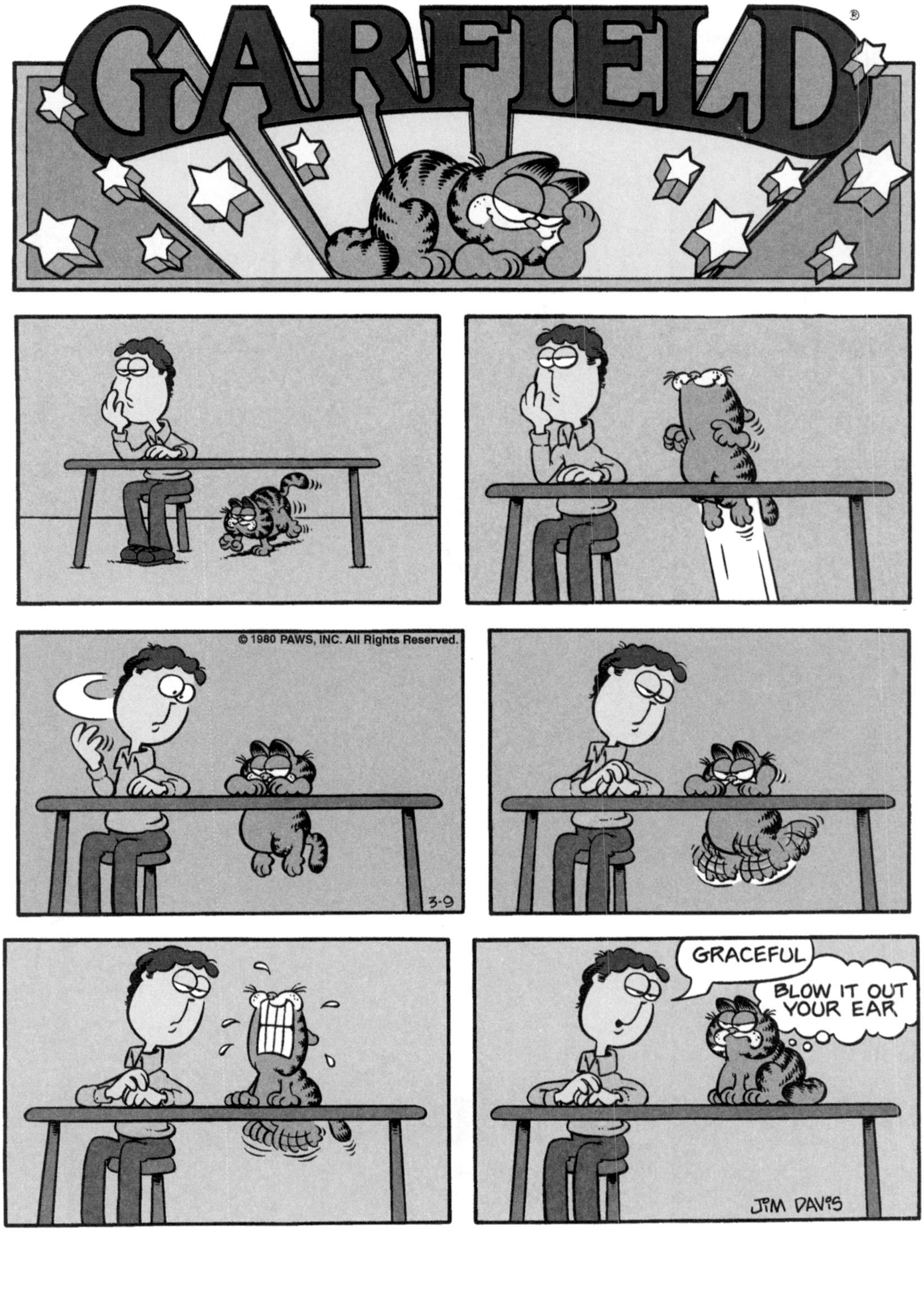
GARFIELD
© 1980 PAWS, INC. All Rights Reserved.
3-9
GRACEFUL
BLOW IT OUT YOUR EAR
JIM DAVIS

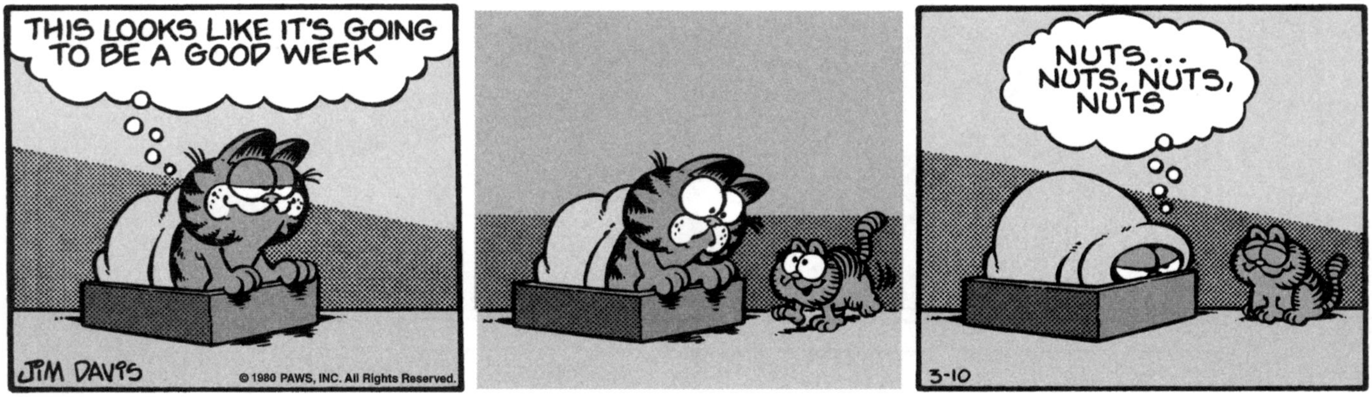
THIS LOOKS LIKE IT'S GOING TO BE A GOOD WEEK
JIM DAVIS
© 1980 PAWS, INC. All Rights Reserved.
NUTS... NUTS, NUTS, NUTS
3-10

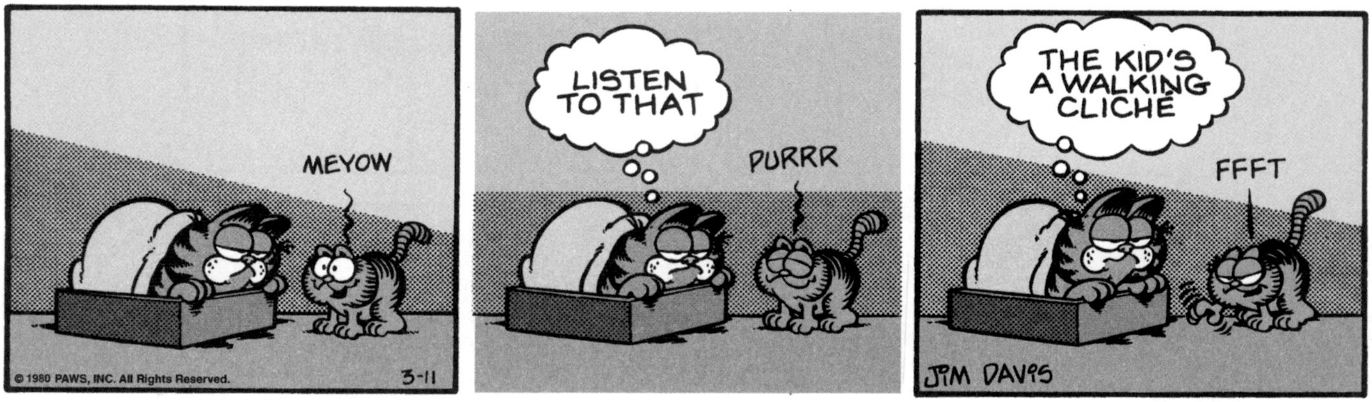
MEYOW
© 1980 PAWS, INC. All Rights Reserved.
3-11
LISTEN TO THAT
PURRR
THE KID'S A WALKING CLICHÉ
FFFT
JIM DAVIS

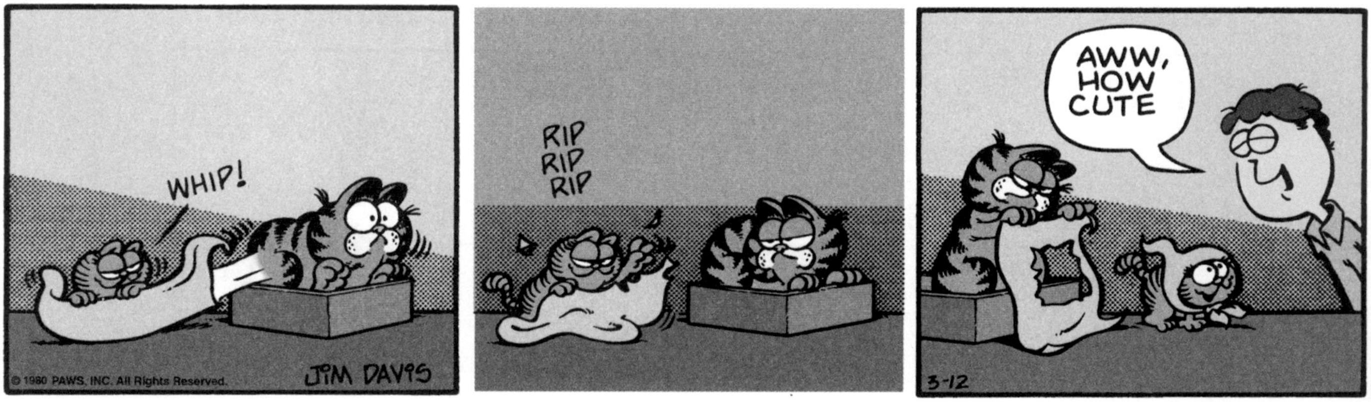
WHIP!
© 1980 PAWS, INC. All Rights Reserved.
JIM DAVIS
RIP RIP RIP
AWW, HOW CUTE
3-12

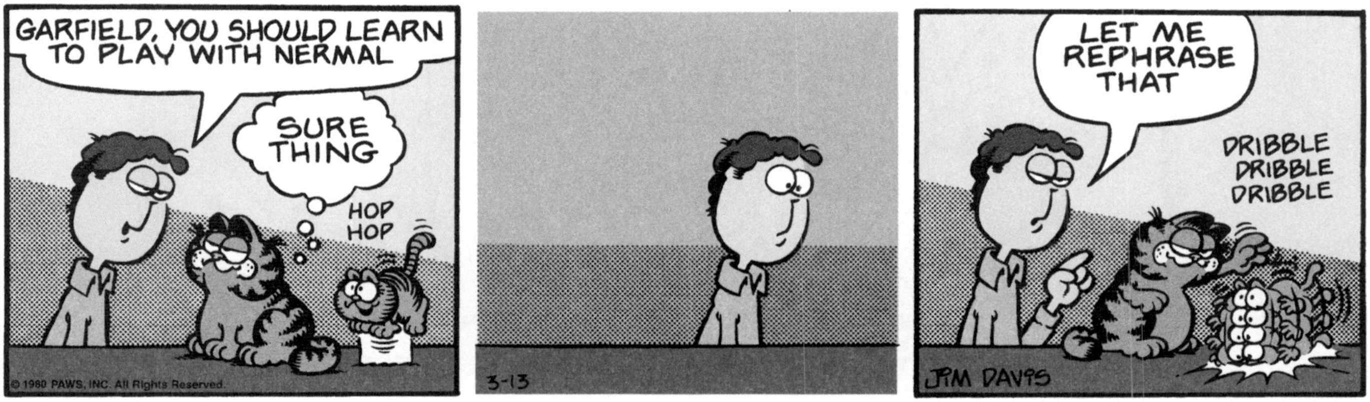
GARFIELD, YOU SHOULD LEARN TO PLAY WITH NERMAL
SURE THING
HOP HOP
LET ME REPHRASE THAT
DRIBBLE DRIBBLE DRIBBLE
© 1980 PAWS, INC. All Rights Reserved.
3-13
JIM DAVIS

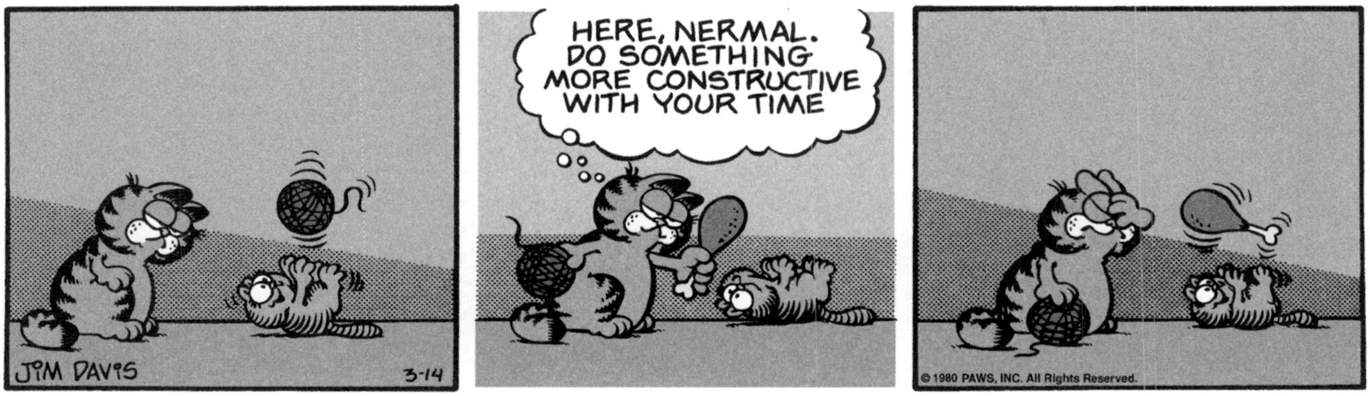
JIM DAVIS
3-14
HERE, NERMAL. DO SOMETHING MORE CONSTRUCTIVE WITH YOUR TIME
© 1980 PAWS, INC. All Rights Reserved.

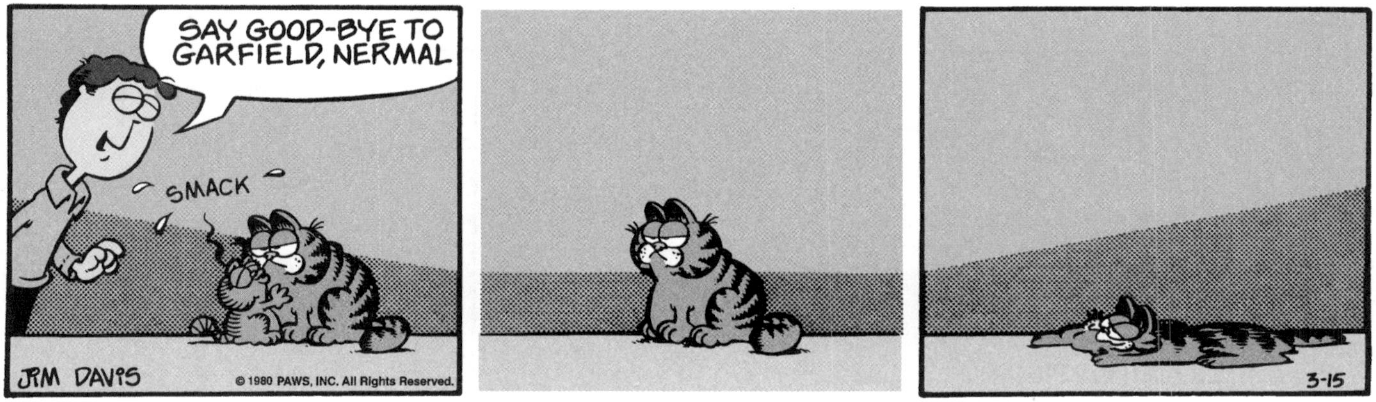
SAY GOOD-BYE TO GARFIELD, NERMAL
SMACK
JIM DAVIS
© 1980 PAWS, INC. All Rights Reserved.
3-15

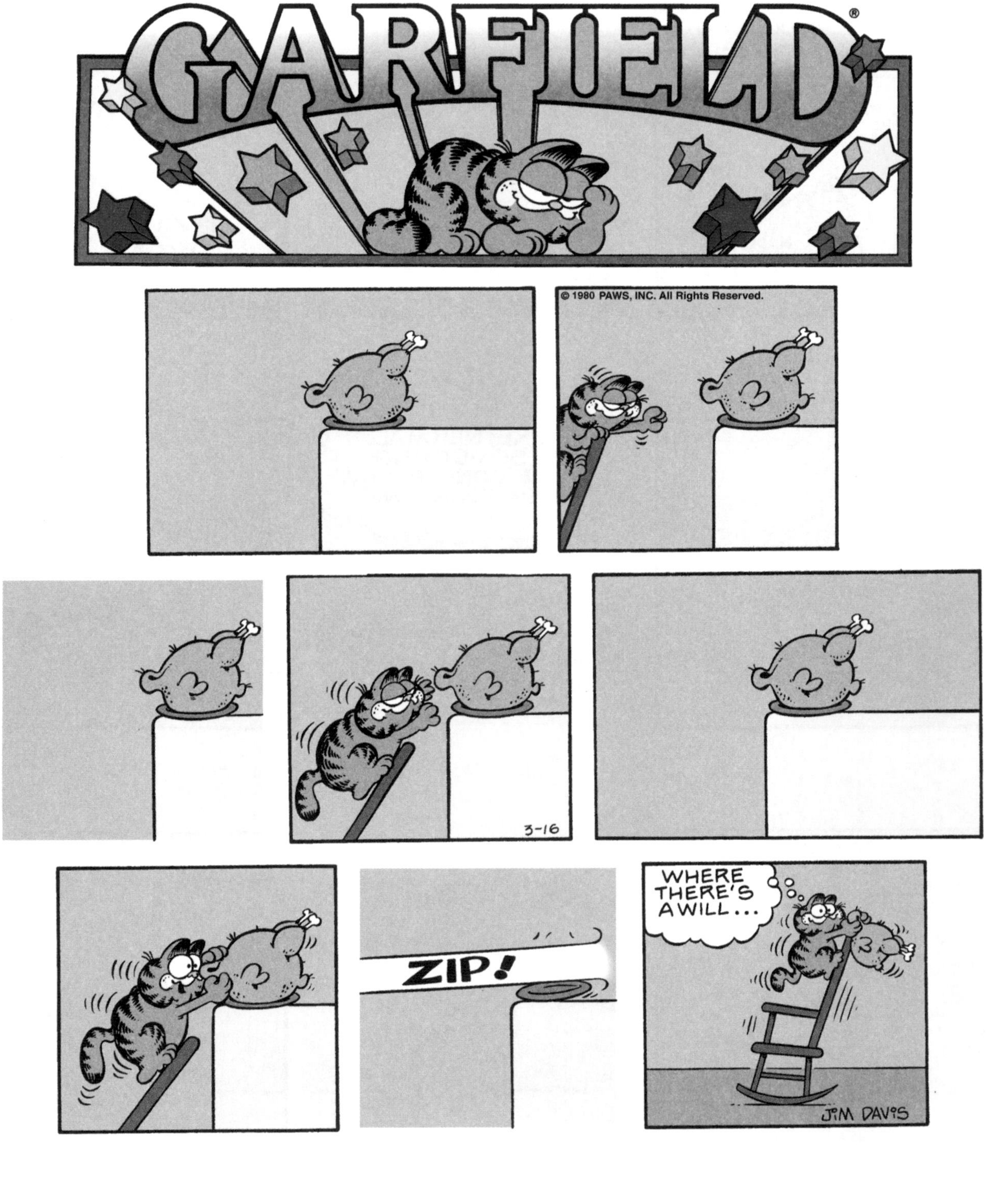
GARFIELD®
© 1980 PAWS, INC. All Rights Reserved.
3-16
ZIP!
WHERE THERE'S A WILL...
JIM DAVIS

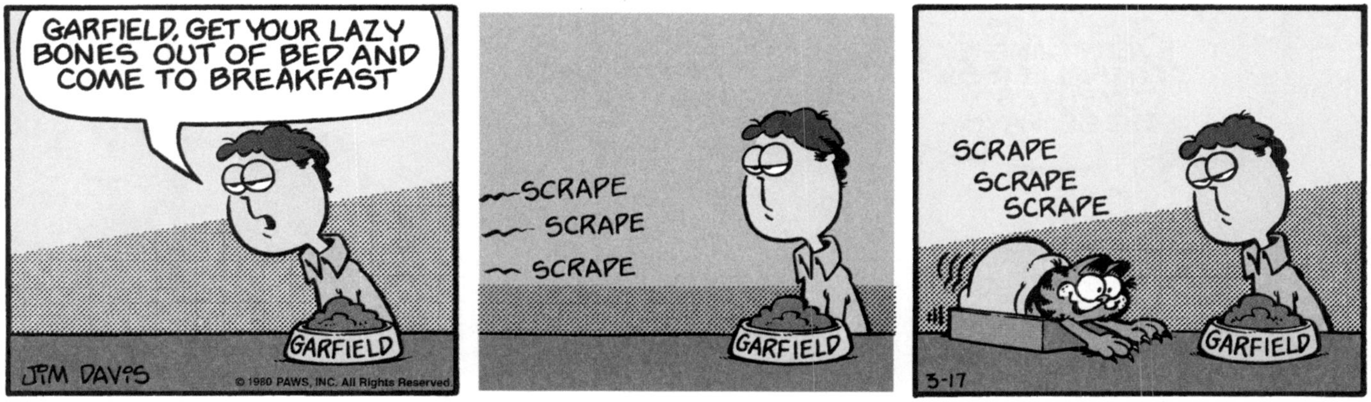
GARFIELD, GET YOUR LAZY BONES OUT OF BED AND COME TO BREAKFAST
GARFIELD
JIM DAVIS
© 1980 PAWS, INC. All Rights Reserved.
SCRAPE
SCRAPE
SCRAPE
SCRAPE
SCRAPE
SCRAPE
3-17

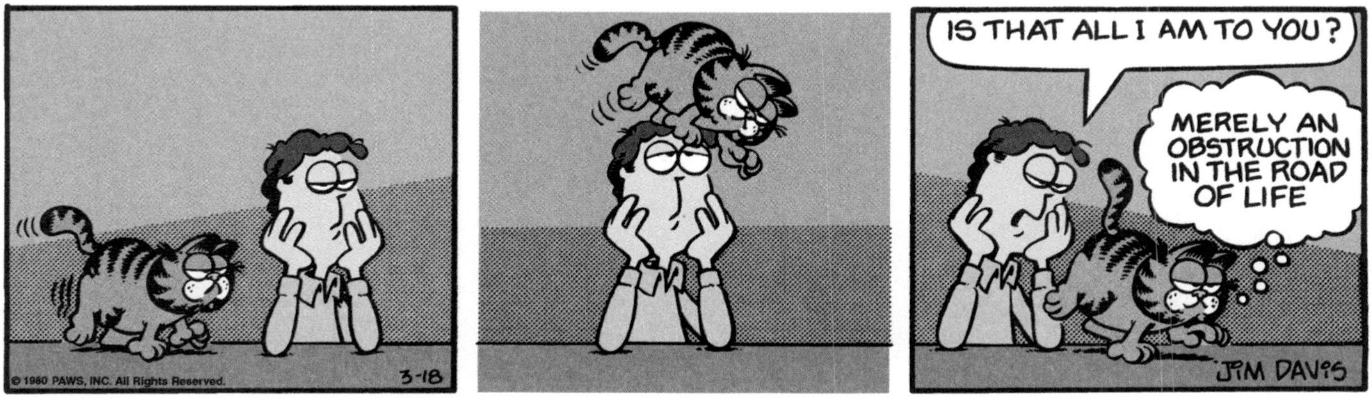
© 1980 PAWS, INC. All Rights Reserved.
3-18
IS THAT ALL I AM TO YOU?
MERELY AN OBSTRUCTION IN THE ROAD OF LIFE
JIM DAVIS

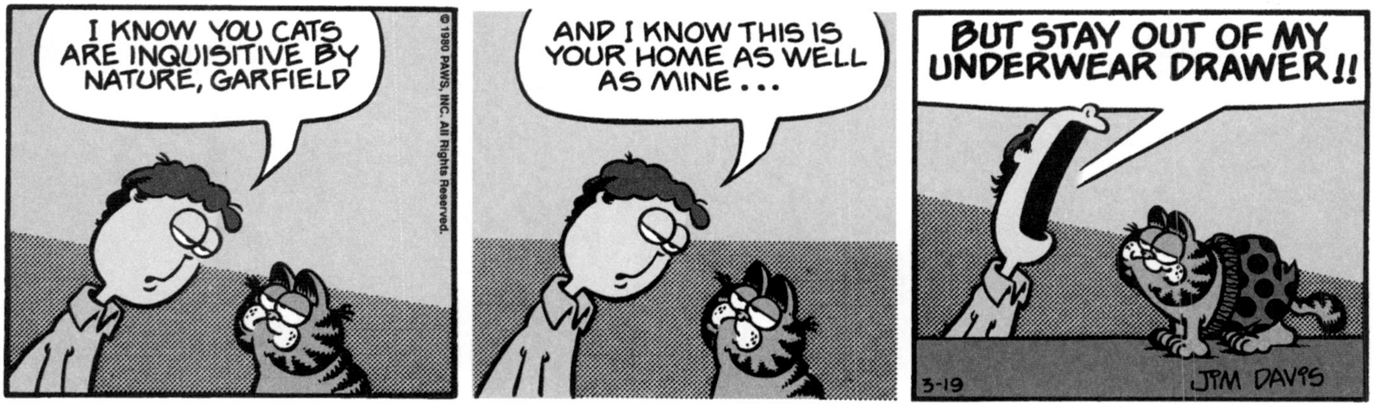
I KNOW YOU CATS ARE INQUISITIVE BY NATURE, GARFIELD
© 1980 PAWS, INC. All Rights Reserved.
AND I KNOW THIS IS YOUR HOME AS WELL AS MINE . . .
BUT STAY OUT OF MY UNDERWEAR DRAWER!!
3-19
JIM DAVIS

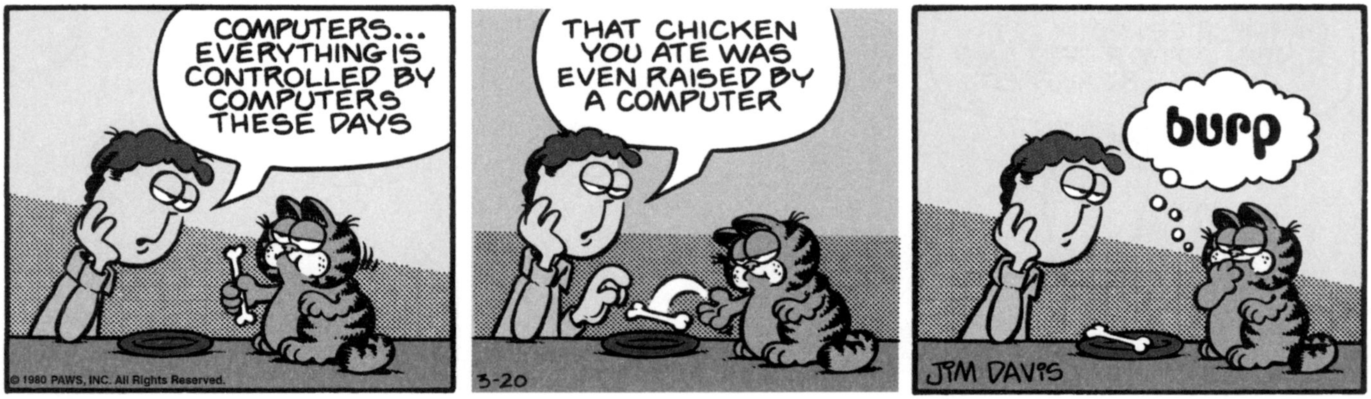
COMPUTERS... EVERYTHING IS CONTROLLED BY COMPUTERS THESE DAYS
© 1980 PAWS, INC. All Rights Reserved.
THAT CHICKEN YOU ATE WAS EVEN RAISED BY A COMPUTER
3-20
burp
JIM DAVIS

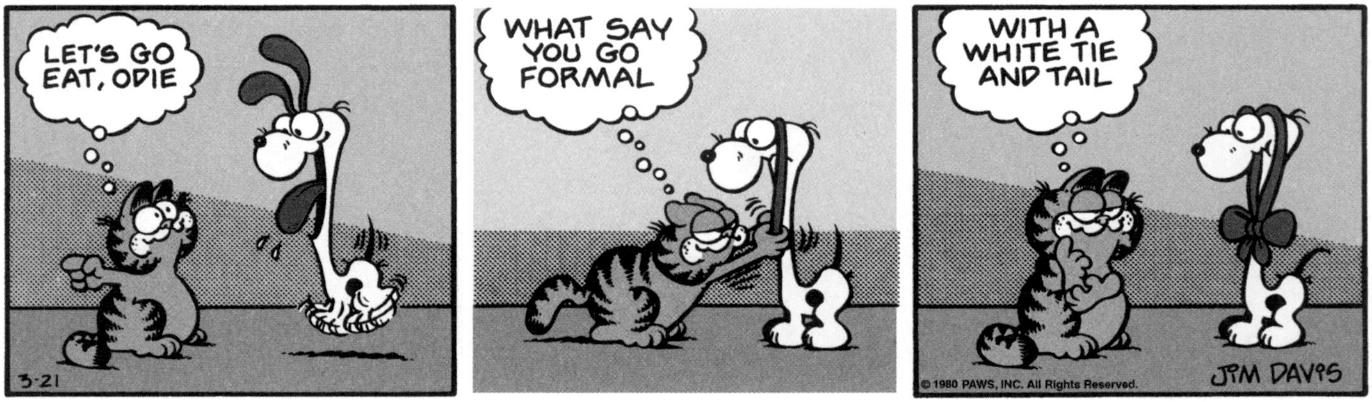
LET'S GO EAT, ODIE
3-21
WHAT SAY YOU GO FORMAL
WITH A WHITE TIE AND TAIL
© 1980 PAWS, INC. All Rights Reserved.
JIM DAVIS

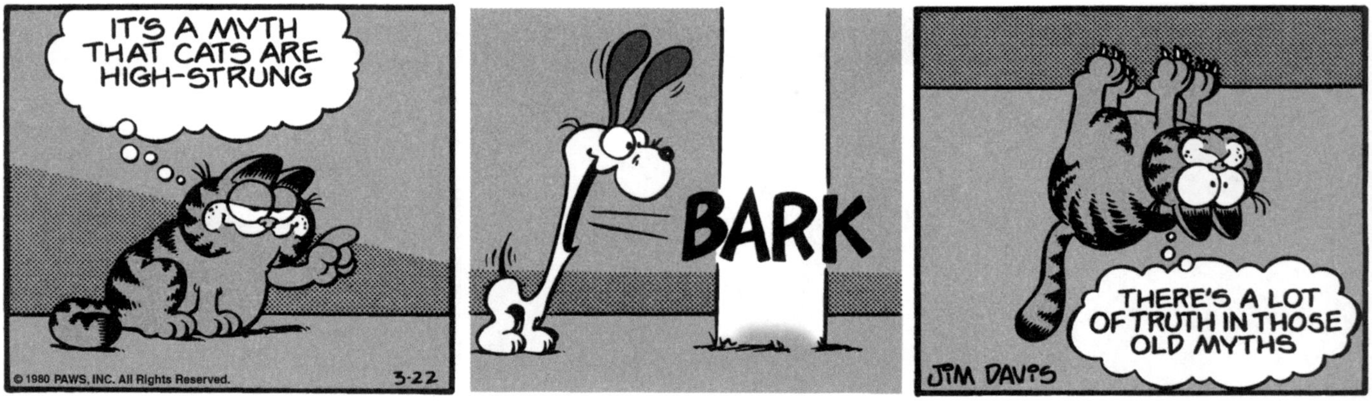
IT'S A MYTH THAT CATS ARE HIGH-STRUNG
© 1980 PAWS, INC. All Rights Reserved.
3-22
BARK
THERE'S A LOT OF TRUTH IN THOSE OLD MYTHS
JIM DAVIS

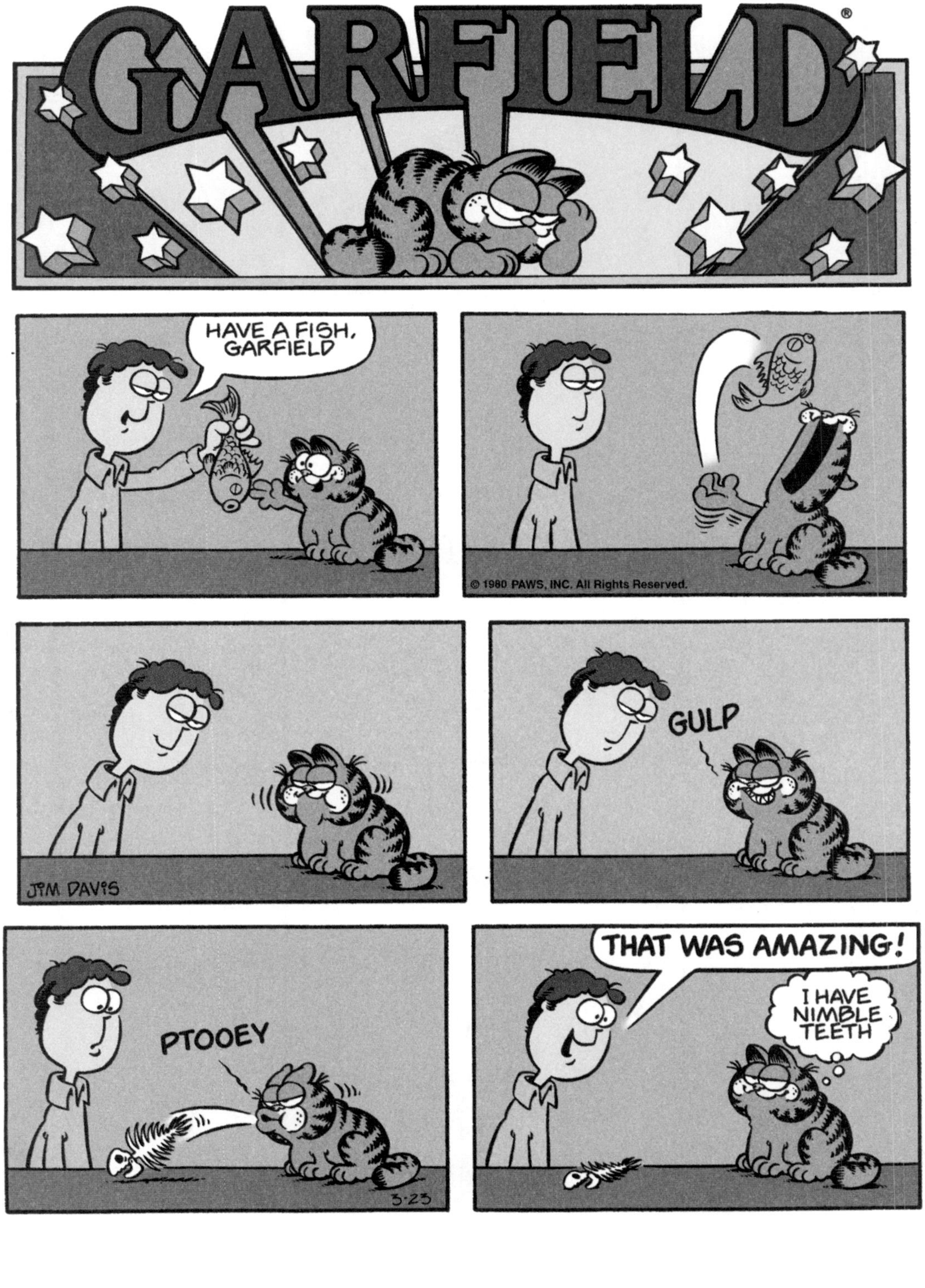
GARFIELD
HAVE A FISH, GARFIELD
© 1980 PAWS, INC. All Rights Reserved.
JIM DAVIS
GULP
PTOOEY
3-23
THAT WAS AMAZING!
I HAVE NIMBLE TEETH

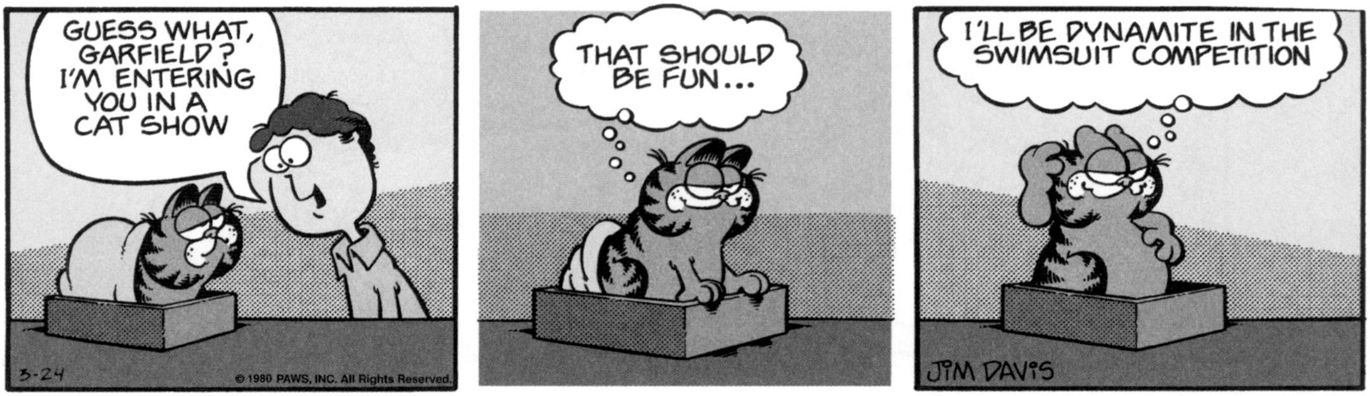
GUESS WHAT, GARFIELD? I'M ENTERING YOU IN A CAT SHOW
THAT SHOULD BE FUN...
I'LL BE DYNAMITE IN THE SWIMSUIT COMPETITION
3-24
© 1980 PAWS, INC. All Rights Reserved.
JIM DAVIS

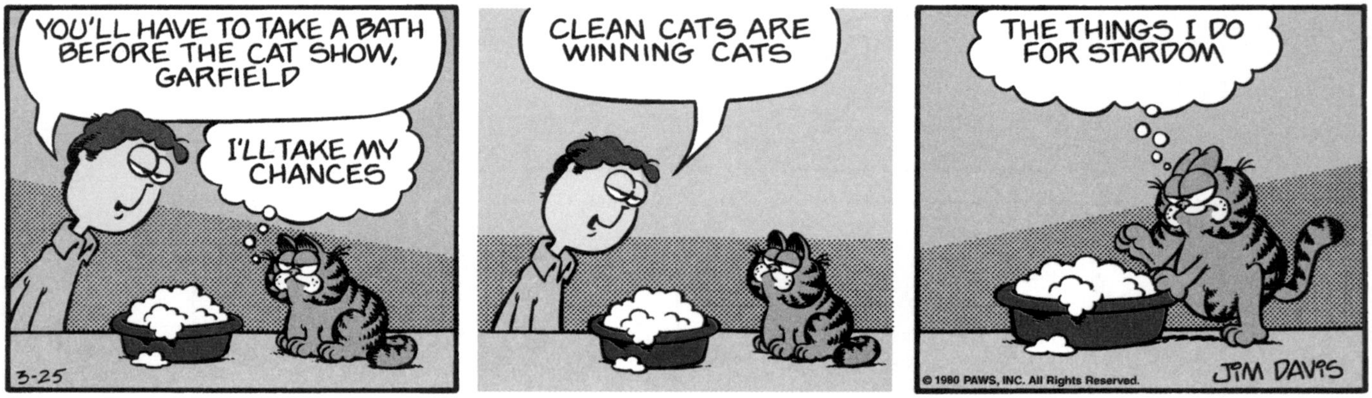
YOU'LL HAVE TO TAKE A BATH BEFORE THE CAT SHOW, GARFIELD
I'LL TAKE MY CHANCES
CLEAN CATS ARE WINNING CATS
THE THINGS I DO FOR STARDOM
3-25
© 1980 PAWS, INC. All Rights Reserved.
JIM DAVIS

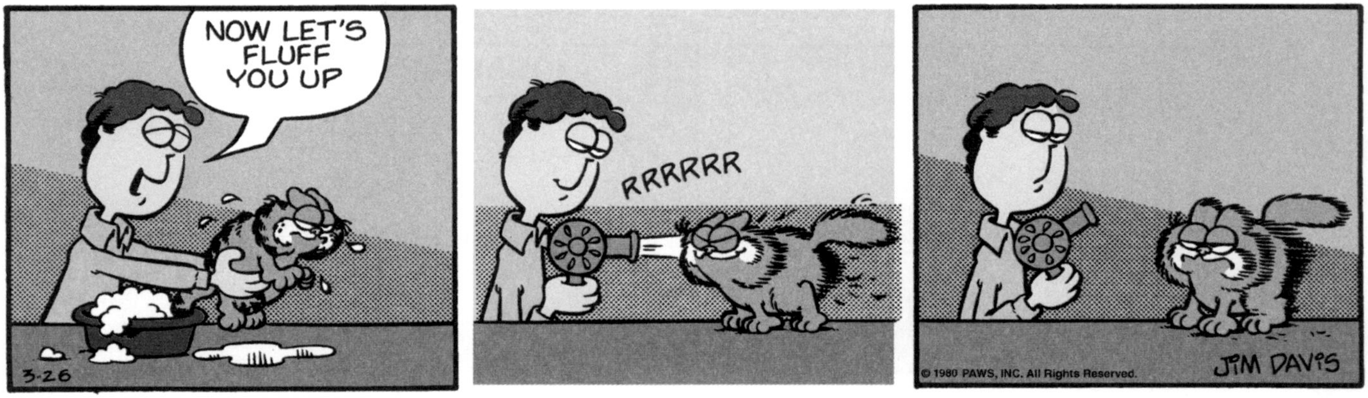
NOW LET'S FLUFF YOU UP
RRRRRR
3-26
© 1980 PAWS, INC. All Rights Reserved.
JIM DAVIS

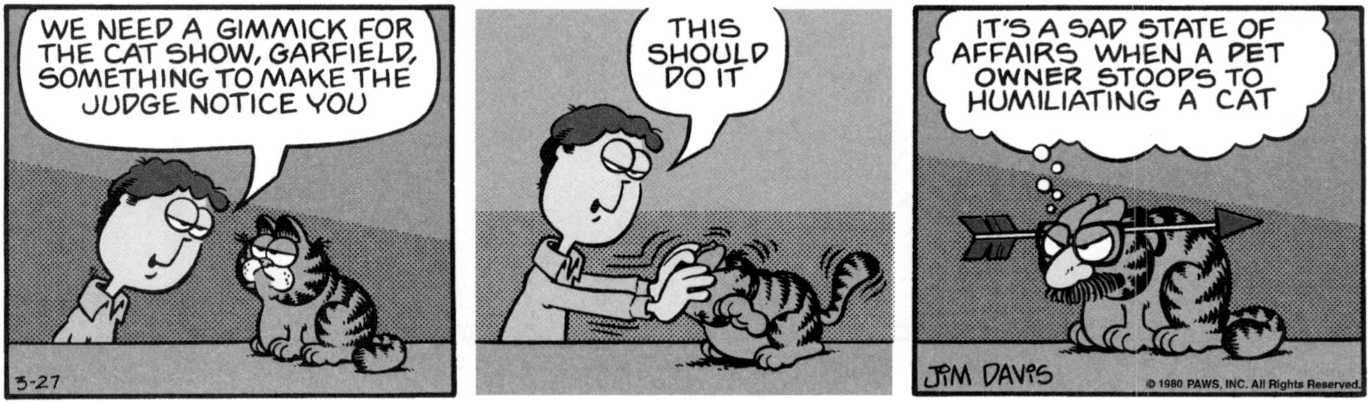
WE NEED A GIMMICK FOR THE CAT SHOW, GARFIELD, SOMETHING TO MAKE THE JUDGE NOTICE YOU
3-27
THIS SHOULD DO IT
IT'S A SAD STATE OF AFFAIRS WHEN A PET OWNER STOOPS TO HUMILIATING A CAT
JIM DAVIS
© 1980 PAWS, INC. All Rights Reserved.

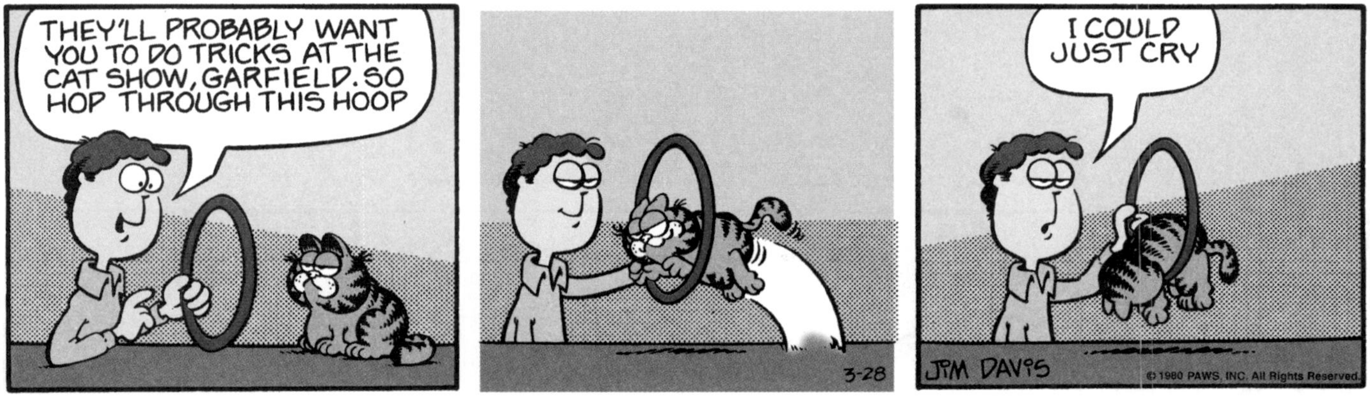
THEY'LL PROBABLY WANT YOU TO DO TRICKS AT THE CAT SHOW, GARFIELD. SO HOP THROUGH THIS HOOP
3-28
I COULD JUST CRY
JIM DAVIS
© 1980 PAWS, INC. All Rights Reserved.

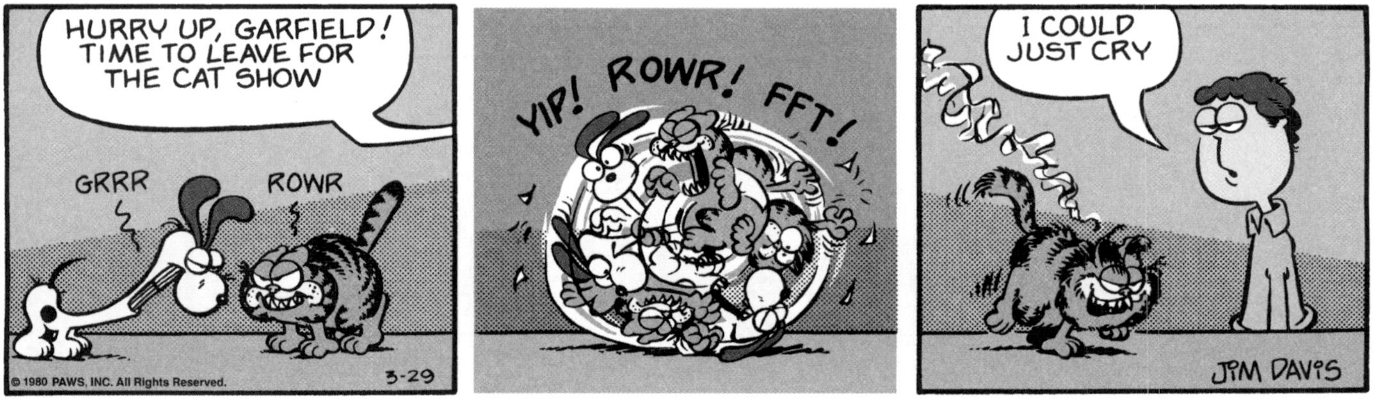
HURRY UP, GARFIELD! TIME TO LEAVE FOR THE CAT SHOW
GRRR
ROWR
© 1980 PAWS, INC. All Rights Reserved.
3-29
YIP! ROWR! FFT!
I COULD JUST CRY
JIM DAVIS

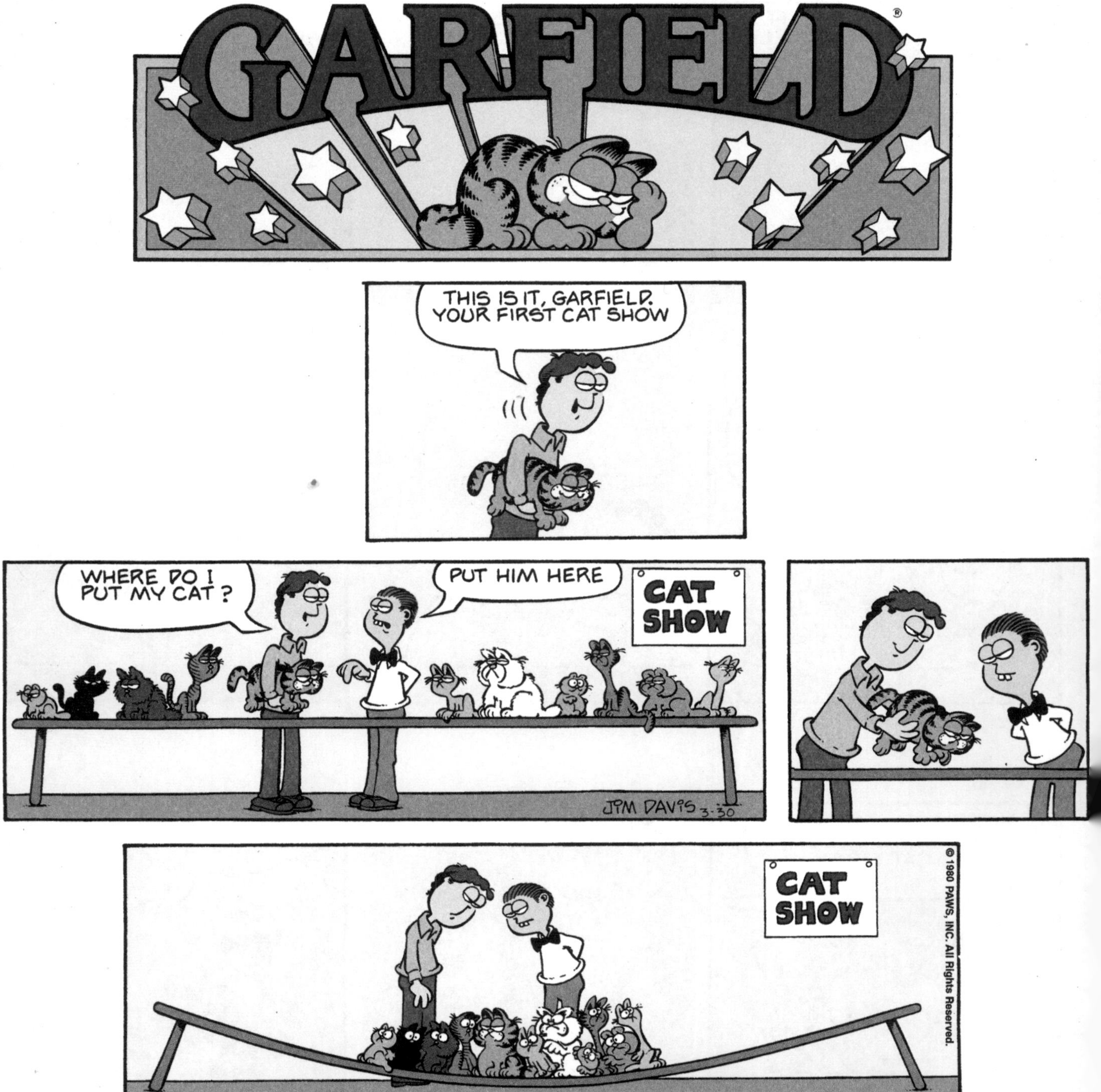
GARFIELD
THIS IS IT, GARFIELD. YOUR FIRST CAT SHOW
WHERE DO I PUT MY CAT ?
PUT HIM HERE
CAT SHOW
JIM DAVIS 3-30
CAT SHOW